Narrative Policy Analysis

Narrative Policy Analysis

Theory and Practice

Emery Roe

Duke University Press   Durham and London 1994

© 1994 Duke University Press
All rights reserved
Printed in the United States of America on acid-free paper ∞
Typeset in Trump Mediaeval by Keystone Typesetting, Inc.
Library of Congress Cataloging-in-Publication Data appear on the
last printed page of this book.

To Louise Palmer Fortmann

and Scott Bradley Fortmann-Roe

without whom, for whom

Contents

Preface and Acknowledgments

"But, Percy, the book should be starting with all these stories, not ending with them. . . ." That's me talking, "Percy" is Percy Tannenbaum, then-director of the University of California, Berkeley's Survey Research Center, and these stories were chapters of a book he was helping edit. The idea behind his book still seems good to me: Get the participants in a major science, technology or environment, controversy—in this case, the California Mediterranean fruitfly crisis of the early 1980s—to put on record their experiences in that controversy, then assemble these pieces into a picture of what actually happened.

But it didn't work out that way. Participants ended up supplying different pieces to different puzzles. Instead of recording what actually happened, the accounts, when considered together, demonstrated just how complex and uncertain these kinds of controversies are for those caught in their midst. As in *Rashomon,* perspective took hold. More formally: Sometimes what we are left to deal with are not the facts—that is why there is a controversy—but the different stories people tell as a way of articulating and making sense of the uncertainties and complexities that matter to them. Percy's view was that the final volume of edited accounts would still serve as a useful reminder to a policy analyst, such as myself. Their message was that in some controversies our tool kit of microeconomics, research methods, law, organization theory, and public management practice ceases to be of any real help. Controversies like the medfly crisis push us to the limits of our competence.

The questions that became *Narrative Policy Analysis* grew out of this interchange with Percy. What would a policy analysis look like if it started with stories rather than ended with them? Can we policy analysts still say something useful about issues of high uncertainty, complexity, and polarization, if the only things we have to analyze are the scenarios and arguments that animate them? These questions proved better than I realized. One conclusion they lead to is that, unless you are able—not just willing, but able—to treat seriously people's stories about those situations where facts and values are in dispute, you are not taking the situations seriously. Contemporary literary theory, especially the analysis of narrative, turns out to be one serious and particularly potent way to treat complex policies. I don't know what Percy thinks of my questions or my answer, but he let me run with the challenge, and I thank him.

"That's the problem," Janne said, tapping the flowchart with his free hand, the other steering our way up I-80 to Sacramento. I looked at the chart closely for the first time. "But this is the solution!" I realized.

Janne Hukkinen had this great idea. He was researching the controversy over salinity and toxic trace elements associated with irrigation in California's San Joaquin Valley. What he had done was to interview major actors in the controversy, code the interviews into separate problem statements, and then analyze the network of relationships that formed when all problem statements of all actors were aggregated together. Once you had mapped this network of interrelated cause-and-effect statements, you could see if there was a pathway that took one from problem definition to proposed solution and that no one interviewee had hit upon alone, but which became visible and useful only when the views of all interviewees were considered together.

That was the idea. What happened was the chart on my lap. Like a plate of spaghetti, arrows crosses arrows and loops looped loops. No dominant pathway this, but rather a mesh of circular networks, where a problem said by one party to cause another was held by someone else to lead right back to the initial problem. So here we were, driving up to meet state officials who sponsored the research, and what were we going to tell them?

The details of that story are in chapter 5. What needs establishing here is my special debt to Janne. Working through our report to the California Department of Water Resources, and then writing the article that is the basis of chapter 5 taught me much of what I know about analyzing policy narratives. Thanks also go to Gene Rochlin, our coauthor for that article, whose almost intuitive grasp of how science and politics intersect cemented much of our analysis.

Other chapters of this book also started out as policy analyses for specific clients. The material on the animal rights controversy (chapter 4) and Native American burial remains (chapter 7) was drawn from work in the University of California's Office of the President, where I analyzed legislation. Much of the discussion on budgeting in chapter 1 as well as on the tragedy of the commons and land registration in chapter 2 came from my overseas advising and consultancy activities in Kenya and Botswana. Also arising out of my work experience is the closing essay on tolerance, indifference, and the need to check the impulse to choose sides in the kinds of controversies studied here, if our goal is policy relevance.

Much of the policy world is not complex; the terrain I know, write about, and write for is. In this region of the world (and to adapt James March), different people at different times and in different ways contribute different things to what we summarily call "decision making." Here and abroad, this decision making is a hodgepodge of muddling through, groping along, opportunistically, incrementally, hopefully by rules of thumb and bounded rationality, in organized anarchies where nothing is ever thrown away but is rarely available or agreed upon when you need it the most. To introduce this book's mantra: the policy world is often quite complex, uncertain, and polarized. Not always, but frequently enough to matter. That's what attracted me to science, technology, and environmental controversies in the first place: they are the most extreme version of the challenge to come up with something useful to advise in the face of many unknowns, high intricacy, and little agreement.

A good number of people believe that the best way to deal with complexity is to focus on what is already simple; with uncertainty the idea is to reduce it or assume that certainty is within reach; and with polarization, to focus on what we agree with already. This belief is understandably human. It, however, robs us—all of us—of our chance to deal with the big issues. What do we do, when we can't reduce the uncertainty, can't simplify the complex, and can't resolve the polarization, yet have to make a decision? How do we deal with major science, technology, and environmental issues whose complexity, uncertainty and polarization are here to stay? This book demonstrates how contemporary literary theory allows us to address the big issues, without assuming away all that makes them big in the first place.

Throughout *Narrative Policy Analysis*, I try to follow a rule of thumb that I learned while working with two very different practitioners, Pat Crecine and Aaron Wildavsky, both of whom were in at the founding of policy analysis. The rule: Never stray too far from the data, if you want to be useful. To that end, I've grounded my analysis in case studies that illustrate how to do a narrative policy analysis for what look increasingly to be intractable policy issues. My thanks to Pat and Aaron for setting the example.

This is a good juncture to introduce some of the concerns raised about my approach to narrative policy analysis and its intersection of literary theory and policy analysis. (These concerns are addressed more fully in the introduction that follows.) For it turns out that the audiences I am writing for (in this case, policy analysts, literary theorists, and scientists, both social and natural) are as divided and polarized as the science, technology, and environmental controversies I study. Some literary theorists expect me to critique the narrative foundations of policy analysis, and since I don't, I have been accused of being neopositivist, insufficiently self-reflective about my praxis, and lacking the conviction of taking narrative analysis to its logical conclusion. (I'm guilty of the first and deserve the Scottish verdict of "not proven" for the others.) Social scientists, on the other hand, by and large dislike deconstruction, think poststructuralism is but one more Continental silliness, and want assurances that narrative policy analysis is not just another adversary culture attack on a status quo that really can't or shouldn't be changed anyway. Natural scientists are quick to conclude that because I'm talking about narrative I must be relativizing science. As for some of my colleagues, the practicing policy analysts, their judgment is loud if not clear: So what? Just cut the theory and tell us what to do! Not for them the postmodern temper of all answers are allowed, no answer is permitted.

Some polarization is very specific. A few of the literary theorists I have talked to privilege irony as a response to uncertainty, undecidability, and pluralism; policy types, by and large, don't find ironists to be of much help in the emergency rooms of contemporary society. Some of these literary theorists privilege the role of culture critique and believe the first duty of the public intellectual is to criticize; the policy types I'm familiar with believe the first duty of the public intellectual is that if you have to criticize, come up with an alternative. A few literary theorists, in turn, see in poststructuralism and postmodernism the first real alternative to science; most policy types would think that's mad. Overall, it's been my observation that literary theorists don't know much about policy, and practicing policy analysts certainly don't know much, if anything, about literary theory.

I do not pretend to have resolved these tensions here. There are, none-theless, readers in each audience searching for cross-disciplinary approaches for improved policymaking, and they are the ones for whom *Narrative Policy Analysis* has been written. I know they are there, because it has been my good fortune to have "test-marketed" earlier versions of the chapters in major journals for literary theory and policy analysis. Moreover, *Narrative Policy Analysis* should appeal to readers not just from literary theory and policy analysis, but also from regional planning, sociology, geography, economics, cultural studies, and ethnic studies. What is presented in the following pages is a new and rewarding way of looking at topics that are in desperate need of being seen afresh by these disciplines.

Literary theorists who helped in the making of this book include Gerry Prince, who invited me to speak on narrative policy analysis for his cultural studies group at Penn, and Ron Schleifer, another narratologist, who extended an invitation to Oklahoma. Seminars on the approach at Tulane and the Institute for the Study of Social Change at Berkeley also contributed. I am especially indebted to Michael Riffaterre, consistently the most challenging and personally most helpful of the literary theorists I have read. I hope some of the scratch-and-itch excitement his work has given me comes through in the case studies on global warming and Native American burial remains. My thanks as well to Jacques Derrida, for his kind words (via Richard Klein) on the article that became chapter 1.

I am also grateful to William Ascher, Ralph Cohen, Janet Craswell, Jeffrey Friedman, Richard Haynes, Richard Klein, Jonathan Morell, and David Weimer for their encouragement and comments as editors of the journals (or special sections) in which the original versions of the chapters appeared. I owe special thanks to the encouragement of Mark Greenberg, Seymour Mandelbaum, and other reviewers of the manuscript, who remain anonymous. This book would not have happened without Reynolds Smith, Jean Brady, and Maura High at Duke University Press.

Support for writing has been provided by the Survey Research Center and the S.V. Ciriacy-Wantrup Postdoctoral Fellowship program, both at the University of California, Berkeley. Additional support has been provided by the Office of the President, University of California, Oakland; Centre for Applied Social Science, University of Zimbabwe, Harare; and the College of Natural Resources, University of California, Berkeley.

Much of the material in this book represents substantially revised journal articles. An earlier version of chapter 1 appears as "Deconstructing Budgets," *Diacritics* 18(2): 61–8 (1988). I am grateful to *Diacritics* and the Johns Hopkins University Press for permission to use this material. Chapter 2 appears as "Development Narratives, Or Making the Best of Blueprint Development," *World Development* 19(4): 287–300 (1991). This material reappears here with the kind permission of Elsevier Science Ltd, The Boulevard, Langford Lane, Kidlington oX5 1GB, UK. Chapter 3 appears as "Narrative Analysis for the Policy Analyst: A Case Study of the 1980–1982 Medfly Controversy in California," *Journal of Policy Analysis and Management* 8(2): 251–73 (© 1989 by the Association for Public Policy Analysis and Management). I am grateful to John Wiley & Sons, Inc., for permission to use this material. Chapter 4 appears as "Nonsense, Fate and Policy Analysis: The Case of Animal Rights and Experimentation," *Agriculture and Human Values* VI(4): 21–9 (1989). I thank *Agriculture and Human Values* for permission to use this material. Chapter 5 appears as "A Salt on the Land: A Narrative Analysis of the Controversy Over Irrigation-Related Salinity and Toxicity in California's San Joaquin Valley," coauthored with Janne Hukkinen and Gene Rochlin, *Policy Sciences* 23(4): 307–29 (© 1990 by Kluwer Academic Publishers). This article won the *Policy Sciences* Lasswell Award. The material is reprinted by permission of Kluwer Academic Publishers. Chapter 6 appears as "Global Warming as Analytic Tip," *Critical Review* 6(2–3): 411–27 (© 1993 by Critical Review Foundation). A shorter version with the same title is to appear in the forthcoming book, *Global Climate Change and Public Policy,* to be published Nelson-Hall. I thank both Nelson-Hall and *Critical Review* for permission to use this material. Chapter 7 appears as "Intertextual Evaluation, Conflicting Criteria, and the Controversy over Native American Burial Remains," *Evaluation and Program Planning* in 15(4): 369–81 (1992). This material reappears here with the kind permission of Elsevier Science Ltd, The Boulevard, Langford Lane, Kidlington oX5 1GB, UK. Material in the conclusion and appendix A appears as "Applied Narrative Analysis: The Tangency of Literary Criticism, Social Science, and Public Policy," *New Literary History* 23(3): 555–81 (1992). I am grateful to *New Literary History* for permission to use this material.

My gratitude goes again to those individuals acknowledged in each article listed above. Finally, I want to thank the two people I love the most and who were instrumental in making this book happen the way it did. To paraphrase P.G. Wodehouse: Without the constant love and attention of Louise and Scott, this book would have been done a lot sooner.

Introduction to Narrative Policy Analysis:
Why It Is, What It Is, and How It Is

The reader implied throughout this book is the practicing policy analyst, but the book should interest anyone who wants to think more intelligently about today's science and technology controversies. The reader is anyone—policy analyst, culture critic, social scientist, or member of the public—who wants to know how the people who are paid to think about such debates could do a better job of analyzing them. This is a book for people who find the latest reports on global warming, pesticide use, animal rights, or any other controversy not particularly useful.

Narrative Policy Analysis applies contemporary literary theory to extremely difficult public policy issues. The objective is twofold: first, to underscore the important and necessary role that policy narratives have in public policy everywhere and, second, to establish the usefulness of narrative analytical approaches that allow one to reformulate increasingly intractable policy problems in ways that then make them more amenable to the conventional policy analytical approaches of microeconomics, statistics, organizational theory, law, and public management practice. By the end of the book, I hope many readers will say, "This is something I might want to use myself."

Much recent literary theory, particularly what is called poststructuralism, has been devoted to applying a set of considerations to a text, and then showing how uncertainty and complexity in that text are to be valued. This book reverses that process: it starts with an undisputed and highly valued uncertainty and complexity (for example, a policy issue like global warming), applies the same set of considerations from literary theory, and then sees what kind of "text" one ends up with (that is, a "text" hopefully more tractable to conventional policy analysis). The contribution this work makes is its repeated demonstration, across the widest set of case studies, issues, and topics yet assembled, that structuralist and poststructuralist theories of the narrative are exceptionally helpful—not just in analyzing difficult policy issues, but also in drawing out their implications and making policy recommendations.

The heart of the book is its case study approach. My operating assumption has been that the applicability of contemporary literary theory to important public policy problems represents information that professional policy analysts, literary critics, decision makers, and the public do not have, but should have, and that the best way to impart this information is through actual policy analyses of specific issues. The case studies elucidate and elaborate the steps to a narrative policy analysis and the policy implications that follow. The material demonstrates that explicit and systematic attention to policy narratives—the scenarios and argumentation on which policies are based—is helpful whether working domestically or overseas, or on issues that span the social, economic, political, scientific, and environmental spectrum.

The key practical insight of *Narrative Policy Analysis* is this: Stories commonly used in describing and analyzing policy issues are a force in themselves, and must be considered explicitly in assessing policy options. Further, these stories (called *policy narratives* in the book) often resist change or modification even in the presence of contradicting empirical data, because they continue to underwrite and stabilize the assumptions for decision making in the face of high uncertainty, complexity, and polarization.

What are Policy Narratives? What is Narrative Policy Analysis? Why is it Needed?

We need an initial description of "uncertainty, complexity, and polarization" before proceeding further. Social scientists typically distinguish *uncertainty* from *risk* and *ignorance*,[1] but for most analysts the three merge into the analyst's lack of knowledge about what matters. What matters, moreover, is often the issue's complexity or polarization. To many analysts, *complexity* is the issue's internal intricacy and/or its interdependence with other policy issues, while *polarization* crystallizes as the concentration of groups around extremes in the issue. What makes special difficulties for the analyst is the interrelation of uncertainty, complexity, and polarization. All too frequently, as we shall see in chapter 5, complexity and polarization cause uncertainty, and efforts to reduce uncertainty or polarization end up increasing the issue's complexity.[2]

What does this mean, practically? Many public policy issues have become so uncertain, complex, and polarized—their empirical, political, legal, and bureaucratic merits unknown, not agreed upon, or both—that the only things left to examine are the different stories policymakers and their critics use to articulate and make sense of that uncertainty, complexity, and polarization. How are analysts to evaluate conflicting stories about highly uncertain policy issues that increasingly dominate political life when their truth value or tractability cannot be established under existing financial and time constraints or through conventional means, like economics, research methods, public management, or the law?

The book's answer is, by narrative policy analysis. To put it baldly and at the risk of making the approach sound hydraulic, a narrative policy analysis proceeds by four steps. (The chapters that follow explain each of the four steps and associated concepts in more detail.) The analyst (critic, social scientist, policymaker, concerned citizen) starts with the conventional definition of *stories* and identifies those policy narratives in issues of high uncertainty and complexity that conform to this definition. If they are stories, they have beginnings, middles, and ends, as in scenarios; if the stories are in the form of arguments, they have premises and conclusions. The policy narratives of interest are those that dominate the issue in question. For the moment, such policy narratives can be defined as those stories—scenarios and arguments—that are taken by one or more parties to the controversy as underwriting (that is, establishing or certifying) and stabilizing (that is, fixing or making steady) the assumptions for policymaking in the face of the issue's uncertainty, complexity or polarization.[3] (Policy narratives are discussed at length in chapter 2.)

Stories are not the only kind of narrative. For the purpose of this book, there are also nonstories, counterstories and metanarratives. The analyst's second step is to identify those other narratives in the issue that do not conform to the definition of story or that run counter to the controversy's dominant policy narratives. The former I call *nonstories*; the latter, *counterstories* (counterstories are introduced in chapter 2 and more fully detailed in chapters 6 and 7). A circular argument, for example, has no beginning, middle, and end of its own, and thus qualifies for narrative analytical purposes as a nonstory. The third step in a narrative policy analysis is for the analyst to compare the two sets of narratives (stories on one hand, and nonstories or counterstories on the other) in order to generate a *metanarrative* "told" by the comparison (the governing precept being that of semiotics and gestalt psychology, namely, a term is defined by what it is not). As the following chapters underscore, metanarratives come in all shapes and sizes. The chapters cover the heightened sense of risk perception on the part of the public (chapter 2), the "nonsense" metanarrative (chapter 4), analytic tip (chapter 6), and the overarching issue of stewardship (chapter 7). In the fourth and last step in a narrative policy analysis, the analyst determines if or how the metanarrative, once generated, recasts the issue in such a way as to make it more amenable to decision making and policymaking. In particular, is the metanarrative more tractable as an issue to the conventional policy analytical tools of microeconomics, statistics, organization theory, law, and public management practice than were the original narratives upon which the metanarrative was based?

The metanarrative is, in short, the candidate for a new policy narrative that underwrites and stabilizes the assumptions for decision making on an issue whose current policy narratives are so conflicting as to paralyze decision making. The comparative advantage of narrative policy analysis and its drive to a policy-relevant metanarrative lies in highly polarized policy controversies, where the values and interests of opposing camps are so fundamentally divided that no middle ground for compromise exists between them. In these cases, the best alternative is to forgo searching for consensus and common ground in favor of a metanarrative that turns this polarization into another story altogether, one that is more pliable to policy intervention, however temporary that intervention may be. It should go without saying there are no guarantees that a controversy will have a metanarrative, or that there will be only one metanarrative and that it will always be policy-relevant.

By making the much more difficult case for a narrative analysis that works within the confines of conventional policy analysis—that is, by claiming that literary theory can help policy analysts, among others, to deal more effectively with policy issues—this book also builds the case for analyzing narratives in related areas, be they the narratives that populate everyday life or those that constitute social science generally and policy analysis specifically. By widening the domains of conventional policy analysis and contemporary literary theory, *Narrative Policy Analysis* represents a significant departure for each.

The Book's Organization

The chapters are organized around explaining and illustrating the four steps in a narrative policy analysis. Each chapter amplifies a particular component of the approach and shows the increasing utility that comes with a progressively formal analysis of policy narratives. Chapter 1 introduces the foundational notions of "text" and "reading" from contemporary literary theory by detailing how they help in better understanding and evaluating the national budget crises of governments around the world. Budgetary effectiveness, a key concept in the field of comparative budgeting, has more to do with reading budgetary texts, the chapter argues, than it does with the more commonly supposed statistical measures of effectiveness.

Chapter 2 moves beyond texts and reading to the policy narratives that combine the two. I show how policy narratives work and what their implications are for policymaking in brief case studies of four policy narratives, including the well-known tragedy of the commons. By establishing and fixing the assumptions for decision making, these narratives enable governments and donor agencies to make and implement developing country policy under conditions of extreme uncertainty and complexity. The case material establishes an important point: the way to undermine a policy narrative is not by trying to subvert it empirically—a tactic that only increases uncertainty and, therefore, the pressure to retain the policy narrative being critiqued. A better way to undermine a policy narrative is by creating a counternarrative (the "counterstory" mentioned earlier), finding ways to "rewrite" dominant policy narratives, or engaging other dominant narratives that happen to run counter to the narrative being disputed. *Narrative Policy Analysis* returns again and again to a central dilemma about policy critiques that only tell us what to be against, not what to be for: while criticisms that undermine a policy are frequently assumed to underwrite and stabilize the taking of decisions against that policy, in practice critiques serve to intensify uncertainty by not providing any alternative. Consequently, pressures increase to retain the now-discredited policy narrative, until something more than a critique comes along to replace it.

Chapters 3 through 5 undertake a more methodical and thoroughgoing analysis of policy narratives by distinguishing metanarratives from the competing stories and nonstories that give rise to them (the role of counterstories is left for later chapters). Throughout, the mantra terms of "uncertainty," "complexity," and "polarization" are explicated and illustrated. As we will see, metanarratives, like policy narratives, come about in very different ways: some are created, others are preexisting, some have to be discovered, and others just aren't there. Chapter 3 introduces the metanarrative and shows how one can be constructed by the public at large. Critiques by environmentalists and others of the scenario favoring aerial spraying of the pesticide malathion to eradicate Mediterranean fruitflies during the 1980–82 California medfly crisis ended up only heightening the public's general sense of risk and uncertainty over that issue. The chapter underscores how understanding the metanarrative of heightened risk perception could have altered the course of that controversy for the better.

In other policy controversies, a metanarrative is not as clear-cut and has instead to be discovered or constructed by an analyst. Chapter 4 illustrates how decision makers can generate a metanarrative from opposing positions in the animal rights controversy so as to address the controversy's more corrosive features. Chapter 5 uses formal computer analysis to identify the major stories, circular argumentation, and metanarrative that fuel an extremely complex policy controversy over toxic irrigation. Without computer analysis, it would have been difficult on the face of it to know just what the competing policy narratives were and the metanarrative they spawned.

In order to demonstrate why narrative policy analysis does not depend on peculiarities in the earlier case studies or on the specific version of narrative analysis applied, two chapters are devoted to applications of the "intertextual reading" model of semiotician, Michael Riffaterre. Chapter 6 relies on Riffaterre's approach to identifying the "intertext"—a notion paralleling that of the metanarrative but relying more on counterstories than nonstories—in explicating the controversy over global warming. The case study shows how a policy narrative about uncertainty itself (in this instance the scenario about global warming's broad but locationally indeterminate effects) is used to underwrite and authorize decision making to mitigate greenhouse climate change. Instead of paralyzing decision making, uncertainty in the global warming scenario is narrativized for the purposes of taking decisions. Chapter 7 applies Riffaterre's model to the general problem of how to choose among conflicting evaluative criteria when undertaking a formal evaluation of any highly complex policy or program. The chapter's case study addresses the especially divisive issue of what to do about Native American burial remains presently housed in museums.

The conclusion marks the ethical implications for tolerance that come with analyzing policy narratives generally and undertaking narrative policy analysis specifically. Whether we use narrative analysis to reflect on the foundations of conventional policy analysis or to address specific policy problems, we end up at the same conclusion: a call for greater toleration of opposing views among analysts, decision makers, and the public at large. What sets *Narrative Policy Analysis* apart from the many other books calling for greater reflexivity in the social sciences is that it gets us to the same end point, but only after demonstrating how potent narrative analytical techniques are in addressing concrete policy issues that trouble us daily.

Finally, appendix A reprises the approach's methodology for the reader who is already or will become familiar with the case material in the chapters. A brief, simplified narrative policy analysis of the Cuban Missile Crisis suggests the approach's wider applicability to other types of science and technology issues.

A Short Digression

If those who have read the book's manuscript are correct, readers at this point will have divided into two groups. One group wants to jump right into the examples and applications of narrative policy analysis. The other wants its questions answered about the approach and the approach's assumptions before going into the examples.

Before proceeding further, readers in the first group should turn to appendix A, which summarizes the points made in this introduction and illustrates the approach and its key concepts. Readers in the second group should find many of their questions covered in the following section.

Questions, Answers, and the Book's Major Themes

In a book as heavily devoted as this one is to application and method, it is essential at the outset to highlight the major themes developed across the chapters.

I have been asked very similar questions by policy analysts and literary critics: Does narrative policy analysis mean that all policy narratives are fiction? What use are policy narratives as stories, the facts of which cannot be determined anyway? Does narrative policy analysis relativize science? Does the approach sufficiently reflect on its own foundations in policy analysis and social science? In the end, isn't it really power and politics that determine what stories are used in policymaking? Lastly, does the approach reduce any of the technical uncertainties driving these science, technology, and environmental controversies?

Let me just say for the moment that these questions strike me as slightly off the mark. In the situations of high uncertainty and complexity for which narrative policy analysis is appropriate, it simply is not possible to decide if the policy narratives being analyzed are fiction, or if the science is right, or what form power and politics are really taking. We just don't know enough. To see why, let us turn to the six questions in more detail. Their answers are the core intellectual agenda of *Narrative Policy Analysis.*

Are Policy Narratives All Fiction? Policymakers and literary critics might well wonder about the rightness of applying to the stories, scenarios, and arguments that populate policy life those analytical techniques originally developed to evaluate fiction. After all, the former make truth claims about reality in ways that fiction typically does not.

Unfortunately, we are continually being asked to take positions on an increasing range of policy issues, to do something about them *now,* even though their empirical and factual merit is in doubt, cannot be determined, or is otherwise disputed. One doctor says you can roll your baby in malathion and nothing will happen; another physician calls that attempted murder. One scientist maintains global warming is not yet proven; another says we cannot wait to see if that's true. One group of animal welfare advocates hold researchers responsible for the mass slaughter of untold millions of animals; another group, among them the terminally ill, claim that their deaths will be on *your* hands if animal experimentation does not continue. In some cases, we even know the policy narrative is factually inaccurate, as with the tragedy of the commons argument of chapter 2. Nonetheless, we keep to the narrative anyway in absence of a better story and because, again, decisions have to be taken now. Waiting is not possible, or when we do wait for better information, as in the irrigation case study of chapter 5, that research all too often raises further questions and problems said to require urgent answers as well.

We are, to put it simply, asked with increasing frequency to take positions on issues about which the only thing we have to analyze are the polarized arguments in favor or against, and for which truth claims cannot be the sole guide in deciding them one way or the other, given their persisting uncertainty and complexity. Against this background, techniques developed for evaluating texts whose truth claims are moot take on considerable appeal. Just how applicable these techniques are depends on what analytical purchase can be squeezed from treating policy narratives first and foremost as stories that can be compared and evaluated. Narrative policy analysis demonstrates that these techniques are highly applicable and useful, and much more so than the analyst might first suspect, given the universal disparagement, "You're just telling stories. . . ."

What Use Are Stories? The belittling term "just telling stories" is discussed at length in an appendix to chapter 3's case study of the medfly crisis. Fortunately, one bridge connecting conventional policy analysis and contemporary literary theory is the importance both place on the role of stories and storytelling in securing and endorsing the assumptions needed to make decisions under conditions of uncertainty and complexity.

Herbert Simon, a major influence on the policy analysis literature, has argued that stories—what he and his students call decision-making rules of thumb, heuristics, or algorithms—allow decision making to take place not only in the face of complexity (that is, when matters are highly interrelated and interdependent) but in the face of uncertainty as well (that is, when we do not know how things are related, if at all). More recently, Richard Neustadt and Ernest May have advised policy analysts that the best way to find out the real problems in a complicated issue of many unknowns is not by asking directly "What's the problem?" but rather "What's the story?" behind the issue.[4]

In fact, few practicing policy analysts and academics in the policy profession would disagree that stories in the bureaucracy can convey a great deal of information and fairly efficiently at that. Certainly, attention to stories and narratives is not new in the literature on policymaking and policy analysis.[5] Also recognized is the fact that public managers must be sensitive to such storytelling and be adept at it themselves if they are to be good managers (a point developed in chapter 3). What has been by and large missing until *Narrative Policy Analysis* is a way of channeling this appreciation into better managing or solving concrete policy problems.

Doesn't Narrative Policy Analysis Relativize Science? For some readers, terms such as "stories," "narratives," and "poststructuralism," along with phrases like "stabilizing the assumptions for decision making," raise the specter of an approach that relativizes science, that implies reality is arbitrarily and in every sense socially constructed. As some poststructuralists would have it, "uncertainty, complexity, and polarization" are just discursive formations, here in one episteme and gone with the next. That is not the position of this book.

The starting point of narrative policy analysis is the reality of uncertainty and complexity in the polarized issues and controversies of today. Readers will differ over the origin of this reality. Its roots may lie in place, personality, politics, or perception; ultimately, it may be socially constructed or exogenously determined. For the purposes of a narrative policy analysis, what is important is that the parties to the controversies take as given the uncertain and complex nature of the topics they are debating and the conflicts over which they find themselves opposed. The only causality of interest to the analyst is that of a proximate nature, namely, the parties to the controversy assume as given a polarization that leads to uncertainty and complexity, or an uncertainty and complexity that leads to polarization, or a combination of both (the dynamic is described more fully in chapter 5).

Some parties are, for example, certain about precisely those matters which others take as deeply disputed, as in the global warming controversy. Or the controversy may involve polarized camps who are absolutely certain about the truth of their opposing positions, as in the debates over animal rights and Native American burial remains. In other cases, disputants find themselves uncertain over specifics, but nonetheless opposed over what to do, as in the medfly crisis. These controversies are, in short, perceived by those most intimately involved as uncertain, complex, and divisive, because the empirical and factual merits are genuinely in doubt or disputed; or because where there is consensus among disputants, there is no unanimity over the points that matter for policymaking; or where there is certainty, it is frequently expressed as expert, but contradictory, opinion. Why disputants believe what they believe is of less interest to the narrative policy analyst than the fact that they believe what they do and the consequences that follow from these beliefs.

Thus, narrative policy analysis is just as compatible with assumptions of realism as it is with relativism. Indeed this is why *Narrative Policy Analysis* can be read by such different audiences. The approach does, however, offer up a reduced prospect for analytic objectivity. To repeat a point highlighted in appendix A, the closest that the analyst gets to objectivity in narrative policy analysis, where conditions of extreme uncertainty and complexity are taken as the point of departure, is identifying just whose uncertainty and complexity is being analyzed. Is it the uncertainty of the disputants in the controversy, as and when they express doubts or puzzlement? Is the uncertainty that of the analyst, when confronted by the conflicting certainties of expert opinion? Or is the uncertainty more systemic and visible only when one considers the controversy in its entirety, as we find in the irrigation case study of chapter 5? One of the strengths of narrative policy analysis is demonstrating how useful it is for the analyst to clarify just whose uncertainty and complexity are at issue.

Is Narrative Policy Analysis Sufficiently Reflexive? Those familiar with contemporary literary and critical theory might well expect narrative policy analysis to critique its foundations in conventional policy analysis and social science. The fact that this book does not provide such a critique does not mean I believe it cannot or should not be done. It means only that I have nothing to add to the many criticisms already out there of conventional policy analysis. *Narrative Policy Analysis* takes instead a radically different tack.

Current critiques of "positivist" social science and policy analysis typically call for greater tolerance of differing viewpoints and ways of doing things professionally. A more self-conscious pluralism, rather than unreflexive positivism, should be a professional's hallmark. This is what Donald McCloskey commends in his *If You're So Smart: The Narrative of Economic Expertise.*[6] Narrative policy analysis makes much the same recommendation, using even some of the same narrative techniques, but reaches this point by way of another terrain. Here it is the high contingency of uncertainty, complexity, and polarization, not just the undoubted pluralism of narratives in everyday life and professional activity, that drives us to tolerance.

But the reader may object: Surely pluralism and contingency are related? After all, we hear repeatedly that pluralism leads to polarization, diversity engenders uncertainty, and plural voices are what makes matters so complex socially and politically these days. Everyday pluralism has been transformed into the exceptional circumstances of high contingency, hasn't it?

I don't accept that. With or without pluralism, global warming would still be a controversial issue full of many unknowns and amplifying complexity. This is true for all the controversies discussed in the following chapters. Of course, there may be instances where value pluralism and empirical contingency are related, but that cannot be settled a priori. It is a matter to be established case by case, controversy by controversy. Of course, narratives permeate everyday life as well as the policy profession and the social sciences generally. But we should not confuse those narratives with the specific subset that are the focus of this book, namely, policy narratives that underwrite and stabilize the assumptions for decision making in the midst of high controversy, particularly in the science, technology, and environment arenas. *Narrative Policy Analysis* takes seriously the need of analysts, policymakers, and the concerned public *to act upon*—not just reflect about, rhetoricize, or disparage, but *to do something* about—what they already recognize to be the scenarios and arguments driving issues of high controversy.

In short, this book starts from a controversy's uncertainty and complexity, not from everyday pluralism. It ends up arguing for tolerating as many voices as possible, not because of some *a priori* privileging of pluralism or the Other, but because it is in these multiple voices that we may find a metanarrative—small *m*, please—to help us deal with our current difficulties. Tolerance is here a methodological, not normative, imperative. Advocates of narrative pluralism have been much too quick in jumping from pluralism to tolerance and then to the conclusion that tolerance is the best answer we have for a polarized controversy. Tolerance comes parlously close to a large-*M* metanarrative in such a leap (right there alongside Science and Rationality). On the other hand, at the core of a narrative policy analysis is the recognition that we tolerate a multiplicity of different and conflicting voices because the more voices there are, the better the idea about the metanarrative, if there is one. We squeeze much more than tolerance from the analysis of plural narratives, and *Narrative Policy Analysis* is a clear—and so far the *only*—demonstration of how potent narrative analytical techniques are in addressing specific controversies. Fortunately, it is contemporary literary theory that shows us the way, and it goes a very long way at that.

Indeed, the case study approach of this book, like narrative policy analyses generally, is empiricist and positivist in the same sense as literary criticism is when explicating and engaging theory in order to analyze a particular text. I see the enterprises as functionally equivalent. Contemporary literary theory is much too useful to let it be limited to the domains of critique, reflexivity, and value pluralism alone.

Doesn't Narrative Policy Analysis Ignore Power and Politics? More damning is the charge that the analysis of policy narratives ignores power and politics in the deployment of those narratives. The conventional power-and-politics argument holds that the way any policy narrative is used, indeed the very way it is read, depends on the ruling ideology (read: power and politics) of the society in question. Since *Narrative Policy Analysis* shows the opposite to be the case—precious few ways exist to analyze the role of power and politics in issues of high uncertainty and complexity without recourse to the kind of analysis of policy narratives proposed here—we must be very clear from the start why this is so. In the process, that other bridge connecting conventional policy analysis and contemporary literary theory comes out of the fog, namely, a reluctance to heed the calls for a more overtly historical approach informing the enterprise of each.

Power and politics can be found operating within any disciplinary frame the narrative analyst is working in, whether it be conventional policy analysis, literary criticism, or the policy sciences and humanities generally. Policy analysis, for instance, is client-based and frequently focused on short-term issues of getting things done without necessarily interrogating the larger, underlying issues of institutionalized power relations. There is, thus, no denying the importance of power and politics within a discipline, even when members of the discipline do not recognize this to be so.

The central question of *Narrative Policy Analysis*, though, is much more daunting: How are power and politics articulated and realized in those controversies and disputes where narrative policy analysis is most appropriately applied, that is, for controversies revolving around issues of extreme uncertainty, complexity and polarization? Power politicians can, of course, obscure matters deliberately and make issues seem uncertain and complex and divided, when they really are not. But these are not the issues treated in *Narrative Policy Analysis*. As the following chapters make clear, the issues for which narrative policy analysis is suitable are those in which each party to the controversy, including the expert, is in the grip of uncertainty and high contingency, where the issue could go either way in the view of the parties concerned, where no one involved knows what really is in their best long-run interests, and where most everyone is playing it by ear, including many, if not all, the so-called power brokers.

Power and politics do not disappear in these issues. Rather, they operate only when access to decision making resources is articulated and differentiated through and by means of competing policy narratives about the issue in question. Unequal power relations work themselves out through the competition and opposition of stories, storytelling, and other policy narratives that get people to change their own stories when conditions are complicated, full of unknowns, and divisive in the extreme (these narrative asymmetries are the focus of chapter 3). Indeed, competing narratives that change peoples' minds and end up "telling the better story" are the primary way we know that unequal access to information and resources among the key parties to a controversy really does matter when it comes to how that issue is perceived, communicated, and managed in situations of high ambiguity. Rather than being absent, power and politics are at the core of the narrative analysis of policy narratives forged under conditions of high uncertainty and complexity. More to the point, I do not know how the role of power and politics in such circumstances could be analyzed without the kind of analysis of policy narratives that is developed in the following chapters. Narrative policy analysis allows one to *reflect* on how instrumental policy narratives are in shaping *and* determining major policymaking controversies today.

This book makes an even stronger case for the central role of narrative analysis in understanding the nature of power and politics. To understand the case, we have first to consider what occurs when one undertakes a narrative policy analysis. As the following chapters demonstrate, the language of story/nonstory or counterstory/metanarrative enables the analyst to cast the controversy and its opposing parties in a different, less familiar context than the parties typically see themselves in. The primary effect of a narrative policy analysis is to defamiliarize and decontextualize what the opposing parties take to be the givens of their controversy by rendering their differences into another story completely, the metanarrative.

Consider now the oft-repeated insight that institutionalized relations of power and politics are only really visible when they are already in decline.[7] Its corollary is that power relations are most effective when transparent, that is, when they are embodied in what we take as the unquestioned givenness of the world, in our commonsense understanding of reality. Thus, when the analyst sets about to defamiliarize and decontextualize the givenness of reality, power and politics are indirectly addressed, as in the case of chapter 1's study of national budgeting, or even directly challenged, as in the irrigation case study of chapter 5. To put it another way, few of the narrative policy analyses of this book have been well received by their intended clients. It is not popular to recommend, as those chapters do, that the pesticide industry fund environmental groups, that universities contract with animal welfare groups to design alternatives to animal subjects, that agribusiness finance environmental organizations concerned with water quality, or that environmentalists abandon the global warming scenario, even if it turns out the scenario is true.

The all-too-common lament that we must first understand power relations in order to challenge them has it backwards. If the above insight and its corollary are correct, we confront power, whether we intend to or not, every time we generate a metanarrative whose claim to policy relevance is that it reconceives the policy narratives of the day as if their time had passed, as if their story is a different story than the one of uncertainty, complexity, and polarization that first interested us. Instead of looking to the past to understand power relations today, the narrative policy analyst looks to the future in the form of a metanarrative that recasts the givens and status quo in a different light, no matter how temporary and transient that new narrative contender may be. As the chapters show, narrative policy analysis does not dispense with historical analysis. Those who say, however, that history is essential to analysis have, in narrative analytical terms, only started the analysis.

Does Narrative Policy Analysis Reduce the Technical Uncertainties Driving a Controversy? Nothing in the approach reduces or resolves the technical uncertainties and complexities underlying the policy narratives that animate science, technology, and environmental controversies. Global warming and malathion applications are still environmentally uncertain, irrigation continues to be technically complex, while animal research and Native American remains in museums persist as polarized issues. A narrative analysis may show, as in chapter 3, how uncertainty is increased at the metanarrative level and thus indicate a way for policymakers to reduce that uncertainty; but nothing in the four steps of the approach guarantees that uncertainty will be reduced, complexity simplified, or consensus reached across polarized groups. What this book's approach does do, however, is identify that other story, if there is one, which turns out to be more tractable to analysis and policymaking. At best, what a narrator seeks in a metanarrative is a way that jump-starts decision making, at least until that time when the metanarrative itself comes under attack by polarizing and complexifying positions.

There are costs in doing so. Objections have been raised to narrative policy analysis, though these objections are the same as those leveled against conventional policy analysis. It is useful here to pursue for a moment some of the more important complaints, as they lead directly to the ethical issues associated with the approach. First and foremost, the four steps of a narrative policy analysis do not free the analyst from sample size and misreporting problems that confound practicing policy analysts and literary critics alike. The approach is not a mechanical exercise of adding story to nonstory (or counterstory) and getting metanarrative. As in the practice of policy analysis and literary criticism, much depends on the analyst. That different analysts could come up with different metanarratives, depending on the type of nonstory or counterstory used, is quite similar to the difficulty analysts have when developing scenarios based on different statistical packages or methods of economic analysis, each of which offers advantages the others do not.

Some have objected to the approach for the same reason they do not like conventional policy analysis or contemporary literary theory: they disagree with the policy implications drawn. Others prefer never to move beyond culture critique, some loathe the thought of sitting down with pesticide manufacturers, military analysts, and agribusiness, while others think themselves above the fray of having to follow up the policy implications of their analyses.

To others, the approach means "working within the system." As one well-known social critic put it when I explained narrative policy analysis, "But, but . . . that just props up the corrupt system that got us into this mess!" Earlier remarks on power and politics, the givenness of uncertainty, and the dilemma of critique show why he is wrong. For a narrative policy analyst, it is the givenness of uncertainty, complexity, and polarization that is the "mess," not a "system" of power and politics. The science, technology, and environmental controversies that are the focus of any narrative policy analysis result not from some kind of systemic corruption that, whether intended or not, has duped us in believing all manner of false polarizations, ersatz uncertainties, and kitsch complexity. In the givenness of everyday life, the truth is not known, the science is uncertain, the polarization is there. And even if there were a system of power and politics at work, we scarcely understand it until it is challenged with an alternative, not with critiques that serve only to reinforce the system because they have no program to replace it.

Just as conventional policy analysis is criticized for being too quantitative, some object to the systematization of narrative analysis into steps, arguing that the analyses of narratives, like narratives themselves, are open-ended and indeterminate. There is no pretension, however, that the approach offered here is High Theory. The book makes no claim that its approach "transcends" the policy narratives it describes. The four steps of a narrative policy analysis, just as its goal of stabilizing the assumptions for decision making, are themselves a narrative. So too at times are the aspects of uncertainty, complexity, and polarization narrativized for the purposes of taking decisions (as in the global warming scenario of chapter 6). This is to say the book's approach is underwritten by the very same consequentialism and pragmatism that drive conventional policy analysis and policymaking: Does the approach offer insights? Does it make the controversy being analyzed more understandable and tractable to decision making? The approach does not guarantee finding a metanarrative, nor, if one is found, is there any reason to believe it will be final, definitive, and totalizing. Today's metanarratives are tomorrow's policy narratives, to be superseded at some later date. Metanarratives are small-*a* answers that give us room to maneuver on an issue that has hitherto been treated as so uncertain, so complex, and so polarized that it affords little or no movement whatsoever.

There is a final cost to narrative policy analysis, if cost is the right word, and it takes us to the heart of the approach's ethical implications. To undertake a narrative policy analysis is not merely to start with the uncertain, complex, and polarized. It is to legitimate and maintain that uncertainty, complexity, and polarization. This ratification goes well beyond the fact that the technical uncertainties underlying a controversy are not reduced: narrative policy analysis *requires* uncertainty, complexity, and polarization as a continuing precondition for analysis.

The approach needs uncertainty and complexity, because without them there would be no policy narratives to underwrite and stabilize the assumptions for decision making. Without policy narratives there is nothing for narrative policy analysis to analyze. The approach needs polarization because without polarization there would be no binary contraposition around which to semiotically frame the comparison of story and nonstory/counterstory into a metanarrative. The spectacle of opposing parties so polarized that one camp defines itself entirely in terms of being opposed to the other—a polarization disabling and paralyzing to so many analysts and critics—is for narrative policy analysts exactly the contraposition with which semiotics and narratology have made them comfortable. In narrative policy analysis, polarization is treated as an opportunity, not a barrier, for further analysis and policy relevance, the chance to reread polar opposites into a different story from the one about the contraposition of opposing parties.

Conventional policy analysis, indeed much of contemporary social and cultural studies, has long needed approaches that do not shy away from uncertainty, complexity, and polarization but in fact thrive on them and see them as the basis for action, not paralysis. Indeed, what appeals most to the average analyst about this approach is the prospect of rendering seemingly intractable problems into ones more amenable to solution (read: uncertainty reduction, complexity simplification, and depolarization) through conventional policy analytical means.

That said, the notion that there are positive, functional, and policy-relevant uses to which uncertainty, complexity, and polarization can be put, even indirectly, is a bitter pill for analysts to swallow. This is especially true for those whose training and professional experience have been centered around the belief that the uncertain, the complex, and the polarized represent the problem, not the means to a solution. Policy analysts, like most readers, believe that the best way to deal with a divisive, ambiguous problem is to compromise, to find some points of consensus with which to bridge differences.

Those who come from such background will find something faintly unprofessional about being told to accept uncertainty, complexity, and polarization and use them more expediently. The hint of unprofessionalism is even stronger when one is told that the narrative policy analyst encourages marginalized voices in a controversy to speak up, to tell their own stories, on the grounds that the more policy narratives there are, the better idea about metanarratives, if any, they generate. That opens the floodgates to even more uncertainty, complexity, and polarization, or so it is claimed.

For those of us on the independent Left, the phrase "to give voice to marginalized groups" has continued appeal. What I have in mind, though, requires a greater tolerance of polarized groups than many along the ideological spectrum want to muster. It means tolerating intolerant environmentalists and animal rights advocates. It means understanding that those who work in agribusiness, the pesticides industry, or national budgeting are more powerless in the face of uncertainty and complexity than most suppose. It means accepting that some military analysts do have a good story to tell and deserve a hearing. For the narrative policy analyst, tolerance is not ideologically pure in its persistent regard for voices that have been marginalized. Tolerance is a position the analyst comes to by treating policy narratives seriously and then has to fight to keep, given the pressure to choose sides and become part of the very polarization, uncertainty, and complexity whose metanarrative the analyst is trying to derive. In no way is tolerance an easy skepticism that starts off each analysis or a comfortable relativism that can always critique any position whatsoever as factually errant, foundationally shallow, and reflexively immature.

Why be tolerant at all? Because the analyst cares enough about uncertainty, complexity, and polarization to want to do something about them, but is wise enough to know that there is no one and true answer. Because indifference is the opposite of tolerance and the analyst cannot be indifferent to the uncertain, complex, and polarized in these disputes. (Who, after all, can run the risk of having one group dominate over all the others in controversies characterized by so many unknowns, so much disagreement, and such high contingency?) Because, in short, the positions taken in a controversy may ultimately represent incommensurable values *and*—this is the important part—because incommensurability does not mean the positions are therefore incomparable. They can be compared and contrasted, at least for the purposes of generating another narrative altogether, one that could be more helpful than any of the positions on their own, but one that in no way slights their incommensurability.

Isaiah Berlin reminds us that the fact "that the values of one culture may be incompatible with those of another, or that they are in conflict within one culture or group or in a single human being at different times—or, for that matter, at one and the same time—does not entail relativism of values, only the notion of a plurality of values not structured hierarchically. . . ."[8] For Berlin, there is "no overarching standard or criterion . . . available to decide between, or reconcile . . . wholly opposed moralities." Yet this pluralism of incommensurable and incompatible values does entail a metanarrative of sorts, and one that speaks to tolerance in the face of uncertainty. The "best one can do is to try to promote some kind of equilibrium, necessarily unstable, between the different aspirations of differing groups of human beings." This

> precarious equilibrium that will prevent the occurrence of desperate situations, of intolerable choices—that is the first requirement for a decent society; one that we can always strive for, in the light of the limited range of our knowledge, and even of our imperfect understanding of individuals and societies. A certain humility in these matters is very necessary.

I would only add, a humility not just "necessary" but actively pursued in the pages that follow.

1

Deconstructing Budgets, Reconstructing Budgeting:
Contemporary Literary Theory and Public Policy in Action

Text and reading. What, you might well ask, do these have to do with making policy and its analysis more useful? The answer: Text and reading are core to contemporary literary theory's focus on the narrative, and this theory and focus prove immensely helpful in addressing the major policy issues of our day. To see how, we consider one of those issues that confronts readers in the United States and elsewhere, namely, the worldwide disarray in national budgeting systems.

This chapter is a first step toward understanding chapter 2's discussion of what a policy narrative is. I show that even a rudimentary understanding of contemporary theory can improve our understanding and making of public policy.

The Problem

It is not just the so-called Third World countries that cannot cope budgetarily, but the United States as well. We here in the States have had an increasingly hard time keeping to the federal budget. "How we Americans used to deride the 'banana republics' of the world for their 'repetitive budgeting' under which the budget was reallocated many times during the year, until it became hardly recognizable. . . . Yet resolutions that continue last year's funding for agencies, for want of ability to agree on this year's, are becoming a way of life in the United States," as Aaron Wildavsky put the problem a decade ago.[1] Since then, Wildavsky has argued that continuously remaking the national budget "has now become standard practice in relatively rich nations."[2]

Descriptions of national budgeting systems occur again and again in the work of Aaron Wildavsky, particularly *The Politics of the Budgetary Process, Budgeting: A Comparative Theory of Budgetary Processes,* and Naomi Caiden and Wildavsky's *Planning and Budgeting in Poor Countries.*[3] These documents are regarded as the most influential post–World War II books on U.S. budgeting and comparative budgeting generally and provided some of the most recent information we have had on national budgeting systems.[4] I have distilled seven major features of current national budgets from this material. After discussing these features, I draw out some of their important implications. The seven features underscore why current budgetary practice has a great deal in common with contemporary literary practice, in particular, deconstruction.

A qualification before proceeding further. What follows is not a comprehensive review of the literature on government budgeting. What is reviewed scarcely touches on the project implementation and program evaluation literatures. The sole aim of the next section is to distill features of budgeting that reproduce concerns in a field we normally in no way associate with budgeting, namely, literary theory.

Key Features of National Budgets

Budgets are, first of all, texts. Usually budgetary figures are "embodied in a document that may be called the budget, but the budget is much more than that. It is the outcome of a process," comments one expert.[5] Yet for all the accent on budgetary process and politics in the political science literature, the budget as written text is virtually always the starting point in that literature. Almost unavoidably, the first chapter of *The Politics of the Budgetary Process* begins, "In the most literal sense, a budget is a document, containing words and figures, which proposes expenditures on certain items."[6] So central is the printed budget to our understanding of what government is all about that the inability to publish a national budget is easily one of the best measures we have of a government whose very existence is under threat.[7] Politically plagued Angola, for example, apparently did not publish a budget for years.[8]

National budgeting extends, of course, beyond the written word. Budgeting is a way to set priorities, a mechanism for expenditure control, a means of staff coordination, and more. Still, the printed budget and its documentation remain core even to these other efforts. The national budget is, in reality, often not just one published text but many. The Government of Kenya's budget, for instance, has been a set of publications covering annually its development estimates, recurrent estimates, supplementary estimates, ministerial budget speech, revenue estimates, and survey of current and future economic conditions. The U.S. federal budget has, in contrast, summarized many of these same topics in two documents, the budget and its appendix. In addition, each of the conventional stages of the budget process—compilation, approval, execution, and audit—requires its own documentation. The more or less dispersed nature of the printed budget within and over its various stages and functions has profound implications for how closely budgets, money, and power are related, as we shall see.

Budget texts are increasingly fictional. National budgets are notorious for trying, by way of figures and statistics, to simplify, quantify, and commodify into commensurable units a reality that revolts against such reductionism. The fictional character of national budgets also derives from areas other than this inherent problem of using numbers on the page to refer to things out there. For Caiden and Wildavsky,

> the failure of budgets to have predictive value, that is, to calculate expected national income accurately, to relate expenditures to it over the year, to allocate these resources to various purposes, and to have them spent as authorized is a noteworthy phenomenon in many poor countries. To speak of a budget as "a great lie" . . . is sometimes no exaggeration.[9]

The description still holds for many Third World countries and now presents a fair picture of parts of the U.S. federal budget as well.[10] The more written texts there are to the national budget, the more the sense of fiction amplifies this sense not of lies or deliberate distortion as much as drastic simplification and inherent nonreferentiality. For instance, substantial differences have existed between what was printed in the five-year National Development Plan of the Government of Kenya (GoK) and what the GoK eventually budgeted in its three-year forward budget, between that printed forward budget and what was eventually budgeted annually in the published estimates, between what the ministries formally requested to have budgeted in the annual estimates and what was finally allocated them by way of official treasury warrants, between that allocation and the documented funds made available to be spent, and between what was available and what audit reports subsequently show was in fact spent.[11]

Budget texts have no author. Casual observers would likely say a national budget is produced by anonymous decision makers on behalf of "government." More fundamentally, though, a national budget has no author. Budgetary priorities are often implicit and emerge from the push and pull of decision making and bargaining.[12] "The budget that emerges from this process is nobody's ordering of preferences," as one long-time observer put it. "It does not conform in all its particulars to any [Congress] Member's comparative preferences, let alone those of a congressional majority."[13] The same point is made by Wildavsky: There "is no one person, the president and congressional leaders included, who is charged with the task of dealing with the 'budget as a whole' and who is able to enforce his preferences." "After a number of entitlements and tax expenditures have been decided upon at different times, usually without full awareness of the others, implicit priorities are produced *ipso facto* [in the budget], untouched, as it were, by human hands."[14] The budgets we are talking about, in other words, have many narrators, but few, if any, authors.

The texts are open to (mis)reading only. There is probably no better or more universal example of the inherent conflict between readerly and writerly versions of a text, to use Roland Barthes' distinction, than national budgets. According to Barthes, readerly texts are those that call for a reader who is "serious," that is, one who is "intransitive . . . [and] left with no more than the poor freedom either to accept or reject the text"; writerly texts, on the other hand, require a reader who is "no longer a consumer, but a producer of the text."[15] When it comes to national budgets, a government's chief executive or treasury would prefer their world to be full of readerly (take-it-or-leave-it) budgets. From the treasury's perspective, its budgets should be unquestioned and unchanged by the audience for which they are intended, namely, civil servants whose task it is to treat budgets seriously by spending only what is budgeted on only those activities budgeted. Such budgets are, in short, "authorized" texts.[16]

In practice, many governments produce writerly (always revisable) versions of a national budget. A host of government departments and decision makers rewrite the budget once it is published, best evidenced by all those "unauthorized" operations found across rich and poor nations alike, for example, widespread misappropriations, underexpenditures, overexpenditures, uncontrollable expenditures, and failed implementation (more about budget-induced implementation failure in chapter 2).[17] Much of this revision is carried out unofficially and in the form of reinterpretation; much is officially sanctioned and in the form of amendment. Both forms go by the name *repetitive budgeting.* Under this budgetary practice, the "budget is not made once and for all when estimates are submitted and approved. Rather, as the process of budgeting is repeated, it is made and remade over the course of the year.... The entire budget is treated as if each item were supplemental, subject to renegotiation at the last minute.... Its most extreme manifestation is as cash-flow budgeting where changes may be made from day to day or even from one hour to the next."[18]

Governments are understandably reluctant to admit how widespread repetitive budgeting is, but one candid admission comes from the Government of Kenya in its *Report and Recommendations of the Working Party on Government Expenditures:*

> Finally, but perhaps most damaging to the effectiveness of Government, many policies agreed by Cabinet have been unnecessarily delayed or distorted during implementation. An examination of the policy chapter in the current Development Plan reveals that little work has yet been done to implement about half of the Cabinet decisions recorded there. Delays in implementation often cost Government millions.... A careful review of the Reports of the Controller and Auditor-General reveals a systematic tendency in many ministries of ignoring financial regulations and instructions from the Treasury. Indeed, the proliferation of Treasury circulars on many aspects of financial management and responsibility testifies to the breakdown in management in the Public Service.[19]

Note the reference to the "proliferation" of budget documents. Each document in this proliferation is itself a reminder of the aforementioned gap between what starts on paper and what ends in practice. The more documents there are, the greater the gap seems, and the greater the sense of breakdown in public management under the writerly revision of national budgets.

Budgets are by definition intertextual. One year's budget infiltrates and is infiltrated by earlier budgets. Vincent Leitch, in his early book on poststructuralist criticism, put the matter generally:

The predecessor-texts themselves operate intertextually, meaning that no first, pure, or original text ever can or did rule over or delimit the historical oscillations at play in texts. Thus all texts appear doubled: they are uncontrollably permeated with previous texts.[20]

The subject of intertextuality is taken up in chapters 6 and 7. Here note only that national budgets are interwoven with many documents in the same manner as Leitch describes. They interpenetrate each other not only because a given annual budget is itself a set of interconnected documents frequently referring to and depending upon the others for that year. Equally important, budgets are publications produced incrementally in a series over time, where in many cases this year's proposed figures are contrasted on the same page with last year's figures for the same item. A national budget is really one long, multiyear compendium, where each new annual budget gives its readers the opportunity to reinterpret it as well as preceding annual budgets in light of each other.

The terms within the text define each other. Budgets live and breathe semiotic contraposition. Each and every item budgeted defines and is defined by all other items through the budget total. More money for x means less money for y, if the two items are to equal the budget total, z.[21] In the past, this contraposition of x being defined by what it is not, namely, y, has been reinforced by a wider contraposition between budget guardians (those conservers of the budget such as the treasury) and budget advocates (those spenders of the budget whose expenditures the treasury was meant to control):

> [A]gencies are advocates of their own expenditures, not guardians of the nation's purse. . . . And the job of the finance ministry is to see that they don't get it. . . . Each role implies its opposite; guardianship expects advocacy to provide a choice among items to cut, and advocacy needs guardianship to supply at least tacit limits within which to maneuver. . . . [These] spending-saving roles are one of the constants of budgeting.[22]

Less constant today, however, under repetitive budgeting. As Wildavsky and his colleagues have made clear, worldwide inflation, recession, and pervasive economic uncertainty have over time fueled the dispersal and erosion of the underlying trust, expectations, and rules of the game that once made budgets predictable, readerly texts.

As a result, a profound gap exists today between what we thought the budget text was and what it now is. Many still expect a national budget to have figures that are more or less accurate, priorities that are more or less deliberately chosen, and an implementation that is more or less as stated. Yet, the reality is that national budgets have been and are now being rewritten in a writerly fashion all over the place. Repetitive budgeting is not merely contrary to the expectation of many, it is at every point orthogonal to that expectation. Published figures, priorities, and plans have no stable interpretation and mean nothing apart from their readers' rewriting, the only constant of this revision being its repetitive nature.

Policy Implications of Repetitive Budgeting

Where do the seven features get us? If the budgeting literature is correct in identifying these features, then repetitive budgeting is a deconstructive practice that treats budgets primarily as texts whose reading is always open-ended, if not undecidable. The political and institutional implications are considerable.

Budgets, Power, and Income. Because repetitive budgeting is an unstable process, the conventional link between money and power is drastically altered. True, the older syllogism still holds: money is power, budgets are money, so budgets represent power. It is realized in a vastly different way than before, however. The power we see in repetitive budgeting is that of different budget (re)writers at different times and in different ways remaking the budget, in whole and in part.[23] Budgetary power is dispersed and fragmented, and the ability to make or influence decisions—that is, to interpret action and act upon such interpretations—is spread through the budget process. Yes, material interests matter, but they matter all over the place and in many competing ways.

Moreover, this interpretative power is dispersed *precisely* in terms familiar to deconstructionists. Contrary to received wisdom, there is no Grand Author articulating national budgets. Instead, budget texts are multiple, intertextual, and constantly revised and altered by their readers. Just as the reader has a major say in what the literary text means, so too for readers of the budget text in repetitive budgeting. In repetitive budgeting, this power of readers to "reinterpret" is quite literally, as the saying has it, "good as money."

One important question to ask is how the fragmentation and dispersal of budgetary power affect a country's distribution of income. Are writerly national budgets with multiple interpretations and revisions more associated with oppression and income inequality than readerly budgets of single interpretations? My several years of advising experience in Kenya and Botswana suggest otherwise. (I once wrote a handbook on Government of Kenya budgeting for its Ministry of Finance and Planning;[24] while in Botswana I guided one district's capital budget over the course of three years.)

Botswana is an African nation whose Ministry of Finance and Development Planning has been able to exercise great control and strict discipline over how the government budget is read and interpreted there. In contrast, Kenya's Treasury has been less successful in controlling the multiple readings of its budget.[25] Although both countries have been fairly stable politically, Botswana has less government oppression and has clearly been more democratic than Kenya (for example, Botswana has a working multiparty political system, unlike Kenya's authoritarian one-party state).

Yet Botswana is considered to have one of the most unequal income distributions in Africa, where a minority of the population owns and controls the majority of the countryside's productive resources (namely, cattle). This is in large part the result of the Botswana elite ensuring that government budgetary expenditures and policies favor its cattle-owning interests. On the other hand, Kenya's pattern of budgetary misappropriations, overexpenditures, and uncontrollable expenditures (particularly the growth in public sector employees and wages) has often been said to have benefited many Kenyans at all levels, urban and rural, rich and poor.

Obviously, data are required to buttress this argument that writerly budgets do not always correlate with economic favoritism and readerly budgets do not always correlate with a fair distribution of income. The more general point here is that Kenya, as indeed many other countries with repetitive budgeting, confirms that the old budget adage, "Whoever controls the budget, controls policy," still holds, but not as before. Budgets shape policies and budgets are shaped by people—only today it is not just the government hierarchs who write the national budget and its associated fiscal, monetary, and income policies but increasingly people throughout government.

Money, Knowledge, and Learning. The generation of knowledge and learning in today's national budgetary process closely parallels a point poststructuralist J.-F. Lyotard has made about money and learning in general:

> It is not hard to visualize learning circulating along the same lines as money, . . . [where] the pertinent distinction would no longer be between knowledge and ignorance, but rather, as is the case with money, between "payment knowledge" and "investment knowledge"—in other words, between units of knowledge exchanged in a daily maintenance framework . . . versus funds of knowledge dedicated to optimizing the performance of a project.[26]

Lyotard's distinction between payment and investment matches the fairly common convention (although not one found in the U.S. federal budget) of dividing an overall national budget into two, one for capital or development (that is, investment) funds and the other for recurrent or operating (that is, maintenance) funds. What occurs in practice, however, is that some well-known "recurrent-maintenance" items show up in the capital budget, while some equally well-known "capital-investment" items appear in the recurrent budget.[27] A national budget, in other words, invariably cites some items "out of context" and in ways we do not usually "know" them. In this sense national budgets illustrate perfectly Derrida's argument that "[e]very sign, linguistic or non-linguistic, spoken or written . . . , in a small or large unit, can be *cited*, put between quotation marks; in so doing it can break with every given context, engendering an infinity of new contexts in a manner which is absolutely illimitable."[28] We at times *learn* something new about budgeting (and its limits) when such budgetary citations occur, that is, when what we have *known* to be typically one budget's item shows up as an item in a different budget. Or to bring the point back to Lyotard by analogy, the narrative economy of that text called "learning" can be conceived as financed and circulated through several budgets, each of which, taken separately, accounts for different kinds of "knowledge," and which, taken together, account for "learning."

Interpreting Budgets as Answers. Repetitive budgeting is not only unstable; some have described it as profoundly destabilizing. It corrodes the commonweal and undermines the fisc, just as deconstruction has been described as "tirelessly on the move, challenging, . . . attacking, unfixing, undercutting, . . . undermining, . . . unsettling, dismantling, . . . [and] subverting" the way we have conventionally read texts.[29] Such a view, however, misses the very equivocal nature of the destabilization at work in repetitive budgeting.

In practical terms, the continual process of rewriting a national budget treats each new revision as "an answer" to the questions posed for budget readers by the previous revision(s). Budgets are answers to problems, but answers that raise more questions, whose answers in turn raise other questions.... Answers, again, are not final. Indeed, within the context of repetitive budgeting, the ability of each new revision to stabilize the assumptions for decision making proves just as destabilizing as the questioning that give rise to that revision in the first place. To revise the budget is to ratify the readers' process of calling it into question, while calling into question is a process that cannot survive without answers. The very act of asserting that questions have answers, that texts have interpretations, that there can be assumptions for decision making, makes that act as subversive as the doubt that precedes and follows it. If an important part of our knowledge of what constitutes a "question" is what would count as an "answer" to it, then repetitive budgeting's elevation of unceasing questioning to the status of a raison d'être entails also a heightened recognition that these questions must have some kind of answers—otherwise they would not qualify as "questions." Repetitive budgeting is equally stable moments, question asking, and answer giving, each constantly destabilizing the other.

History and Repetitive Budgeting. "History," as Leitch puts it, "is substitution."[30] So too for the role of history in repetitive budgeting. Drawing "the lessons of history," in our budget example, assumes only that other times held other persons in other circumstances that we can think of as alternative to the current situation and which, because they are alternative, entail consequences for the present.[31] History, that is, is only useful if we think it full of alternatives to our own present. If it weren't, then history is literally "of little or no consequence." Let me give a brief illustration.

One of the more dismal findings of the last twenty-five years of social science evaluation of major, government-sponsored development programs is that they all too often do not perform as planned. The gap between a program being proposed and its actual initiation, between its getting started and its completion, and between its having been completed and its utilization as planned is wide, particularly in countries with repetitive budgeting, as mentioned earlier.[32] Two findings from this history of program failure are frequently offered up as necessary, though not sufficient, conditions for increasing the chances that a program will be realized as initially proposed: program design should be kept simple, it is said, and the number of steps in program implementation should be minimized.[33] If this is the case, then at a minimum these lessons of the historical record provide selection criteria for choosing programs worth evaluating. After all, so the argument goes, why waste time evaluating programs that do not have in place even one important necessary condition for improved project implementation?[34]

Many donor agencies and governments believe otherwise. They conclude that every major development program should be evaluated "in light of history." They would rather believe that "history" determines the course of development programs than that it provides alternatives to the way we select programs whose course is worth determining. For if what is really important about history is that it provides us alternatives, then the corollary is that the present itself becomes an alternate reading of what could have happened instead.[35] This is a conclusion that many government and donor officials simply will not accept (at least, such has been my experience working with some dozen of the major lenders and donors). It is unacceptable to them that any specific evaluation criterion, as with any interpretation of any text, is but one draw from a set of all possible criteria or interpretations of that text, such that each criterion or interpretation in that set has a number of possible alternatives. Thus, were the alternative criteria recommended above actually adopted as proposed, doing so would in no way erase other alternatives to it, including the ones its adoption displaced. Evaluative criteria, as such, necessarily conflict, though that conflict itself need not be intractable. All this should become clearer in chapter 7.

Contrary to the view of historical determinists, it is precisely history, or at least history as the repository of alternatives, that gives the present its sense of contingency. It is this sense of high contingency that is expressed so clearly in the givenness of extreme uncertainty, complexity, and polarization that are the starting points of the controversies analyzed in *Narrative Policy Analysis.*

The Major Policy Implication of Deconstructing Comparative Budgeting. Understanding the nature of repetitive budgeting helps us better address at least one important issue currently facing the field of comparative budgeting. As almost anyone who has worked with the major donors knows, a particular budgetary preoccupation has been to identify measures with which to compare the effectiveness of national budgets across governments or across ministries within a government. To date, the search has focused on indices such as the percentage of the national (ministerial) budget devoted to government salaries or to all operating costs, the assumption being that the higher the former percentage, the less effective the budget (that is, more money for salaries means less money to support those services supplied by the salaried). For a variety of reasons, widespread adoption of these measures has not occurred, and the search for alternatives continues.

If the above analysis is correct, then the analyst would be advised to spend less time trying to find effectiveness measures and more time on how "effectiveness" is interpreted by those undertaking the search. The very word, *effectiveness*, gives the game away. We are back once again to the command model of Grand Author, with the executive, be it the treasury, the president, or parliament, determining the one-and-only reading of the text. In this take-it-or-leave-it model, an effective government budget, whether one likes it or not, is a budget whose documentation is open to only a few interpretations, is read seriously, and has figures that are reiterated with little or no alteration. Consider each feature in turn. "Effectiveness" is where readers read the budget in the same way and where that reading, while it may not be definitive, is final; it is a budget whose readers treat it seriously, since what good is having one agreed-upon interpretation if the interpretation says the budget is a fraud or the wish list not worth the paper it is printed on? An effective budget is one whose documentation repeats the same or similar sets of figures. Factors may necessitate changing the budget figures, for example, a shortfall in revenue, but the principle holds even more in such circumstances. The more a given year's estimates change over time or between documents—that is, the less predictable the authorized, command model—the less effective the budget perceived by the Grand Author is.

"Making a budget effective" in these three senses stands as the polar opposite to the practice of repetitive budgeting with its multiple interpretations and its ultimate dismissal of anything like a Grand Author. Budgetary effectiveness is, in other words, a kind of readerly (not writerly) reading, having much less to do with percentages and indices than is commonly supposed. This, in turn, entails a radical reorientation in comparative budgeting. Budgetary effectiveness is a way of reading budget documents. Comparative budgeting is an exercise less in quantification than in textual or narrative analysis.

How does this help budgeters? If budgetary effectiveness and "authorized" readerly budgets go hand in hand, then changes in the kinds of "authors" imply changes in the way we see effectiveness. Government budgets could, for example, be read as if they were national intelligence estimates and government budgetary crises as if they were the intelligence failures to which governments around the world are prone.[36] Determining what it means to fail to read intelligence information "correctly" helps us in turn to understand better that just as intelligence failures are inevitable, so too are "lapses" in budgetary effectiveness. That is, even in readerly budgeting, lapses in effectiveness are possible. Lapses are also possible simply because budgets are in the first instance quite literally read as a system of accounts, and, as March and Olsen remind us,[37] "any system of accounts is a roadmap to cheating on them." In short, readerly budgets are programmed for lapses; they are their own guide to ineffectiveness. As such, the problem with readerly and writerly budgets is not their lapses in effectiveness (we see now that readerly is a guide to writerly) as much as the fact that writerly budgets are tolerant of multiple interpretations, while readerly ones are intolerant of conflicting interpretation. Tolerance, not effectiveness, is the real issue. We return to the wider implications of this point for tolerance in the conclusion of this book.

Final Point

Major policy issues, if national budgetary crises are any guide, provide fertile ground for poststructuralist literary theory, such as deconstruction. As we will see in later chapters, structuralist theories of narratology and semiotics also prove highly applicable. In both cases, policy implications can be drawn and recommendations made, a point we return to throughout this book.

The combined focus on "texts" and on multiple "readings" directs us to those areas of structuralist and poststructuralist literary theory more intimately concerned with the analysis of narrative. What narrative analysis has to offer conventional policy analysis is best introduced by demonstrating how analysts can more usefully examine the many policy narratives that populate policymaking, a topic to which we now turn.

2

What Are Policy Narratives?
Four Examples and Their Policymaking Implications

Let us start by defining "public policy" broadly, to cover not just macro-level planning and decision making, but other public sector interventions, including field projects, departmental programs, sectoral strategies, and bureaucratic reform. If we take this to be policy, then policy narratives are the armature of everyday life in government.

What, though, are policy narratives? The short answer is that for our purposes policy narratives are stories (scenarios and arguments) which underwrite and stabilize the assumptions for policymaking in situations that persist with many unknowns, a high degree of interdependence, and little, if any, agreement.

There is no better way to start understanding the role and function of policy narratives than by exploring those flash points where policy narratives are criticized most vehemently. No one, for instance, has a good word for blueprint development. The notion that Third World rural development policy can be cut whole-cloth from already available plans and scenarios (narratives, if you will) has been taken to task by many critics.[1] Invariably, the remedy recommended is to abandon blueprint development in favor of a learning process approach, one that conceives development not as already established narratives, but as trial and error, where policies are hypotheses and what is called "failure" is part of a broader learning curve.[2] The comparative advantage of the learning process approach is said to be its flexibility and adaptability, given that, in Goren Hyden's words, the "probability of planned actions going wrong is high in an environment characterized by instability and uncertainty," as is the case for much of the developing world.[3] Unfortunately, the last point undermines, rather than reinforces, the purported advantages of the learning process approach.

The reasons why we do not learn more from past rural development plans and policies are precisely the same reasons why we cannot plan better policies for the future. If planning and policymaking are difficult, so too must be learning, and the performance record of rural development points overwhelmingly in one direction: planning and policymaking have left much to be desired.[4] The preconditions for successful policymaking—low environmental uncertainty, stability in goals and objectives, institutional memory, and redundant resources—are also the preconditions for "learning better from experience," and it is these preconditions that are woefully lacking across wide parts of the developing world.[5] In fact, learning more and more and consequently planning better and better are exactly what has not happened in many places. Learning less and less over time while being more and more vulnerable to error characterizes some thirty years of sub-Saharan livestock policymaking, for example.[6] Those caught in its clutches find little consolation in being told that they should "embrace" error in order to learn better.[7]

The learning process approach, or some other remedy, could of course win the day. But what do development practitioners do, if blueprint development is here to stay for the time being? How can they make the best of those narratives that underwrite this development? These are the questions addressed in the case studies below. Rather than focus on how one might improve the learning process approach, this chapter argues that attention must be given to ways in which practitioners can better utilize the policy narratives that motivate blueprint development.[8] In so doing, the reader will take away from the case material a much greater appreciation of the role that policy narratives have in government. Considerable attention and detail are given in what follows to how they work, and why.

Four Policy Narratives

Our starting point is the recognition that blueprint development persists for exactly the same reason said to warrant the learning process approach: rural development is a genuinely uncertain activity, and one of the principal ways in which practitioners, bureaucrats, and policymakers articulate and make sense of this uncertainty is to tell scenarios and arguments that simplify or complexify that reality. (We will see why policymakers might want to make their narratives complex.) Indeed, the pressure to generate policy narratives about development—where, again, policy is broadly defined—is directly related to the ambiguity decision makers experience over that development. Other things being equal, the more uncertain things seem everywhere at the microlevel, the greater the perceived scale of uncertainty at the macrolevel and the greater the perceived need for explanatory narratives that can be operationalized into standard approaches with widespread application. (The Kenya land registration example below illustrates this dynamic quite nicely.) Thus, the failure of field blueprints based on policy narratives often serves only to reinforce, not reduce, the appeal to some sort of narrative that explains and addresses the persisting, even increasing, uncertainty.

These considerations raise the question, Can rural development be improved by identifying ways to make better use of those narratives that underwrite and stabilize the blueprints? To see how this is done, four policy narratives, each cast in a story format, are examined below. The examples are out of Africa, but could be from anywhere. Each narrative has persisted in the face of strong empirical evidence against its story line, and it is this persistence that can and should be exploited. The chief lesson of chapter 2 is this: when an empirically discredited policy narrative persists, efforts should shift to creating or engaging counternarratives to the more objectionable narrative or modifying that narrative to make it less objectionable. To strengthen this argument, the four examples below have been chosen because they appear at first glance to demonstrate the absolute worst in blueprint development. The blueprint persists even though (and precisely because) it has been evidentially undermined and seems to cry out for rectification through a learning process approach. In arguing that the blueprint development in question can be improved by more effectively manipulating the policy narratives upon which it is based, the examples underscore that practitioners should be giving much more attention to those narratives they know than to a learning they do not.

But, again, just what are "policy narratives"? Save for the policy critiques discussed below, our discussion is devoted to those types of policy narratives that conform to the common definition of "story." Each of the four has a beginning, middle, and end (or premises and conclusions, if cast as an argument) and revolves around a sequence of events or positions in which something is said to happen or from which something is said to follow.[9] Less hortatory and normative than ideology, policy narratives describe scenarios not so much telling what should happen as about what will happen—according to their narrators—if the events or positions are carried out as described. Even when their truth value is in question, these narratives are explicitly more programmatic than myths and have the objective of getting their hearers to assume or do something. And as already indicated, the policy narratives, at least the four discussed below, are treated by many of their narrators as continuing to retain some explanatory or descriptive power, even after a number of the points or assumptions upon which they are based are understood to be in doubt and subject to serious qualification.[10] As is the case throughout this book, how these and other features of policy narratives operate—particularly their key role in establishing and fixing the assumptions for decision making under conditions of high ambiguity—is best made clear through working out examples. We turn to four of them now.

The Tragedy of the Commons. There are a number of explanations of why people use common property resources the way they do, the most tenacious and prominent account being the tragedy of the commons. The obvious feature of the tragedy of the commons is oddly the least commented on, namely, its status as narrative. The scenario's famous expositor, Garrett Hardin, goes out of his way to tell the tragedy of the commons as a story having all the classic properties of a beginning, middle, and end. "The tragedy of the commons develops in this way. Picture a pasture open to all . . . ," begins Hardin in what must be the most-quoted passage in all of the common property literature. Soon we are in the middle of things—"the rational herdsman concludes that the only sensible course for him to pursue is to add another animal to his herd. And another. . . . But this is the conclusion reached by each and every rational herdsman sharing a commons"—and the end comes rapidly and palpably into sight: "Ruin is the destination toward which all men rush, each pursuing his own best interest in a society that believes in the freedom of the commons."[11]

Reality and story coincide imperfectly, however. When the tragedy of the commons argument is probed empirically—for example, just what evidence is there for desertification caused by overgrazing?—the data turn out to be much more ambiguous or downright contradictory.[12] Even where people agree with Hardin that range degradation is taking place and that many commons today are open-access free-for-alls, they part company over causes. For these critics, long-term climatological changes along with expanding and competing land uses have led to degradation more than has the commons. A commons which, the critics hasten to add *contra* Hardin, was frequently managed in a restricted-access, not open-access, fashion until these outside pressures of climate and competing land uses undermined local management efforts.[13]

Hardin, however, merits closer reading than some of his critics give him. "It must not be supposed that all commons are bad in all situations," he tells us; "when there were only a few million people in the world, it was all right to run the hunting grounds as a commons, though even then an area was no doubt often managed as tribal property."[14] Hardin is not saying the commons cannot be managed. Rather, "the commons, if it is justifiable at all, is justifiable only under conditions of low-population density."[15] The crux of his argument is that herders find it to their individual advantage not to cooperate in limiting herd numbers or ensuring range quality *even when* each and every herder recognizes that the overall stocking rate on the commons exceeds its carrying capacity and that range deterioration and liveweight loss are on the rise.[16] In such a situation, corrective measures are largely outside the initiative of the individual herder. Either the commons has to be legislated as private property or other coercive devices, such as taxes and user regulations, have to be instituted from the outside.[17]

If we subscribe to Hardin's full-blown argument, we should then expect to find at least two states of affairs when a rangeland tragedy of the commons is said to exist. First, even where herders agree that the range is in poor or already heavily stocked condition, they still act in a non-cooperative, competitive fashion; they evince few if any collective practices for managing that commons, which, in turn, encourages its further overutilization. Second, a tragedy of the commons supposes that a privatized rangeland will be better managed (for example, have a better range condition) than if it were a commons, other factors being equal.

The most thoroughgoing test of Hardin's full-bodied version of the tragedy of the commons is found in a series of publications based on data collected during the 1979/80 Botswana Water Points Survey.[18] These data allow us to address how applicable, if at all, each element of Hardin's argument is to rural eastern Botswana, an area of the country that has repeatedly been described as undergoing a rangeland tragedy of the commons. First, do rural Batswana themselves perceive overgrazing to be taking place? The evidence here is mixed. While the range condition was found to be at low levels in much of the heavily stocked eastern communal areas where assessed by standard range ecology measures, a number of survey households indicated that lack of rainfall, rather than increase in livestock numbers, was the major culprit in overstocking and overgrazing.[19] Yet there are sufficient grounds—in the form of acknowledged findings of low cattle carcass weight and other interview information—to suppose that a significant proportion of rural Botswana, albeit not a majority, did in fact believe that increasing numbers of livestock were leading to overutilization of the range in the 1970s and early 1980s. It was at that time, for example, that the Government of Botswana enshrined the tragedy of the commons argument as the reason for its national grazingland policy.[20]

If overgrazing is taking place, do rural Batswana cooperate in the management of their communal resources and do they have management practices to do so? An in-depth survey by Louise Fortmann of communal dams constructed in eastern Botswana between 1974 and 1980 found that this was indeed the case. Of the twenty-four dams surveyed, twenty-one had some sort of collective management, be it in the form of maintenance, regulation, and/or revenue collection. All twenty-one dam groups had users who jointly regulated the use of these dams; and restrictions on numbers of users, types of use, the manner of use, and/or the time of use were found as well.

Did communal management have a positive effect on the surrounding range condition, and if so, how did this compare to privatized resource management? An analysis of grazing conditions around a sample of forty-six water points found that those water points owned or managed by government or groups had *better* dry season range conditions than privately owned water points.[21] No one-to-one correlation was found between private ownership, private management, and the actual restriction of livestock watering access, as one might suppose to be the case from the tragedy of the commons argument.

Indeed, the finding that private rights and better range condition do not go hand in hand has been confirmed on a number of occasions in Botswana. Only three years after the first leasehold fenced ranches were occupied under the World Bank's First Livestock Development Project, two-thirds of them were already overstocked.[22] Conditions did not improve under the Bank's Second Livestock Development Project. Bekure and Dyson-Hudson found that range management and condition on these leasehold ranches was often no better than in the communal areas.[23] Also, roughly fifteen years of government grazing trials undertaken periodically from the 1950s through the 1970s could show no significant difference in range conditions between those found under various fenced rotational systems and observed under a continuous "single paddock" grazing regime approximating the communal system.[24] Moreover, communal management of the dams studied in the Water Points Survey was found not only to be *ecologically* efficient relative to the next best private alternative, but cost figures indicated that this management was *economically* efficient as well.[25] In sum, the evidence is far from conclusive that privatization of the Botswana commons increases the likelihood of improving range conditions there.

These and other negative findings have been around for some time and it is increasingly tempting to dismiss the tragedy of the commons as some kind of old-fashioned tale. To do so would be misguided. In fact, it misses the point altogether. As a policy narrative, the tragedy of the commons story continues to have considerable staying power, because these negative findings and critiques in no way dispel the chief virtue of that narrative. Like the policy narratives discussed throughout *Narrative Policy Analysis*, this one helps to underwrite and stabilize the assumptions for decision making. Policymakers resort to the tragedy of the commons model in order to understand what is going on and what must be done in lieu of more elaborate and demanding analysis, particularly when such analysis leads only to doubts and uncertainties about just what the story is behind rural resource utilization. Critiques of the tragedy of the commons are doubly troublesome for the decision maker, since they generate, rather than reduce, uncertainty when they undermine the assumptions of decision making, while at the same time leave that decision maker without the means to make the transition from the discredited narrative to whatever is needed to replace it. In fact, the more the tragedy of the commons is critiqued and found substantively wanting, the more uncertain policymakers become—Why indeed did Batswana manage their water points collectively?—and the more pressure they feel to hold onto what scenarios they have, no matter how worn around the edges they now appear. A critique, like that based on the Botswana data, never tells its own story—its point-by-point rebuttal does not have its own argument, its own beginning, middle, and end—and serves only to raise doubts that the critique itself cannot answer. (How it is that critiques are taken to be the basis for making decisions against a policy, and yet increase uncertainty and complexity in the process, becomes clear in chapter 3.)

What displaces a policy narrative like the tragedy of the commons argument is not a negative finding that seems to refute it. Refutation of a decision maker's argument for action doesn't mean you have taken away her or his perceived need to act. Rather, displacing a discredited narrative requires an equally straightforward narrative that tells a better story. The appeal of the tragedy of the commons story to livestock rangeland project designers has been its blueprinted design implications for privatizing the commons and legislating stock controls. If project designers are to reject the blueprint, they must have another story whose design implications are equally clear. If decision makers are to move beyond the model of an entirely unmanaged and open access commons, they will do so not merely by being told that reality is more complex than has been thought but also by having a counternarrative that can predict when common property management will take place and whose implications are clear to them.

Moreover, the counternarrative will have to be as parsimonious as the tragedy of the commons argument, but comprehensive enough to explain not only when management of the commons occurs but also when the tragedy takes place instead. Indeed, the ideal counternarrative for the project designer and policymaker would be like the tragedy of the commons in having to rely on nothing more sophisticated than introductory microeconomics.[26] While this conclusion will offend the social scientist intent only on undermining conventional wisdom by showing how complex the world is, dismissal of the conclusion is surely premature, as we all wait for a counternarrative—*any* counternarrative—to the tragedy of the commons that is more robust than the critiques offered up so far.[27] (Policymakers do sometimes want more from their policy narratives than just comprehensiveness and parsimony, a topic discussed and illustrated at length in chapter 7.)

Land Registration and Increased Agricultural Productivity. For the past thirty-five years or so, a potent policy narrative in Kenya and elsewhere has been that land registration leads to increased agricultural productivity. Once land is adjudicated and registered, so the argument goes, the landowner will be in a position to use the title deed as collateral for securing credit with which to invest in improving and intensifying agricultural production on the land concerned. Dating from (if not before) the blueprint laid out in the government's 1954 Sywnnerton Plan, the argument has remained extremely popular among Kenya politicians, senior civil servants, and social scientists.[28]

Empirical studies have repeatedly failed to find a positive causal link connecting the government's land registration program to expanded credit opportunities and thereby to increased agricultural productivity. Over the years, the effects of land registration in one district (Embu) have been studied in detail by different researchers, while others have undertaken point-in-time research on the same topic—much of it in the form of household surveys at the farm level—for localities in at least thirteen other districts (Meru, Nyeri, Kiambu, Kwale, Kisii, Murang'a, Taita-Taveta, Kisumu, South Nyanza, Nakuru, Kericho, Machakos, and Kakamega) covering much of the country's most agriculturally productive cropland. *All* the studies have failed to confirm or have raised serious doubts about the scenario linking land registration to agricultural production.[29] This robust finding is made even more striking by the equally demonstrated interregional ethnic and socioeconomic diversity of the country's rural households.

In contrast to the policy narrative, the cumulative picture left by research suggests that once landowners are registered, many do not bother to obtain their title deeds (they would never risk losing them on anything as uncertain as loan defaults); of those landowners who do obtain titles, not all of them do so to obtain credit (they may have to sell their land or parts of it to meet school fees and other household expenses); of those who want to use their titles to obtain loans, not all actually receive credit (farmers may not know where to go for credit or may not meet other requirements of the lending institution, which in turn might not have the funds to lend); of those landowners who actually succeed in using their titles for securing credit, a number of them use the loans for nonagricultural investments (for example, their off-farm businesses); of those new landholders taking over after the registered owners die, few reregister; and those who do not reregister or who could not legally register in the first place—mostly women—have been ineligible under the law for title-secured loans.

Nor has the problem only been one of a low conditional probability that, once registered, credit will be obtained and agriculture intensified. In some cases, land registration and increasing agricultural production may actually be negatively related. When registered, some landowners feel that (1) they can leave the land idle without fear of someone else invoking a use-it-or-lose-it principle; (2) they now have the "freedom" to sell land without real consent from those dependent on it and whose labor makes it productive; and (3) they can enter land transactions for speculation purposes only. As a result of these and other factors, several experts conclude Kenya's land registration program has increased insecurity, rather than security, of tenure in many parts of the country.[30]

Yet the recurrent finding that registration does not increase production via the credit mechanism has not changed one iota the belief of many respected Kenyans that registration has a positive and widespread effect on agriculture. What then is the policymaker to do if she or he feels compelled to pursue the topic of land registration's supposedly positive impact on agricultural productivity? One could, of course, continue to analyze the subject of agricultural credit on the hope that land registration will indeed intensify agriculture if only credit is made more timely, convenient, and adequate to more smallholders. Unfortunately, pushing credit has proven to afford about as much leverage in Kenya's agricultural sector as pushing string.[31] Another option is to explore other links between registration and agriculture that appear to have potential in offering up a counternarrative relevant for policy and program development. Land registration, for example, seems to have influenced shifts in crop mixes, land concentration, and fragmentation, and the utilization of both nonfarm income and credit for nonagricultural purposes. Nevertheless, if past research is any guide, this option will also yield mixed signals for the policymaker. Land concentration boosts agricultural productivity in one study, while another finds otherwise; some researchers describe fragmentation as an ecologically valid, risk-averse response of farmers, while other researchers focus on what they see as increasingly subeconomic holdings.[32] The policymaker who chooses this research option will have to balance the findings of increasing complexity at the microlevel with the widening scale of land problems that seem to demand standard approaches to their management.

A very different option suggests itself, however, if the operating assumption is that both the popular narrative linking registration to production and its blueprint, the government's land registration program, will persist for the foreseeable future in the absence of any viable counternarrative and regardless of empirical findings that erode their credibility. The question then becomes one of focusing the policymaker's attention on those few topics where land registration offers up some promise of actually expanding agricultural production.

One prospect stands out for many of those familiar with Kenya, namely, estimating the extent to which the implementation of a land tax could intensify agricultural production by discouraging land speculation, absentee management, uneconomic fragmentation, and nonproductive large holdings. The argument runs something like this. Existing records of the land registration program as to who is registered or holds title deed will greatly facilitate the operation of such a tax, if and when it is introduced. Moreover, it is difficult to conceive of a more efficient way to update these records for the unregistered subdivisions mentioned earlier; that is, the levy would serve as an incentive for the reregistration of land currently registered in the names of former owners, since the tax would presumably be assessed on those whose names show up in the records. Even though land taxation is controversial in Kenya, a focus on the promising positive links between registration and agriculture has the considerable merit of being consistent with the policy narrative that has hitherto resisted all manner of empirical assaults on it. Indeed, the narrative's blueprint becomes one way of altering rather than displacing the narrative itself: the existence of a huge government bureaucracy, staff, and budget, all committed to ensuring that land registration is blueprinted across the country, will inevitably increase pressure to find ways to justify their purported programmatic effect on intensifying agriculture, even if the specific mechanism for linking registration and production is no longer principally that of title-secured credit.[33]

Systems Analysis and Sectoral Integration. Systems thinking suffuses the practitioner's approach to rural development. Livestock rangeland development provides an especially good illustration of this policy narrative. Few specialists, for example, would quarrel with the following:

> Pastoral production is normally and correctly part of wider production systems; changes in any element have ramifications in all others.[34]

> Livestock production is a very complex system which has many interrelated components, such as climate, soil, plants and obviously animals operating with a high degree of interaction within a certain economic and social environment.[35]

> The fact that pastoralism needs to be seen in a regional perspective rather than an isolated production system for an understanding of the changes in living conditions of pastoralists has been pointed out.[36]

But why stop at "region"? The system entails, after a point, supraregional levels in a long chain of behavioral links which

> starts with land managers and their direct relations with the land (. . . stocking densities . . . and so on). Then the next link concerns their relations with each other, other land users, and groups in the wider society who affect them in any way, which in turn determines land management. The state and the world economy constitute the last links in the chain.[37]

Once something has evolved into this narrative of a long linked "system," description frequently becomes prescription. "A local systems approach holds the best hope of success in development for pastoralists," recommend two social scientists.[38] "The Panel recommends a *systems approach* to all phases of project planning and execution," advises a U.S. Agency for International Development (USAID) taskforce on rangeland/livestock projects.[39] For Sidahmed and Koong the moral of their systems approach is clear, that is, "any attempts towards [livestock] development should be preceded by the construction of a mathematical model which should contain all the essential elements of the current production system."[40]

As this last statement should indicate, undertaking a systems narrative can be easier than living with its implications. A development syllogism in the policy narrative seems inescapable: integrated system, integrated intervention, right? Yet as some readers well know, integrated rural development programs (particularly in the agricultural sector) have all too often been "disintegrating agricultural development."[41] Ministerial portfolios, based on apparent sectoral divisions in the political economy, do not readily accommodate the need for intersectoral coordination and integration. Moreover, once one accepts the validity of a narrative that posits a long chain of putative causality between the international economy and the local herder, the probability of finding something wrong along the way increases exponentially. Critics continually find projects that are local successes, but system failures, in a world where localized interventions, such as projects, provide little leverage in correcting what are perceived to be systemic dysfunctions. Nothing works right as a system because the conditional probability of doing so approaches the vanishing point. Development syllogism thus becomes development tautology.

Yet practitioners who object to the systems narrative in rural development risk having to retract their objection. Those who do not believe that cause gives way to effect which gives way to cause could well end up like the recanting Bishop Cranmer at the stake, saying, as he stretched his writing hand into the rising flames, This is the hand that hath offended and it shall be the first to burn. After all, what rural development practitioner is foolish enough to operate as if cause and effect had been repealed?

One recent and salutary development in systems analysis has been to introduce the distinction between tightly and loosely coupled systems. Many early integrated rural development projects were designed as tightly coupled systems, that is, everything had to occur in a sequence of steps, there was only one way to achieve the desired objective, little or no slack existed to do otherwise, and any delays or missteps rippled throughout the rest of the project cycle. What has not been sufficiently observed, however, is the loosely coupled nature of many rural develop- ment systems that set the context in which project cycles have to oper- ate, that is, environments in which delays have to be accommodated, where the order of sequence often changes, and where slack is partic- ularly evident.[42] Moris and Thom argue, for example, that irrigation scheme managers in many parts of Africa have to contend with what is best characterized as a loosely coupled system where a myriad of agen- cies, levels of authority, and formal as well as informal networks of com- munication are relevant to the manager's activities but are not coordi- nated for the purposes of management.[43]

In fact, many rural development processes are best understood as a *mix* of tightly coupled and loosely coupled systems. Another livestock range- land example from Botswana illustrates how this can be so.[44] Research found three tightly coupled levels of water use and management govern- ing any given rural water point there: the site immediately surrounding the water point, the locality in which the water point is found, and the compound locality in which the water point is located (that is, the set of different localities over which the users of that water point typically reside and work during the year).

When rural Batswana are physically at the water point, they are keenly aware of the physical condition of adjacent land as well as the physical type of water source in question (for example, boreholes, because they are mechanized, are operated differently from open wells). At the locality level, how a water point is managed and used is in turn affected by (to list several factors) the availability of labor for fetching water, which varies by locality (some household members move to the cropping fields for planting, while others, such as children who would otherwise fetch wa- ter, remain in village schools); by the locality's topography and hydro- geology; and by the locality's prevailing land uses (for example, in Bo- tswana, villages and grazing areas are typically dominated by borehole development, while mixed cropping and grazing areas frequently have had a greater variety of sources). Equally important, the operation of a specific water point has to be seen within the context of the availability and accessibility of alternative water sources in the locality.

Because members of rural households in Botswana have often shifted their household compounds over the course of the year—in the cropping season, they have gone to the "lands" where their field homes are and, after harvest, they have returned to their village homes for the rest of the year—one finds that the demand for and supply of water has shifted as well over the course of the year across the localities concerned. It is at compound locality level that the specific water point operates as part of a sequence of water points over time and space, with households falling back from many, often surface, water sources at their lands in the wet season to fewer groundwater sources in the home village during the dry (postharvest) season.

These three levels are tightly coupled when compared to those larger regional, national, and international domains pertinent to rural water use and management. The specific water point is at a site, in a locality, and within a compound locality at the same moment. Indeed, these three levels are able to be identified precisely because they share the same unit of analysis at the same time. This is not true for other levels. No one can doubt national considerations affect rural water use, for example, Botswana has relied on boreholes much more heavily than, say, has Kenya in many of its arid and semiarid lands. Similarly, international considerations clearly affect water use conditions in a given county, for example, European Economic Community (EEC) price subsidies on beef exports—which Botswana had taken advantage of, but which Kenya had not because of its relatively weaker veterinary control efforts—helped make livestock investment in Botswana a much more profitable enterprise than it had been in the comparable areas of Kenya. Yet, when moving to these higher levels, it becomes very difficult to keep as the unit of analysis the specific water point fixed in view by the three more local levels. Just how Botswana's being a borehole culture and the beneficiary of international price subsidies affects, say, one of the thousands of open wells in eastern Botswana is certainly not clear to its average user, let alone its outside observer. These other levels are, to put it another way, connected to rural water use and management, but in a loosely coupled fashion when compared to the tightly coupled processes governing the operation of any specific water point. We return to the discussion of local versus more global levels of analysis in chapter 6's case study of global warming.

What such discriminations allow one to do is to adhere to the narrative of rural development as a long linked system stretching from the local to the international, but to recognize that some systems are so loosely coupled that practitioners can treat them *as if* they were not coupled systems at all. From the standpoint of many herders, the health sector is not "integrated" with the agricultural sector, which in turn is not integrated with the wage sector . . . no matter what the government planners say or believe or feel should be the case. Indeed, much of the failure of tightly coupled integrated rural development projects becomes perfectly intelligible the moment we assume that for the typical project beneficiary, "sectors" are not integrated at all, or at least not at the local level(s) relevant to the people concerned. Ironically, this is exactly the reason why "multisectoral" programs are so needed in parts of the developing world: not because project activities are tightly coupled and functionally integrated at the sectoral level, but because multisectoral projects are in practice frequently loosely coupled and are thereby better able to adapt to the "unintegrated" nature of development. Multisectoral projects at times have had more flexibility at the local level in undertaking different projects over different geographical areas and better chances in exploiting new opportunities as and when they arise—both major advantages in an environment characterized by the uncertainty of multiple actors, objectives, and criteria for evaluating program performance.[45]

Repetitive Budgeting by National Governments. As discussed in chapter 1, disarray in government budgeting is international. Repetitive budgeting seems to be everywhere, as is the gap between what was initially budgeted and what is ultimately implemented. Indeed, it is this gap that motivates many critical accounts on why large-scale government programs fail, both here and overseas. Repetitive budgeting has itself become a policy narrative explaining all matter of "failures" from top to bottom in a country.

Facts, again, do not always accord with this narrative linking repetitive budgeting at the national level to poor project implementation at the local level. It simply is not the case, for example, that sub-Saharan governments all budget or implement alike, notwithstanding blanket phrases like "the financial crisis in Africa." As noted in the preceding chapter, the government of Botswana appears to have budgeted differently than Kenya, whose repetitive budgeting in government has not been as severe or disabling as it has been in, say, Nigeria.[46] Similarly, as difficult as budgeting has been in Kenya or Nigeria, these countries have been able to produce yearly budgets in contrast to some more politically troubled governments, like Angola. Such discriminations should be extremely important for those who believe that rural development depends in some significant measure on governmental budgetary behavior.

More empirical work on these intercountry differences is needed and would, I believe, go some way in undermining the grim narrative's depiction of chaotic national budgeting and a failed south of the Sahara. Are there other ways to weaken the narrative? Several options have already been suggested. In theory, one could try to create a counternarrative (as in the tragedy of the commons example); or use the blueprints generated by the narrative to alter it (as in the case of land registration); or fill in the "details" of the narrative in order to make it less misleading (as in the systems approach example). There are many instances, however, where the practitioner has little leeway to be creative. The best she or he can do is to engage another already-existing narrative, which, once engaged, conflicts with the more objectionable one.

A U.S. example illustrates how this has been done.[47] The California Department of Motor Vehicles (DMV) has had a reputation for long lines and slow service. The narrative of a government department palsied by red tape and paralyzed by inaction was and is still popular to some extent in the media and the public's mind. Senior DMV managers have reacted by engaging two other preexisting narratives that are also widely accepted in the United States and elsewhere, namely, the scenarios in which "computerization improves bureaucratic efficiency" and "personalized service is what really makes bureaucracies effective." In this case, the managers had DMV field operations computerized and initiated a program whereby service by appointment could be provided to those who before had to wait in line. The issue here is not whether these other narratives are accurate—in this example computerization and service by appointment did lead to some improvement—but that their story lines ran against the dominant narrative of a government bureaucracy mired in its own indifference to the needs of the people it is meant to serve. The temptation is to think of the actions of these senior managers as "public relations," but to do so would deny the highly circumscribed nature of the public arena in which they had to make decisions. That the managers maneuvered at all is a credit to them, as we will again see in chapter 3's case study of the medfly crisis.[48]

Parallel developments can be observed in government budgeting overseas. Computerization of the Government of Kenya's budget was introduced when budgeting and financial management there were widely considered to be at a low point. Pinckney, Cohen, and Leonard recount how the introduction of microcomputers into the Ministries of Agriculture and Livestock Development improved the efficiency and effectiveness of scarce, skilled managers in their budgetary process.[49] They add that "the presence of the microcomputer visibly changed the technology of financial decision-making. . . . [It] legitimized a role in financial decision-making for those who could use it, therefore making it easier for new, reform-minded individuals to participate actively."[50] Further legitimation came from the World Bank in the form of one of its elect "box" case studies for the 1988 *World Development Report:* "Overall the Ministry of Agriculture developed better management tools and information systems, aided by the introduction of microcomputers. The overall quality of agricultural programs improved markedly during this period."[51] This technology subsequently became an important part of the budget preparation exercise of the Government of Kenya treasury and the government estimates for 1985/86 were the first to be produced by microcomputer.[52] Once again, the impression, certainly among members of the donor community, was that this extension in the use of microcomputers had increased the budgetary and financial management capacity of Treasury officials and advisors.[53] While Kenya's budgeting is still acknowledged to have problems, reforms such as the introduction of microcomputers certainly helped alter its image of a repetitive budgetary process that could not be improved.

Final Note

It should be clear that blueprint and learning are not mutually exclusive, at least to the extent the latter operates within the context of the former. Counternarratives to the tragedy of the commons, for example, can and have been based on what has been learned in the field about common property resource management.[54] Also, no one is arguing that, since budget computerization seems to have worked in Kenya, it should be copied to Bolivia without learning to what extent, if at all, "computerization improves budgeting" is even a policy narrative there. The argument is not that blueprint development that suits one country suits them all, but rather the more modest claim: blueprint development can be made more suitable to the needs of a given country by first learning how to manipulate better the policy narratives that motivate these blueprints.

Such a conclusion should not be taken to mean that policy narratives are to be evaluated solely on the grounds of how well learning introduces a measure of realism into them. In the four cases discussed above, it is not a question of which narratives are more accurate or have greater verisimilitude.[55] Rather, the issue is the extent to which the policy narratives were successful in underwriting (that is, establishing or certifying) and stabilizing (that is, fixing or making steady) the assumptions needed for decision making in the face of what is genuinely uncertain and complex. As such, policy narratives can be representationally inaccurate—and recognizably so—but still persist, indeed thrive. In fact, when one narrative more than any other becomes the way we best articulate our "real" feelings or make sense of the uncertainties and ambiguities around us, then we are often willing to put up with that narrative, no matter how empirically objectionable it is in many other respects. The day may dawn when rural development and public policymaking become less uncertain and divisive. Until then, we must think more positively about how to make the best of what we already have, meager and troubling as it often is.

Identifying one way for analysts to proceed more positively is the main assignment of *Narrative Policy Analysis.* The challenge is to extend the above analysis into a systematic approach to the study of policy narratives generally. To see how, a detailed discussion of the formal analytics of narrative policy analysis follows in chapters 3 through 5. We begin by introducing the key notion of metanarratives in public policy.

Stories, Nonstories, and Their Metanarrative in the 1980–1982 California Medfly Controversy

Preliminaries

Metanarratives have gotten a very bad press lately. They are corroding and corrosive, as Lyotard and others inform us, especially if writ large—as in the Enlightenment, Science, and Rationality. *Narrative Policy Analysis*, however, is about small-*m* metanarratives, ones that do not seek to homogenize or stifle conflict. Small-*m* metanarratives are those policy narratives in a controversy that embrace, however temporarily, the major oppositions in a controversy, without in the process slighting any of that opposition. To revert to policy terminology, a metanarrative is not "consensus" or "agreement," but rather a "different agenda," which allows us to move on issues that were dead in the water on their older agendas.

This chapter and the following two deal with one kind of small-*m* metanarrative, namely, those resulting from the comparison of stories and nonstories that frequently dominate policy controversies. The case study below illustrates how the semiotic dynamic of contraposition of story and nonstory works in practice, producing a metanarrative that the public recognized but whose implications were not then fully appreciated. Chapters 4 and 5 show how contraposition can be used to create a metanarrative where one does not exist, or to discover one that is otherwise obscure. Finally, chapters 6 and 7 address a different kind of small-*m* metanarrative, ones arising from the contraposition of stories and counterstories, such as found in the global warming controversy and the debate over Native American burial remains.

What I show in this chapter is an example of people already working at the metanarrative level and the implications of this practice for policy. The best place to begin our analysis is those policy narratives that populate the lives of policymakers and analysts worldwide and which were the focus of the preceding chapter. Again, these narratives by and large follow the conventional definition of *story*. Each relates a succession of events, real or hypothetical. Such accounts of government bureaucrats and decision makers, as Martin Krieger reminds us, typically have beginnings, middles, and ends, and include plots, characters, and frequently recognizable styles of storytelling.[1] Other types of narratives, however, circulate in government which, while still called stories by their narrators, do not meet this conventional definition.

Bureaucratic critiques and circular arguments are often cast in a story format. Yet the latter have no beginning or end in a strict sense. Circular arguments look like conventional stories (they relate a succession of events and frequently specify actors), but their structure is decidedly different and to significant effect.[2] So, too, for another type of narrative, the critique, which was introduced in the last chapter and is the subject of this one. Frequently critiques of complex and uncertain policy issues take the form of point-by-point rejoinders of other, more conventionally structured scenarios and arguments about a policy issue. While critiques may have the outlines of a conventional story (the criticisms typically stay quite close to the sequence of reasoning set out in what is being critiqued), one would be hard-pressed to say they have plots or arguments of their own. If an argument is, following Bernard Shaw, the standard means whereby one discovers what one thinks by repudiating what others think,[3] then critiques are incomplete stories or, better yet, *nonstories*. They tell us what to be against without completing the argument as to what we should be for. Critiques, to put it sharply, simply don't have their own beginnings, middles, and ends.

Such comments are not intended to disparage the role of critiques or, for that matter, circular arguments in public decision making. Not every policy-relevant narrative need be conventional in having a beginning and an end or premises and conclusion. What is of more interest are the implications an analyst can draw when the issue she or he is analyzing involves policy narratives structurally different from each other. What follows is a case study of an important policy issue—the 1980–82 Medfly Controversy in California—that was dominated by two competing narratives asymmetrical in terms of their structure—one a policy narrative that closely approximated the conventional form of story, while the other was essentially a nonstory in the form of a set of critiques of the former. The specifics of the case study illustrate a more general proposition for the analysis of a complex and uncertain policy issue: although one cannot say a priori what is signified when such an issue is governed by different types of narratives, one's knowledge of these structural differences can make the issue more tractable and its policy implications clearer, even when the technical uncertainties associated with the issue continue.

Analysts taking their first look at the Medfly Controversy need only rely on their knowledge of politics, bureaucracies, and interest groups to predict, perhaps accurately, the controversy's eventual outcome. On the other hand, had the analysts actually involved in the controversy been familiar with this book's analytical approach, they would have understood better how these narratives were used to articulate the risks associated with interventions to handle the medfly. In so doing they would have identified the area where conventional policy analysis could have made a contribution to reducing that controversy's complexity and uncertainty, but did not. More generally, the significance of the Medfly Controversy lies in how its major participants, under considerable political, economic, legal, and bureaucratic pressures, used narratives, including policy narratives, as their primary means of grappling with the problem of ascertaining risk in the midst of many unknowns, high complexity, and widespread division.

My introduction touched on the ambivalent attitude many analysts and policymakers have to stories and storytelling in public life. Certainly, stories are important, even essential at times, but how do they help better address the policy problems of the day? This chapter takes us to the heart of a debate on this question.[4] Thomas Kaplan, in "The Narrative Structure of Policy Analysis" and Martin Krieger in his "Big Decisions and a Culture of Decisionmaking," both in the flagship *Journal of Policy Analysis and Management*, reaffirm the centrality of stories and the telling of stories in policymaking and the profession of policy analysis. Kaplan in particular maintains that narratives and appeals to narratives must play an important role in the profession specifically. Gideon Doron, in the same journal, disagrees: the "potential contribution of these ideas to the understanding of [the] policy phenomenon is rather small, in my opinion. . . . Krieger's and Kaplan's ideas could come only *in addition* to and not *instead* of the conventional practice" of policy analysis.[5]

This chapter, like *Narrative Policy Analysis* as a whole, proposes a different tack. Irrespective of one's views on storytelling in policymaking, the analysis of public policy must be broadened to include systematic ways of *analyzing* such storytelling. Since stories are a fact of life for practicing policy analysts, some form of rigorous narrative analysis should be available for them. This is especially so where the storytelling at issue arises largely or solely in order to articulate those recognizably complex and uncertain issues that otherwise continue to defy adequate specification by precisely those other elements found in the analyst's tool kit, namely, microeconomics, statistics, organization theory, legal analysis, and public management practice. We return to this point at the end of the chapter.

Background to the Case Study

The 1980–82 California Medfly Controversy provides an especially well-documented case study of a policy issue sufficiently complex and uncertain that its proposed "solutions" were generally acknowledged to be scenarios about what might possibly happen rather than predictions about what would happen.

Synopsis of the Controversy. In June 1980 several Mediterranean fruit flies ("medflies") were found in two widely separated counties of California, Los Angeles and Santa Clara. A Medfly Project was immediately created in the California Department of Food and Agriculture (CDFA) to deal with the outbreak. The following month a technical review committee, later known as the Technical Advisory Committee (TAC) and consisting largely of professional entomologists, was established to advise the project and the public on eradication efforts. A ground program was initiated, eventually consisting of fruit-tree stripping, localized application of pesticides, and the release of sterile medflies (known as the "sterile insect technique," whereby young male medflies were sterilized through irradiation, released as adults, and mated with wild female flies to produce nonviable eggs).

The ground program was applied to nearly 500 square miles of Los Angeles County, and eradication there was declared by mid-December, 1980. The Santa Clara infestation, however, continued to grow throughout that county and into adjacent areas, spreading from some 150 square miles at the end of September 1980 to over 200 square miles by the end of November that year. By late 1980, officials in the United States Department of Agriculture (USDA) and CDFA were maintaining that aerial spraying with a malathion and bait mixture was necessary to eradicate this infestation, which was probably more extensive than official estimates indicated. The aerial spraying proposal was strongly opposed by environmental groups, politicians, scientists, and academics (including members of the TAC), and CDFA eventually agreed to postpone action. A formal risk assessment undertaken at this time by the state's Department of Health Services (DHS) concluded, however, that the chances of such spraying causing cancer in an exposed infant were in the order of one in a million.

The ground program appeared to be effective throughout the winter, but June 1981 brought an unexplained outbreak of medflies in Santa Clara County. On 8 July, Governor Brown made the politically controversial announcement that the ground-spraying program would be greatly expanded in order to deal with the reemergence. The U.S. Secretary of Agriculture responded by threatening to quarantine the state's fruit exports if aerial spraying was not begun forthwith. On 10 July Brown gave the order to begin spraying malathion by air. Some state and international quarantines on California fruit were imposed, but eventually lifted. In September 1982, CDFA and USDA held a joint conference to declare that medfly eradication had been achieved in California. For ease of reference, a chronology of these events has been provided in appendix B.

Over $100 million was said to have been spent by federal and state authorities in eradicating the medfly during this period. Another $40 million was estimated to have been lost by state growers when other countries and states rejected California fruit. More than 1,300 square miles were sprayed weekly with malathion, and several deaths resulted from accidents attributed to or because of the aerial spraying program.[6]

Relevance of the Controversy. Apart from its high cost, the major feature of the Medfly Controversy was that there were no widely accepted or clear-cut technical and scientific reasons to favor or oppose the ground-based program, the aerial spraying program, or some combination of both. As the state's comanager of the Medfly Project put it,

> In the medfly public policy debate, the . . . technical information available to both the public and project management was constantly changing throughout the life of the project, and it was difficult or impossible for advisors and managers to accurately assess the risks and benefits associated with various technical components of the

program. . . . [Nor was the public] able to evaluate the severity of the problem or assess the degree of risk associated with the various solutions.[7]

In such a highly uncertain project environment, stories took the place of evidence and proof. Storytelling and scenarios pervaded all aspects of the controversy, a sample of which is provided in appendix C.

The focus of following sections is on an analysis and comparison of the two narratives that the key participants to the controversy considered to be central, namely, the cases put forth (1) in favor of the spraying of malathion by air and against the expanded version of the ground program and, conversely, (2) in favor of the expanded ground program but largely in opposition to the aerial spraying proposal. Although the aerial spraying program had a ground-spraying component and the ground program, some contended, should have had an aerial spraying phase, for expository purposes, I call the pro-aerial and antiground argument the "Aerial Story," while the proground but largely anti-aerial analysis is termed the "Aerial Critique." It is important to underscore that calling them a "story" or "critique" is not meant to criticize them. Rather, so much uncertainty existed over the merits of the proposal to spray aerially, the case against aerial spraying, *and* the proposal to expand ground spraying that competing scenarios for program implementation became the key mechanism whereby the major country, state, and federal players in the controversy could compare and choose between the ground and aerial intervention alternatives. Just what the Aerial Story and Aerial Critique had to say specifically becomes clear below.

Those who approach the Medfly Controversy by way of trying to determine how the Aerial Story and its critique were different from each other in terms of their structural features as narratives will readily see that the former followed a more conventional story format. Its implementation scenario had a beginning, middle, and end, all centering around an argument both for aerial spraying and against an intensified ground program. Moreover, the Aerial Story eventually became *the* policy narrative most favored by a powerful coalition of politicians, government officials, and agribusiness interests on how to get back to the premedfly *status quo ante* in California. In contrast, the Aerial Critique had no real story of its own, it being primarily an extensive criticism of the Aerial Story's argument for spraying aerially rather than more intensively on the ground. A variety of groups and policymakers (some of whom were politically powerful or scientifically influential) were more united and forceful in their opposition to aerial spraying than they were in their support of the ground-spraying component. Proponents of the Aerial Critique offered up, as we shall see, a world *without* excessive chemicals, *without* intrusive technologies, *without* the need to eradicate, but made few arguments in favor of the "something else" that would replace it.

This asymmetrical opposition between the two structurally different narratives—one a full-fledged story, the other its critique—was reinforced by two other asymmetries that also had nothing to do with the putative truth value of either narrative. Not only was the Aerial Story an argument in a way that its critique was not, but the latter was at critical times literally impossible to read (unlike the story). Moreover, the Aerial Story was the policy narrative that more and more people were telling when the telling mattered. This does not mean that the Aerial Story was "more logical," "better reasoned," and "less contradictory" than its critique. How the rules and standards governing argumentation, readability, or storytelling work is not the issue here. Rather, the absence or presence of such rules was what set these two narratives apart. One was an argument while the other was not; one could be read where the other could not; one was what important actors were telling when the other had no such storytellers. In the absence of both evidence and the means of proof to establish the merits of either narrative, these differences gave the Aerial Story an advantage over the other, and in this controversy—indeed in any complex and uncertain policy environment where policy narratives are all one has to underwrite and stabilize courses of action—such an asymmetrical advantage proved decisive. Let us now examine these differences and their impact in detail.

The Imbalance between the Two Narratives' Argumentation

The first asymmetry: The proground spraying and anti-aerial spraying components of the Aerial Critique were not counterpoised in the way that the two components of the Aerial Story were. The critique's case for ground spraying centered on how Governor Brown's intensified ground program would lead to the eradication of the medfly by means of substantially expanding the efforts of the Medfly Project at fruit stripping, release of sterile flies, and localized application of chemical sprays. Put that way, the critique would seem to have had a conventional beginning (start with fruit stripping . . .), middle (expand these efforts . . .), and an end (eradication). Yet several factors quickly worked to undermine this story line and reinforce the critique's status as criticism of aerial spraying only. While the release of sterile medflies appeared to have led to the successful eradication of medflies in Los Angeles in 1975 and 1980, over-all the proposed expansion in the ground program placed many of the supporters of the Aerial Critique in an awkward position: a number of them were antieradication or antipesticide, whatever the pesticide, wherever the application.

Some of the critique's supporters argued that the effort should be one of controlling the medfly, not eradicating it. As one proponent said, "[I]t might be far cheaper to learn how to develop a mix of strategies to control [the medfly] below an economic threshold. . . . Once you learn how to live with it you may decide that it's not a bad thing after all. The world had to live with it; and, by the way, most of the world is living with the med-fly."[8] Those critique supporters who were antipesticide endorsed the ground-spraying program largely because the alternative—aerial spraying with malathion or, if that failed to eradicate, utilization of the much more toxic pesticide and potent carcinogen, ethylene dibromide (EDB), to fumigate fruit for export—was so unacceptable to them. According to the representative of the environmental interest group actively opposing aerial spraying, "A lot of our members don't use pesticides in their gar-dens, yet we have been in the position of encouraging them to tolerate the repeated ground applications of pesticides. . . . We supported eradica-tion from the beginning because we did not want all those additional pesticides [like EDB] to be used."[9] Similarly, the university entomologist who turned out to be one of the more important supporters of the inten-sified ground program had an orientation that was on the face of it at odds with the pesticide applications proposed even in this program: "I just hate for chemicals to be put on an inch of land, quite frankly, I just hate it!" is how he summed up his feelings on the matter.[10]

The double bind felt by antipesticide supporters of ground spraying component in the Aerial Critique was exacerbated by the fact that fen-thion and diazinon, chemicals that are far more hazardous than mal-athion, were used in the project's ground program prior to its shift to aerial spraying. Moreover, some argued that the release of sterile flies, a major feature of the ground-spraying program, had to be preceded anyway by aerial spraying of malathion. Dr. Knipling, considered to be the "fa-ther" of the sterile release technique,[11] was "aghast that the area hadn't had aerial spraying before the sterile flies were released,"[12] according to an informed observer. In short, the pro-ground-spraying component of the critique, with its technological scenario of pesticide applications and release of steriles all in the name of medfly eradication rather than control, frequently had attenuated support among the critique's more fervent proponents.

The anti–aerial spraying component thus dominated the critique. All manner of criticisms were leveled against the Aerial Story. One of those familiar with the controversy characterized as "sheer propaganda" the story put out by supporters of aerial spraying to the effect that some $300 million would be lost if the medfly were allowed to be established.[13] The representative of the environmental interest group doubted the Aerial Story being put out by its supporters: "People . . . were saying that medfly was going to destroy California's agricultural industry—billions and billions of dollars down the tubes. But medfly can't destroy our entire agricultural industry. Only a small proportion of the industry would be susceptible."[14] Moreover, the way malathion was applied on the ground prior to its proposed expansion had caused concern over its application by air: "One of the frequently asked questions from the public was, 'If malathion is so safe, why do your employees look like they are dressed for a moon walk?'" reported the project's state comanager.[15] Anti–aerial spraying critics in addition faulted the Department of Health Services' risk assessment on several grounds, for example, the assessment had not considered the wide range of possible hazards associated with malathion and had initially failed to take into account higher-than-expected dosage rates of malathion spray.[16] The predominant feature of the Aerial Critique, in other words, was its focus on undermining the argument for aerial spraying while maintaining lukewarm or divided support for ground spraying.

The proponents of the Aerial Story were, in contrast, equally vocal in stressing both the pro-aerial and antiground arguments of their story (though of course these arguments were criticized by supporters of the Aerial Critique). To Aerial Story proponents, not only were the logistics of the proposed expansion in ground spraying implausible, but aerial spraying—albeit the tactic of last resort—had a proven track record in eradication. As the former chair of the Technical Advisory Committee put it to Governor Brown, the expanded ground program "just wasn't logistically feasible"; more to the point, that strategy "has never been known to eradicate medfly, while the aerial bait spray program had been effective in other states."[17] "Even if it were possible to get the necessary equipment and carry out such an extensive ground spray program," he went on, "there were not enough sterile flies to cover the area."[18] On the other side, aerial spraying with malathion was not a new story. Florida and Texas over several decades had such programs that seemed to work.

Malathion has also been one of the most tested pesticides on humans available and was said to have no proven acute or toxic effects at the dosage levels utilized by the project.[19] Last but not least, most of the controversy's key participants, including members of the major environmental group involved, agreed that aerial spraying was acceptable for eradication purposes as the measure of last resort.

The Difficulty in Reading the Aerial Critique

The second asymmetry: The critique was at times unreadable in comparison to the Aerial Story. The term "read" is meant quite literally. The widespread uncertainty that turned the Medfly Controversy into many smaller controversies was due not simply to the lack of pertinent information needed to establish the merits of either policy narrative, but also to the extreme difficulty of interpreting the information that people already had. Several factors, however, made the critique considerably more problematic to read than the Aerial Story.

From the very beginning, a major and continuing source of controversy was the difficulty in interpreting the implications of medflies caught in traps specially constructed to monitor the spread of the infestation. While trap finds confirmed the presence of the adult medfly, they did not indicate the depth of the infestation, particularly for medfly larvae (in fruit) or pupae (in the ground). But the problems of interpretation went much further and were more pervasive, especially in the areas of medfly detection, sampling, and the project's management of both.

In the opinion of one informed source, the local officials who had not treated the original medfly finds as a matter of priority did so because they misread the implication of the finds: "they didn't know the true meaning" of the flies they had trapped.[20] So too for CDFA's initially slow response to these finds, at least according to its principal staff entomologist: "We didn't realize the significance of those two flies combined with that low a trap density in Santa Clara . . . so we didn't take the action we should have."[21] Trap records were incomplete and, according to a top USDA entomologist, not "summarized in a useful fashion, so the guy looking at the overall strategy of the program [could] analyze it."[22] Some traps appear to have been sabotaged.[23] Also troublesome was the fact that project technicians were unable to distinguish trapped sterile and wild medflies from each other. Why only female flies continued to be caught in the traps that relied entirely on male attractants was as well never fully explained. A different type of trap had to be introduced because the original type "loaded up like a piece of fly paper" with steriles after their release.[24] More disturbing was the fact that no one was able to decide whether the trap finds at the outset of the mid-1981 reemergence of medflies were in reality due to (1) the release of "steriles" left fertile because of improper irradiation, (2) the survival of medflies over winter, which earlier research had concluded was not possible under Santa Clara conditions, (3) the project's defective medfly monitoring and detection procedures, or (4) a combination of these factors and others.[25] Finally, the eventual absence of any trap finds by September 1982 could be explained, according to the university entomologist, by several scenarios other than the one claiming eradication had been achieved through aerial spraying with malathion.[26] That widespread malathion spraying and the disappearance of infestations have been correlated in the past was just that, a correlation and not proof of effectiveness, according to this scientist.

Both the critique and the Aerial Story relied on this imperfect information. Yet in the midst of all the uncertainty, the proponents of the aerial spraying had a story line, the analogue of which their opponents did not have. Earlier on, project management and the TAC came to consensus over what kind of trap finds would be interpreted as reflecting a medfly outbreak sufficiently severe to warrant aerial spraying of malathion.[27] The criteria agreed upon were recognized by these decision makers to be arbitrary, but necessary. In addition, while the project managers—who were eventually the major proponents of the Aerial Story—were often at a loss over how to interpret trap information accurately, they did have a computer model that told the story of the medfly's life cycle in fairly useful ways for them (in particular, it helped them to explain how the medflies could overwinter, contrary to previous research findings). As the project's federal comanager put it, "one thing that really gave our program credibility towards the end . . . [was the] computer model for calculating the medfly life cycles under San Jose climatic conditions. It was a godsend to us and made what we said acceptable to the Japanese, the Floridians, and to whoever else [wanted to quarantine California produce]."[28] Finally, after resistance by some of its parties, a written protocol specifying how the aerial spraying was to proceed was hammered out and agreed upon in July 1981. The protocol kept the project on track and "was our bible," according to the project's federal comanager.[29] In sum, the outbreak criteria, computer model, and protocol allowed many key participants to take action *as if* they knew whether or not the empirical merits of the situation warranted that spraying.

Reading the Aerial Critique, particularly its "case" for more ground spraying, proved much more difficult. The major feature of the ground program, namely, the release of sterile flies, had many methodological problems that reduced the ability of the critique's proponents to interpret basic information provided by the trap finds. One was the already mentioned difficulty in distinguishing steriles from wild medflies; other problems emerged that were even more intractable. The head of the project's quality control unit, for example, complained about the unfeasibility of meeting acceptable sampling standards. When a professional statistician indicated that a 10 percent sample of each sterile fly container was required, she pointed out that

> on the average, we received 68 million flies a day. It would take one technician 262 years of 94,586 technicians working twenty-four hours to sample ten percent of a mixed population. That is impossible. . . . A decision was never reached about sample size, so I used my judgment.[30]

On the face of it, the "arbitrariness" of her decision was no different from that of the outbreak criteria, computer model, or protocol just mentioned, save in one crucial respect. It turns out the project's sampling techniques provided trap information in a form that was of more use to the supporters of the Aerial Story than it was to the supporters of its critique. Bait spray programs, such as that for aerial spraying of malathion, rely on discrete data that are demonstrably measurable, while sterile fly release programs are based on continuously variable data, having probability limits that are less well defined. One entomologist member of the TAC explained the difficulty and difference this way:

> The high quality of data for bait sprays lies in their discrete testable elements. The toxicant, the bait, the dosage, and the formulation are all testable individually. . . . Ultimately, our "comfortableness" with the data derived from the bait spray experiments comes from the fact that it is quantal, based on dead flies with yes or no data. Thereby you get yes or no advice. . . . The [sterile insect technique] data are, by nature, variable and incomplete, and they don't give yes-no answers. Decisions about sterile flies always involve trade-offs.[31]

Note the issue here is not that the sterile insect technique produced results that were necessarily less believable than the bait spray experiments but rather that the latter provided results that could be acted upon more easily. "Actionability," not believability, was the problem.

Difficulties existed in reading not only the proground spraying com-

ponent of the Aerial Critique, but also its anti–aerial spraying component. Much of the opposition to aerial spraying with malathion was
fueled by media reports of dissent within the Department of Health Services over the methodology and conclusions drawn in its risk analysis of
such spraying. The assessment was based on the "worst case scenario"
thought possible under aerial spraying and eventually concluded that
there was a one-in-a-million chance of an exposed infant developing cancer from the aerial spraying of malathion. Yet, one of the DHS officials
who undertook the probability assessment also concluded that its methodology had important limitations. He complained that "[t]here is no
consensus on a methodology for [treating] . . . events where the initial
event may have been improbable, but it sets up greater probabilities for
secondary errors."[32] Supporters of the ground program had, in brief, extreme difficulty in reading just what the story being told was at the tail
end of the probability distributions for acute and chronic effects, if any,
associated with malathion.

To summarize, while the greater difficulties in reading the critique did
not make it any less plausible in terms of putative truth value than
the Aerial Story, they did serve to reinforce the asymmetrical status of
the critique as nothing more or less than a critique. The problem with the
critique was not that it was unbelievable or implausible because of data
shortcomings; rather, the shortcomings made it difficult to read the critique as the basis for action. Being less readable, the critique offered a
weak defense against those detractors who characterized it as "only" a
set of disparate complaints from skeptics having little in common but
their opposition to aerial spraying.

Narrative Shift

Finally, several of the key participants altered their story during the
Medfly Controversy, and these shifts were in the same direction, from
the critique to the Aerial Story. Certainly when one particularly well-
known USDA advocate of the sterile insect technique argued in favor of
aerial spraying once the medflies reemerged in mid-1981, the Aerial
Story gained credibility.[33] The public's unexpected but continued acceptance of aerial spraying once it finally started also did much to keep the
Aerial Story the only one worth telling by its proponents until eradication was declared.[34]

Yet two other shifts were probably more important, because they happened at a strategic point in the controversy. After aerial spraying began,

the press, which had been critical of the project, changed its story to one of largely being in favor of the project. High officials in USDA also took steps to ensure their own story in support of aerial spraying became the project management's and the TAC's version as well. These shifts came at the moment when it mattered and the timing of these changes was in no small part the result of the storytelling abilities of the project's state and federal comanagers. Although documentation is scant on how these narrative shifts took place, we do have direct accounts of some of the major participants involved, particularly with respect to the shift in press coverage.

The media influenced not only the public's perception of the Medfly Project, but also the key participants in the controversy, especially project managers and politicians.[35] Media reports were thus crucial to the course of that controversy. The decision of the project's state comanager to allow the press open access to project staff proved to be one decisive reason why members of the press became considerably less critical of project activities. According to a reporter who covered the controversy for the state's best known newspaper, the Medfly Project was in great turmoil on the day before aerial spraying commenced. One of her colleagues was running around trying to figure out how the spraying program would work. Because no one on the project had time to explain, project staff told him to sit in on their meetings and pick up what he could from what was said. "He listened to everything," she said, adding

That would scare the beans out of 99% of the world's bureaucrats to let a reporter listen as they worked things out. . . . That night, when they started spraying, the pumps broke. . . . The AP [Associated Press] put out a bulletin saying that the initial spraying had failed. Well, they weren't wrong. The pumps broke and they didn't get it sprayed; so, yes, they failed. . . . [O]ur story was a little bit different. All it said was that they began the spraying but failed to complete it because a pump broke. . . . [W]e gave them [i.e., the Medfly Project] the benefit of the doubt. Since we operate the *Times-Post* wire service, all of our clients' readers got this story also. I felt our story was fair and accurate; and it happened because of the project's openness.[36]

The project's state comanager, in turn, saw this press turnaround precisely in terms of shifting the stories they reported,

[T]he pumps jammed closed and when the helicopter went over nothing came out. The press and public said, "Jesus, is that all there is to it? I thought there was going to be more than this." The news stories the next day said, "Is this all there is?" and overnight public reaction changed. [One San Francisco newspaper] did a poll at the end of that week and 73% of the people were in favor of aerial spraying. The week before you couldn't have found two percent in favor. . . . [T]he media was seduced by our candor. We let them have the run of the project. They got to talk to anybody they wanted to. I think they are not used to that, and as a result they were much more fair, even biased in our favor than you would normally find. There were a number of incidents where [project] employees . . . took the day off at the beach . . . or tipped over a spray rig. It was not a big story, because the media was living with us on this project. There was all this complexity and they said, "Well, hell, with this many people you are going to have those kinds of problems; that is not news." I really think that a policy of openness changes their approach to the story.[37]

The other critical shift in support from one narrative to another came through the turnabout in the USDA's advisory role to the project. In the early stages of the controversy, USDA's influence on the project, while large, was diluted because of its policy of rotating federal managers on the project every thirty days. Moreover, USDA was not the project's chief technical advisor and in consequence found itself sometimes at odds with the Technical Advisory Committee (for example, some members of the TAC did not support aerial spraying in the winter, a strategy USDA by and large strongly supported). This position changed considerably after aerial spraying of malathion was initiated. A permanent USDA project co-manager was appointed, another USDA official took over from the CDFA's principal staff entomologist as the new TAC chair, while his boss within the USDA hierarchy, a senior USDA official, was appointed a member of the TAC. As a consequence, "the USDA exerted a much stronger influence on the running of the project and the Technical Advisory Committee" according to the TAC's former chair.[38] The TAC shifted its role from one of at times lukewarm supporter that questioned some project management decisions to one of project rationalizer that rubber-stamped the Aerial Story of project managers. "The committee was used to validate the decisions the project leaders wanted to make. It was a back-up and excuse-giver" is how one informed source put it.[39]

This transformation of the TAC was in large part due the skills of the USDA managers and advisors on the Medfly Project. According to the former TAC chair, "The Committee was revamped and [a USDA official] replaced me as chairman. [He] was a good showman, a loyal soldier. He reported to project leadership to find out what they wanted and he came in and sold it to the Committee. They put several other USDA people on the Committee; the most unfortunate choice was [the senior USDA official mentioned earlier]" who was a strong supporter of aerial spraying with malathion.[40] According to the former chair, this senior official "rammed . . . through" the TAC one particularly contentious recommendation involving this aerial spraying.[41] Another TAC member described the effort in the following terms: "we [on the TAC] were told very directly, 'I don't care what you decide you're going to recommend. We're going to do it this way.' "[42] "I felt that [this senior USDA official], particularly, had an overall control of what came out of that Technical Committee" is how the newspaper reporter described the matter more generally.[43] The reorganized TAC, in short, was now able to better toe the USDA line.

Whatever the relative merits of the critique and the Aerial Story, this ability of the project managers to shift its story from one to the other at a strategic time in the Medfly Controversy was crucial to the rise of the Aerial Story and the decline of the critique. Project managers did not create the scenario supporting aerial spraying of malathion. It came to them largely already written by past eradication efforts and by preexisting organizational imperatives. Still, the managers proved capable of displacing one story with another more favorable to the project and to these managers.[44] Their narratives may have come to them already scripted, but their skills as narrators were more their own. What first appeared to some observers of the controversy as the decisive effect of unique and forceful personalities on events[45] was in reality not that, but rather the activities of quite effective public managers.

Asymmetrical Narratives and the Metanarrative of Increased Risk

What should these asymmetries between "story" and "critique" have signified for analysts involved in the Medfly Controversy or observing it from the outside? What do asymmetries between policy narratives mean generally for analysts who have to examine an important policy issue so uncertain and complex that all they have to work on are stories whose truth value cannot be ascertained? Alternatively, what implications could the analyst draw if the relationship between narratives was symmetrical along the dimensions examined above rather than asymmetrical?

Policy narratives, like the Aerial Story, are one signal way that public managers, government policymakers, and politicians transform issue uncertainties and complexities into perceptions of risk. Policy analysts are trained to distinguish between risk and uncertainty (only the former is said to have a probability distribution). In narrative-analytical terms, some stories circulating in government attempt to give to uncertainty something approximating just this kind of distribution. Had the policy analysts involved in the medfly crisis fully appreciated how essential policy narratives are to sculpting risk out of uncertainty and complexity, they would have pursued the one area that might well have helped resolve some of the controversy. To see this, we need go no further than that formal definition of risk frequently used in policy analysis.

Risk has been defined as the product of the severity of the hazard associated with an event and the probability of that event occurring. In the Medfly Controversy, the hazard was taken to be acute and chronic maladies, particularly cancer, arising as a result of the widespread spraying of this pesticide, malathion, by air. The nature and severity of these hazards, along with the probabilities of their occurrence, were at the core of the differences between the Aerial Story and its critique.

Supporters of the Aerial Story by and large took their low estimate of the health risks attached to malathion spraying from the DHS report. Proponents of the critique, for their part, did not use an analogous estimate of the risks associated with ground spraying chemicals. Such a figure may have been computed and even discussed, but it never played the central role in the critique that the DHS estimate had in the Aerial Story. Nor is this surprising, given that the critique never really moved beyond finding fault with the various figures and estimates proposed by supporters of the Aerial Story. Not once in the recorded accounts of key participants does one find the critique's proponents arguing that they had done their own estimation of the likelihood of cancer caused by ground spraying or that such an estimate was lower than the DHS figure.

Yet without this estimate of risk associated with the ground program, which was presumably not zero as well, the policy analyst would have had no way to address the major policy-relevant question it raised: Could supporters of the Aerial Story have redesigned the aerial spraying program in such a way as to have reduced its level of perceived risk to the level of risk thought associated with the ground-spraying component of the Aerial Critique? Such a task would itself be a matter of great uncertainty, but specifying the question in this way would have had the virtue of transforming the narratives into a testable hypothesis. While "real" probabilities and risks may well be different from those estimated by either policy narrative, at least having two estimates of risk—one associated with aerial spraying, the other with ground spraying—would have put the analyst in a better position to ascertain whether or not the structurally different Aerial Critique and Aerial Story could have been treated *as if* they were one and the same policy narrative, both structurally and substantively, at least when assessing risk.

This, in turn, raises a more general point for the practicing policy analyst confronting any complex and uncertain policy issue. While she or he might first think that having to recommend one of two or more equally "compelling" scenarios is the more difficult and uncertain task, in practice such structural symmetries between stories need not be as much a problem for the analyst as their asymmetries are. The presence of asymmetrical narratives in an important policy issue tells the analyst that the issue is considerably uncertain, if not risky. Two equally plausible stories, after all, have the chance of being the same story when it comes to risk assessment in the manner just described. Contrast this to the situation where the main policy narratives remain asymmetrical. Rather than reducing uncertainty or transforming the policy issue into one of risk assessment, the critique, when contrasted against Aerial Story, actually increased uncertainty. The public's comparison of the critique and the aerial spraying scenario effectively created a metanarrative about how that critique heightened people's sense of risk and uncertainty associated with the medfly infestation. The critique raised a host of questions about the Aerial Story without having an alternative to replace it, and the primary effect of the critique's criticism of the Aerial Story was to heighten and amplify at the metanarrative level the overall sense of uncertainty and risk attending the Medfly Controversy. Thus, the central dilemma in so much of policy critique: the extent to which a critique is effective at the narrative level in overthrowing a policy is often the extent to which it undermines at the metanarrative level its own ability to underwrite and stabilize the assumptions for decision making in the face of complexity and uncertainty.

The context in which uncertainty is heightened is paramount here. In judicial proceedings, the role of the defense can be one of critique, raising in the minds of the jury a reasonable doubt about the prosecution's case. According to the judicial "rules of the game," reasonable doubt is sufficient basis for bringing in a verdict of not guilty. In controversies such as the medfly, an increased sense of "reasonable doubt" over a scenario like the Aerial Story occurs within a context where there are no "rules of the game" to settle the matter one way or the other. As noted before, the Medfly Controversy (as well as the other science, technology and environmental controversies discussed in this book) are controversies precisely because of the absence of rules and standards to settle what is the "better" narrative, in this case the story or its critique.

Such insights hardly help the analyst who continues to face persisting asymmetries between dominant narratives, even after attempts to equate them in terms of risk assessment. What the analyst should do in such situations depends on a fuller appreciation of the sources of these asymmetries.

The Role of Politics, Power, and Interest Groups in Policy Narratives

The focus on asymmetries between critique and story inevitably begs the issue of what causes them, which in turn raises the question, Why use policy narratives at all as the unit of analysis when one presumably could appeal instead to other, more readily apparent causes? For example, Hilary Lorraine notes about the controversy,

> Evaluating economic impact, identifying alternatives and evaluating their projected impact take place in an asymmetrical decision context. Agencies and the industry have full access to the relevant information and can come to a decision through a process which is usually hidden from public scrutiny. Third-party interests face high information costs, are often not aware of their possible stakes in the decision and seldom have ready access to the decision process.[46]

Appealing to such resource differentials in politics, economic power, and interest groups to explain policymaking has a long tradition in the policy sciences. Why then do we need another decision variable called "different types of policy narratives"?

Clearly, a full appreciation of how the Medfly Controversy unfolded requires understanding something about California state and national politics at that time. Governor Brown's handling of the medfly crisis was one reason why state politicians and agribusiness interests sought to bring impeachment charges against him, thereby seeking to thwart his senatorial and presidential ambitions. The extent to which Brown's perceptions of the risks attached to the two major eradication proposals were influenced by these and other political considerations is less clear. Brown is on record saying he decided to expand the ground program in July 1981 in spite of "the serious political consequences," and he seems to have expressed such sentiments privately as well.[47] After working with him during this period, the project's state comanager came to a similar conclusion about the governor's motivations: "I believe that Brown felt deeply that spraying with pesticide was wrong, no matter how he analyzed the problem he came back to that end and said, 'It is wrong and I don't care what the political risks are.' "[48]

Yet some of these very same advisers paint a more complex picture of Brown and his actions. When the project's state comanager tried to impress upon the governor how the decision not to go for aerial spraying could well hurt his electoral chances with other California voters, Brown snapped "I'll worry about the politics, you worry about the medfly."[49] And worry about the politics of medfly Brown did, at least according to the former Democratic chair of the California state assembly's agriculture committee who also worked with Brown during this period:

> After the helicopters were in the air [spraying malathion], some of us visited [the governor] and advised, "Jerry, for God's sake, just stay out of it. Don't make another damn remark." But he thought the medfly was the hottest issue in the world at the moment and he wanted to capitalize on it for a while.... I think Jerry, above all people, wanted eradication as soon as possible, because this was to his political gain. He knew he had an albatross around his neck if the ground program didn't work, but he didn't want aerial spraying because he felt that 90% of the people in the Santa Clara area would react negatively to helicopters flying over them.... I think Jerry knew that he was going to have to order the helicopters into the air, but he wanted to cover himself and make it look like President Reagan forced him because they were going to quarantine the whole state.[50]

The commonly perceived "proenvironment" Brown had not endeared himself to the "antienvironmentalist" Reagan administration. The Medfly Project was said to have been denied the use of a major government airfield for the aerial spraying because of the governor's comments about the president.[51] Apparently only after enormous pressure from the state's Farm Bureau and other farm organizations on Secretary of Defense Weinberger did the airfield become available for project use.[52] These agricultural groups had exerted their political influence in Washington in other ways that worked in favor of the Aerial Story and against Brown's stated position in favor of the expanded ground program. In the judgment of the project's federal comanager, "the agribusiness interests [in California] are what finally triggered the aerial treatment" by bringing pressure on the

Secretary of Agriculture to call for immediate aerial spraying in July 1981.[53] In contrast, the alliance of interest groups and individuals in favor of the Aerial Critique was less influential and coordinated, consisting primarily of a diverse set of politicians, environmental groups, physicians, government officials, scientists, and academics. For this group whose access to resources, data, and shared values was limited, it proved easier to coalesce around the critique of what they were against (albeit for different reasons) than to come to some consensus over what they should be for.

In short, differential access to economic and political power had an undeniably important role in the medfly crisis. Reconfirming the importance of that role is not, however, the aim here. The question of interest is when and how this importance is established under the kinds of uncertainties and complexities that preoccupied the Medfly Controversy, and indeed those other controversies discussed in *Narrative Policy Analysis*. This book's argument is that, under conditions of extreme issue ambiguity, differential access to decision making resources operates for a policy issue only when that access is realized through and by means of competing policy narratives about the issue. For policy issues so complex and uncertain that it is not possible to determine what are the "objectively weaker arguments," asymmetrical narratives used to make sense of these issues are the only index we have that unequal power relations are working themselves out through these policy narratives, through their asymmetries, through getting people to change their stories. Competing and asymmetrical stories are in such cases our primary way of *knowing* that unequal access to resources among the key parties to the issue really does matter when it comes to how that issue is perceived, communicated, and managed.

It is important to be clear about these points. The argument here is not that policy narratives are insignificant for determining analysis, argumentation, and power relations in most situations, namely, those that are not complex, uncertain, or divisive. Policy narratives are found all the time working to underwrite and stabilize the assumptions for decision making, including but in no way limited to times of high issue ambiguity. In those latter cases, though, such as those found in the Medfly Controversy, it is only by watching who ends up "telling the better story" or "making the better case"—that is, who ends up on the side of the scenario that actually underwrites and stabilizes the decision making in the face of controversy—that we come to any kind of understanding as to who has more or less power in getting people to "change their stories," when changing them matters for decision making. In such circumstances, asymmetrical narratives do not reflect or mediate power relations; rather, they instantiate them. It isn't that what is "behind" narratives are the power relations that form them as much as what is "in front of" us is power in form of winning and losing narratives. When all else remains uncertain in a controversy, our knowledge of asymmetrical narratives is our knowledge of power.

This argument's implication for the analyst investigating complex and uncertain policy problems is straightforward: because differential access to resources operates through policy narratives, then people should be empowered to tell their own stories. Why? Because it would be ludicrous for the analyst to advise that only one narrative should have hegemony within a context of high complexity and uncertainty. To the extent that the inability "to tell our own stories" is a function of unequal access to information used in decision making, as Lorraine implied for the Medfly Controversy, then differential access itself must become the focus of intervention and rectification. Those who want to move beyond policy critique should be encouraged to do so, and it is in the interest of both those who critique and those who are critiqued to want that movement. For the analyst to recommend otherwise is to advise living with considerably more uncertainty than may be necessary if the major competing narratives in the public realm were all to have their own scenarios, their own arguments, and their own estimates of risk.

Thus, it is not at all counterintuitive to argue that CDFA, USDA or the TAC itself should have financed environmental groups to come up with their own estimate of cancer risk associated with the intensified ground spraying program. So too should universities pay animal rights groups to assist in the design and management of animal alternative centers on their campuses (chapter 4) and agribusiness fund environmental organizations to come up with their own implementation proposals for what they see as environmentally unsound irrigation (chapter 5). In so doing, the analyst is not recommending that the "powerful" (read: government agencies) try to coopt the "powerless" (read: environmental and animal rights groups) or that the latter pander to the former. Power is being worked out in these controversies; it is open-ended and not perforce a zero-sum game. Government officials and their ideological opponents need not be compromised by working with each other, when opposing parties are telling functionally the same story—a story that in turn empowers all concerned to the extent it reduces uncertainty and complexity at the metanarrative level.

Summary

From a narrative-analytical viewpoint, the more the asymmetries between narratives in difficult policy issues, the greater the uncertainty and risk associated with those issues. The potential for uncertainty or risk increases when one or more of the competing narratives is not really a conventional story at all but rather a critique. At best, critiques leave unaddressed the palpable need of government officials and politicians to have a story line when faced by what they do not know or cannot otherwise analyze and justify. At worst, critiques serve only to intensify the ambiguities of an issue.

Potential for policy ambiguity also increases when analysts and others have difficulty in actually reading one or all of the competing narratives. To the extent that policy narratives center around methodologies that are not well understood or comprehensible, then the sense of risk and uncertainty increases with respect to the issue concerned. The ability of public managers to tell a good story about a policy issue and their ability to manage the perceptions of issue uncertainty and risk are directly related. The perception of ambiguity involved in any public policy issue increases to the extent that public managers lack the narrator's skill, craft, and flexibility to move the issue from one agenda to another and shift the issue's "real" story in the process. Finally, the analyst who wants to identify the risks associated with a complex and difficult policy issue is well advised to spend less of her or his time on determining the putative truth value of the issue's major policy narratives and more on investigating the narratives' structural differences and possible equivalence in terms of some shared index.

The introduction notes that treating an argument as "just another story" is the time-honored way that bureaucrats and others demean the often very real merits of their opponent's case. Indeed, most policy analysts have seen cases where organizational storytelling has hindered rather than helped the analysis of policy issues. As such, the kind of narrative policy analysis discussed above and in subsequent chapters is intended for those policy problems recognizably so complex and uncertain that stories, scenarios, and other policy narratives become of necessity the way these problems are articulated. Indeed, the absence of adequate statistical, methodological, or legal specification does not permit otherwise.

Lastly, while different approaches to narrative analysis exist than the one presented here,[54] they by and large converge on one point: the structure of narratives can be formally analyzed and compared across narratives in such a way that the analysis and comparison are themselves a metanarrative. The asymmetries discussed above tell their own story and that metanarrative can be called, as we just saw, "a heightened sense of risk and uncertainty" with respect to the policy issue concerned. Thus, narrative policy analysis is not completely free of its own kind of storytelling, but neither—fortunately—is the conventional policy analysis of microeconomics, statistics, legal analysis, organization theory, and public management practice.[55]

4

Constructing the Metanarrative in
the Animal Rights and Experimentation Controversy

Not all controversies come to us with neatly defined policy narratives from which a publicly recognized metanarrative arises for use by the analyst. What I develop in this chapter is the recognition that there may be circumstances under which the analyst is able to construct a policy-relevant metanarrative, as long as she or he finds a way to recast the contending narratives into the story/nonstory contraposition sketched in the medfly chapter. How this can be done is explained and illustrated through a case study of the controversy over the use of (nonhuman) animals in research.[1]

The Controversy and the Proposal

According to many animal researchers and their opponents in the animal welfare movement, everyone—including those reading *Narrative Policy Analysis*—is part of the animal rights controversy and implicated in its unfolding. Let's assume this is so and undertake a thought experiment. Assume you are an analyst working in the administration of a major university. You have been assigned the task of preparing a proposal to establish a university center on the use of alternatives to animals in research, teaching, and testing.[2] Assume as well that popular or legislative pressure has mandated the center's establishment, so that the exercise is one of design rather than of deciding whether or not to create the center in the first place. Assume finally that the university administration sees its role as one of promoting the use of animal alternatives in university research, while at the same time buffering its science faculty and researchers from attacks by what it perceives to be militant animal rights activists.

Three considerations rapidly come into view. First, the university administration faces a highly polarized issue. What looks to animal rights advocates like the mindless slaughter of millions upon millions of animals in the name of dubious research goals has to be weighed against what many university researchers consider to be the unconscionable vandalism, bombings, and death threats of an animal rights movement actively working against the betterment of humankind. From the perspective of the university administration, there is considerable merit in developing a proposal that tones down the discord between the opponents and proponents of animal research, even if the proposal cannot hope to resolve the fundamental differences dividing them.

The differences are over not only values but facts. The second principal feature of the animal experimentation controversy is uncertainty regarding the empirical merits of the competing positions. Since this statement is hotly contested by both the proponents and the opponents of animal research, it is important to establish the case in some detail. A late 1980s publication of the University of California provides a representative compendium of statements cataloguing the contrary evidence said to support each camp.[3] Differences between the proponents and opponents of animal research are often cast in terms that range from cost to structural factors.

Cost. According to the Animal Protection Institute of America, animal alternatives "tend to be more cost-effective because they do away with the costs of animal procurement, housing and care." On the other hand, according to a head of the University of Wisconsin's Research Animal Resources Center, "because equipment, expertise, and money to change technologies to use [an animal alternative] may not be available . . . [they] may not be cheaper."

Scientific Evidence. Issues of cost and availability revolve around questions of scientific evidence. The head of one anti–animal research group, In Defense of Animals, speaks for other groups when arguing that "modern data on public health and disease show that animal experimentation is not the cheapest, most effective, most successful, or most appropriate approach." This conclusion is countered not only by proponents of animal research, but by some groups sympathetic to aspects of the animal rights case, for example, the director of the Scientists Center for Animal Welfare maintains that, while "many animal rights activists claim that much animal experimentation could be eliminated or reduced, experience has shown this to be exceptional."

It is important to underscore just how much of the animal research controversy is framed as a matter of science by both the opponents and proponents of animal research. Claims such as "I have found it is much better science to . . ." or observations prefaced with "As a scientist, I . . ." are common, particularly from scientists allied with animal welfare organizations.[4] Animal rights groups such as the Association of Veterinarians for Animal Rights, the Physicians Committee for Responsible Medicine, and the Medical Research Modernization Committee have marshalled a wealth of scientific evidence in favor of their positions and have referred to extensive bibliographies of research relevant to animal alternatives.

Behavioral, Attitudinal, and Structural Factors. According to the head of In Defense of Animals, use of animals for research has "more to do with tradition, habit, conceptual confusion, economics and legal considerations than any real advancement of science or medicine. . . . [I]mprovements in academic rank, prestige and salary often depends [*sic*] on the number of research papers published, which usually means animal research grant applications." In the view of the Medical Research Modernization Committee, the "lag in utilizing [animal alternatives] is most attributable to the educational and training backgrounds, centering on animal models, of persons in the federal bureaucracies who have the power to determine projects and methods." Legal considerations play no small part in this regard: many proponents of animal research "fear such regulations [as the federal Animal Welfare Act] would make current levels of animal research too expensive," according to the Animal Protection Institute of America.

In contrast, some proponents of animal research regard opposition to animal use as "an invasion of academic freedom and unnecessary bureaucracy," according to the director of the Scientists Center for Animal Welfare. Proponents frequently try to take the high road: "We at the American Diabetes Association are not for indiscriminate research of any sort; we are *for* the ethical use of all research subjects, animals and computers and cells and, for that matter, humans." Thus, "it is misleading—and often impossible—to characterize many vocal groups either as simply 'proanimal' or 'proresearch,' " according to the California affiliate of the American Diabetes Association. A related tactic of animal research proponents has been to question the distinction between animal research and animal alternatives by appealing to the interdependence of the two. Computer modeling, for instance, is often touted as an alternative to animal use, but the data used in these models come at times from the results of direct experimentation with animals. Moreover, bioengineering work on tissue cultures (another favorite animal alternative) will undoubtedly lead to increased experimental work with animals, as in the case of transgenic mice. Other tactics of animal research proponents include (1) treating the development of animal alternatives as primarily a funding problem—such alternatives, for instance, should "not deplete funds from present and future allocations for [animal] research projects but should be based on additional funding," in the view of the California affiliate of the American Heart Association; and (2) focusing, as does the director of the University of Wisconsin's Research Animal Resources Center, on the antipoor and anti–Third World implications of stopping animal research in certain diseases having the highest incidence among people of color in the developing world.

While sympathetic to the position of animal rights advocates, some nonetheless see the necessity of selective animal use in research as fundamentally a matter of avoiding what society considers unacceptable risks both to humans *and* nonhuman animals. According to the director of the Center for Alternatives to Testing at Johns Hopkins University, "in excess of 100,000 chemical compounds are currently in the market place for which we have little, if any, data on which to assign risk. . . . [T]o eliminate animal testing at this time would constitute an abrogation of the toxicologist's responsibility to insure safety and will pose a risk to human health that government, industry and the public will find unacceptable." Animal rights activities counter by arguing that the assignment of risk would not be necessary if we were operating under a different model of medicine. As a representative of the Medical Research Modernization Committee puts it in a newsletter of In Defense of Animals: "The truth is that experimentation is inextricably linked not to health, but rather to disease. Unfortunately, it is this disease-orientation of American medicine that is responsible for the misplaced priorities that result in de-emphasizing prevention techniques, ignoring personal responsibility for one's health, and the belief that the omnipotent medical profession has the potential to, and ultimately will, remedy anything and everything—provided we continue endless, repetitive, redundant, irrelevant and wasteful animal experimentation."

Such disagreement and uncertainty, along so many dimensions, comes about not merely because conflicting facts and values ensure that animal research means different things to different people. Widespread topsy-turviness pervades the controversy as well, and this topsyturvydom is the third and chief feature of the debate. From one camp, we hear calls that lab animals should live even when their death would save the lives of humans. On the other side is the prospect of endless animal experimentation breeding ever more animals for destruction: "One thing we DO know for certain—cancer causes mice" reads the caption of a cartoon showing two researchers looking at row after row of caged mice.[5] One animal rights group speaks about the need to stop the "barbaric practice of animal experimentation in the name of human health" (the Medical Research Modernization Committee), while stopping such research would be considered even more barbaric by other groups, such as the Incurably Ill for Animal Research, a national organization representing those who suffer terminal illnesses.[6] A pro–animal research advertisement shows a picture of animal rights activists protesting behind police barricades, with the headline "Thanks to animal research, they'll be able to protest 20.8 years longer."[7] Further, the more animal alternatives there are, the fewer animal alternatives there may be in practice. Animal-dependent toxicity testing has been reinforced because the relatively few funds and staff to validate proposed alternative tests have become even more limited as the number of potential alternatives have increased over time.[8]

Anecdotes best convey the controversy's topsy-turvydom. A university proponent of animal research, whose research was compared to that of the Nazis by one animal rights advocate who had had family in the concentration camps, felt compelled to point out that Hitler himself was an antivivisectionist, and an ardent one. Yet these proponents of animal research give the controversy its most visceral upside-down character by their professional euphemisms. Instead of being killed, animals are "sacrificed," "euthanized," or have "gone to death"; body parts are "harvested" like crops and thereafter economically and judiciously used; experimentation on animals becomes "testing on animal models"; and keeping an animal comfortable becomes a form of "environmental enrichment and enhancement."

It is precisely this topsy-turvydom combined with the controversy's polarization and multiple uncertainties that provide the analyst—you, the reader—with the key point of departure in writing the university proposal for an animal alternatives center. Conventional wisdom and practice would advise you try to reduce the uncertainty or, barring that, suboptimize by focusing only on those few aspects of the controversy that can be dealt with, even if this leaves the larger controversy unresolved (see the next chapter for a discussion). That is to say, design the center around those already available alternatives to the use of animals in teaching or testing, thereby avoiding the much more difficult task of developing alternatives to animal research. However, unfortunately for you, testing of alternatives is already taking place (at Johns Hopkins University), and legislators have made it abundantly clear they want universities and their faculty to deal with the research issue much more directly, no matter how perplexing it is university administrators, researchers, and students.[9]

Rather than try to create a middle ground between parties so fundamentally divided, the analyst is better advised to stress the metanarrative elements in the controversy that complexify the divisive lack of middle ground and in so doing neutralize concern over the divisions or at least promote the parties' tolerance of these differences. You do this by accentuating those technical elements of nonsense that dominate the controversy, that is, its topsy-turviness, polarization, and uncertainties.[10]

The Proposal's Specifics

Nonsense "balances a multiplicity of meaning with a simultaneous absence of meaning."—Wim Tigges

The objective would be to design a center whose core agenda revolves around the metanarrative that, on one hand, a multitude of different interpretations exists over the facts and values that make animal research the controversy it is today, while on the other hand this multiplicity is balanced against the very real absence of meaning that the controversy has for the nonhuman animals that are its object. Few, if any, animals, "want" to be in pain, but the point here is the obvious one: animals do not know or understand or interpret their "right" not to be tested, at least in the same sense that the "right" of human beings not to be tested has semantic and interpretative meaning for humans. And, of course, the varying interpretations as to just what a "right" is, whether ascribed to humans or nonhumans, is part and parcel of the multitude of views just mentioned.

In narrative-analytical terms, the "multiplicity of meaning" in the animal rights controversy revolves around the differing stories that the opposing camps tell in order to articulate the controversy and the philosophical issues these stories raise, while the "absence of meaning" that the controversy has for the animals that are its object represents that controversy's central nonstory (because, unlike the stories, the "absence of meaning" has no beginning, middle or end). In other words, "nonsense," as the balance between the multiplicity and absence of meaning, becomes the metanarrative told by the controversy. *Nonsense* is used here in a technical, not pejorative, sense, and it is the accentuation of these technical elements that should be advanced in the design proposal.

First, the multiplicity of views should be institutionalized. One aim of the center could well be to prepare a series of workshops and position papers designed to itemize and then detail the differences between and within the groups supporting or opposing animal research. Resolution of differences would be ideal, but the best the center can hope for is documenting and cataloguing the divisions in much more detail than has been done in this chapter. The catalogue, when compiled, would stand in stark contrast to and thereby help subvert the policy narrative currently underwriting much of the controversy, namely, that the debate is between two equally homogeneous camps, each with a straightforward scenario, only one of which is right and the other wrong.[11] Differences within camps are profound, complicated, and are to be exploited as such.

An important feature of institutionalizing the complexity of the animal research issue is that it widens the debate's terms. Opponents and proponents of animal research are only two among many camps taking opposing positions. One must also distinguish between those who are not against animal research and those who are not in favor of animal research. Those not against animal research of course need not be for it: some groups may be so opposed to human subjects experimentation that they do not object to (nonhuman) animal research, albeit they do not necessarily support it either (as, for example, some consumer product testing proponents). As for groups not in favor of animal research, they include people and organizations who object to research on all living beings. Accordingly, one major objective of the center would be to provide a forum for an ongoing and fully publicized debate among *all* opposing groups over the advantages and disadvantages of human and animal research.[12] The need to widen the animal research controversy by including those for and against human subjects experimentation deserves underlining, since such experimentation was and still is in many quarters just as contentious as animal research currently is.[13] To these ends, the center could offer periodic conferences or one-year appointments to visiting scholars, scientists *and* representatives of animal welfare groups representing the full range of views, the proceedings of which would then be widely circulated.

After having complexified the animal research issue in terms of its multiple perspectives, the next step for the center's designer would be to highlight the truly problematic nature of the animals' "perspective" in the controversy. This goes beyond epistemological and ethical questions about whether or not animals have any "thoughts" or "feelings" on the matter. Also involved are the perennial questions of ontology: What is an animal? What is a human being? And what "rights," if any, do either have? These are the contested terrain at the core of the animal research debate. Accordingly, one of the major objectives of the alternatives center would be to involve bioethicists and philosophers of all stripes in the center's activities so that its visiting practitioners, particularly university researchers and animal rights advocates, are prodded into reflecting on issues they otherwise ignore, if not actively avoid.[14]

What are the advantages and disadvantages associated with such a proposal for an animal alternatives center? The cost to the university administration is fairly obvious: institutionalizing a forum for the discussion of such widely opposing viewpoints would keep in high profile a set of extremely divisive issues. Equally important, every year is a bad year for university budgets, and this center might well be an expensive enterprise. The benefits are more subtle, but compelling after their own fashion. An understandable concern of administrators and faculty is that a center, once established, would become the focal point for subsequent efforts by legislators and animal rights groups to regulate, oversee, and centralize animal use in university research. But what legislature would assign regulatory responsibilities to a center having the explicit goal of encouraging, even if it can't hope to resolve, the debate over animal research? The best legislators could expect from such a center would be to treat each instance of animal experimentation on a case-by-case basis (a general point developed more fully in chapter 7). Another potential benefit of such a center would be that its establishment puts the university on record as supporting both animal alternatives and animal welfare groups, though the center does so within the same context of seminars, conferences, and appointments it uses to support the airing of all opposing viewpoints.

Is this reasoning cynical? Undoubtedly some university administrators and faculty would like nothing better than to accentuate the divisions among animal rights advocates as a way of neutralizing the threat they pose to animal-based research. But you are the analyst in this example, and policy analysts by and large proceed on the assumption that consequences, not the intentions that give rise to them, are what really matter. From the perspective of conventional policy analysis, what motivates the creation of a policy or program is rarely as important as the consequences that follow from its implementation. Fortunately, one of the primary consequences of establishing the proposed center, irrespective of the animus of its initiators, would be the empowerment of hitherto marginalized groups having little voice in the controversy but who are nonetheless at the heart of it. In a conflict of such high uncertainty and polarization where the stakes are so considerable, who can risk having to choose only between those who say they know that the future shall hold us accountable for our wholesale slaughter of animals and those who would blame us for the human deaths they say will surely follow when we do not allow that slaughter? Who can afford to have one group dominate over the other in circumstances characterized by so many unknowns and so much division? The differences within the animal rights community and among university researchers should be exploited by the university administration—exploited in the sense that the issue of human subjects experimentation will surely come back to haunt the university community in an even more virulent fashion, if it is not dealt with in tandem with the animal research issue.

Final Point

High-risk, high-tech, and high-cost controversies frequently present what seems at first a truly vicious double-bind: not only can the questions you don't ask kill you as much as the answers to questions you do ask, but equally destructive can be those unwanted answers to questions never raised and those questions that should never have had answers in the first place. The double bind appears central to the animal welfare controversy. Appeals to long-standing "models" of research that are taken to predicate and distinguish fields from each other—biochemistry admits animal experimentation in a way that chemistry does not—are as much a way of avoiding question asking as they are the con-ventionalized search for the "right" kinds of answers. Similarly, the un-anticipated consequences of animal research—the bovine growth hor-mone, for example, is belatedly seen as threatening one kind of animal industry, while another industry has arisen to supply lab animals—underscore some of the unwanted research questions and unintended research answers that animal experimentation has engendered. In these kinds of double-bind issues, you're damned if you do and damned if you don't.

A less pessimistic view has been offered in this chapter. We certainly do not know the final answers to major policy issues for which no middle ground seems possible, but we can defend the search for metanarratives that put us in a position to provide some kind of answer. Treating an issue as nonsense at the metanarrative level can be defended as the position an analyst takes in order to analyze what seems to be an irreconcilably contradictory issue without at the same time making the analysis itself contradictory and thereby also a piece of "nonsense."[15] We will return to the narrative features of this "positioning" in chapter 6's case study on global warming. It need only be noted here that there is no guarantee a metanarrative can be constructed or is always policy-relevant. Certainly some metanarratives are extremely difficult to see or read, as policy nar-ratives can be much more obscure and complexly interactive than in the case of the animal rights controversy. We turn to one such example now.

A Salt on the Land: Finding the Stories, Nonstories, and Metanarrative in the Controversy over Irrigation-Related Salinity and Toxicity in California's San Joaquin Valley

With Janne Hukkinen and Gene Rochlin

Introduction

Some policy controversies are so uncertain and complex that the major policy narratives driving them are not at all evident. In such cases, the temptation is to try to reduce the uncertainty and simplify the complexity directly. Unfortunately, that option is not always available or even possible. Moreover, as we saw in the last chapter's case study of the animal rights controversy, the underlying premise that well-defined options in and of themselves promote improved policymaking cannot be assumed. Issue uncertainty and lack of agreement may reflect both the tortured evolution of policy analysis efforts to deal with the problem and the positive role that uncertainty and disagreement can play in policymaking and analysis. In either case, attempts to systematically analyze the underlying reasons for persisting uncertainty and lack of agreement may be deliberately frustrated by bureaucratic and policy actors.

Where imprecision has become functional to the actors, the tangled scenarios and arguments they tell can be the best (sometimes the only) means to expose issues of high uncertainty or little agreement in ways that make them more amenable to conventional policy analytical tools. Narrative policy analysis provides a procedure for integrating such narratives, which identifies not only the issues at stake, but the causes, modalities, and purposes of their systematic obfuscation. In particular, we use a computer program based on network analysis and a fairly sophisticated semiotic approach to better elicit the dominant stories, non-stories, and metanarrative that otherwise remain obscure to many, if not most, of the major participants in what has been a highly contentious and costly environmental issue in U.S. agriculture: the problem of irrigation-derived salts and toxics in the San Joaquin Valley of central California. This chapter offers the reader a detailed example of the ideal method-ology for a narrative policy analysis, an application of those methods, and a client's response to that application (much of which is reprised in appendix A).

The results of this chapter's case study can be summarized succinctly. In their efforts to deal with the valley's agricultural drainage, local, state, and federal irrigation agencies are caught in a dilemma little recognized or articulated by irrigation officials. On the one hand, despite consider-able social and political pressures to solve or mitigate the problems of toxicity and salinity in agricultural drainwater, persistent uncertainty about the risks and efficacy of competing methods has prevented prog-ress in rectifying these problems. On the other hand, solutions that allow irrigation to continue unabated in the valley will exacerbate the ongoing controversy over the provision of subsidized water for the subsidized crops of a few highly subsidized agribusiness firms.

In short, irrigation agencies need to reduce uncertainty about treat-ment methods, while reducing uncertainty could further polarize the controversy. Identifying the dilemma helps us understand the underly-ing reasons why policymakers have been reluctant to move in any direc-tion that forces action but increases their political costs and have instead continued to request additional study in the face of a manifest and grow-ing problem.

This chapter demonstrates how narrative policy analysis identifies such blocks to effective policymaking and these areas of contention that must be addressed before conventional policy analytic tools can be effec-tively used. It also describes our experience in presenting the results of our analysis to irrigation officials and their disappointing response.

Background on Irrigation Toxics and Salts in the San Joaquin Valley

The Setting. According to estimates published in the early 1980s, ap-proximately 8 million of the 11 million crop-producing acres in Califor-nia are under irrigation.[1] The San Joaquin Valley has accounted for over half of the irrigated acreage[2] and well over half of the state's $15 billion annual gross agricultural production.[3] Among the ten highest producers of agricultural commodities in the United States are five valley counties.[4] The State Water Project and the federal Central Valley Project, which are the valley's main suppliers of irrigation water, account for over a quarter of the water used annually in California.

In addition to the obvious problem of salinization, potentially toxic trace elements have been found in the drainage water from irrigation. Soils in some parts of the San Joaquin Valley (and in particular along the western slopes) have relatively high concentrations of selenium (a naturally occurring trace element that washes out of farm soils) as well as other potentially toxic elements. The valley's salinization problem is due to an underlying layer of clay, which restricts the proper drainage of irrigation water. As a consequence, widespread and continuous irrigation has led to high water tables and heavy salt accumulation. These problems afflict some 500,000 acres of irrigated land, and it has been estimated that between 1 million and 3.6 million acres of valley farmland could eventually be affected by salt buildup and inadequate drainage.[5]

In an attempt to resolve the salinization problem, subsurface drains have been constructed to remove the drainage water from beneath the fields. For more than thirty years, a master drain, either to the San Francisco Bay and Delta Region or directly via pipeline to the Pacific Ocean, was considered to be the best way to dispose of the drainage out of the valley. As neither has been constructed, drainage has been discharged primarily into the San Joaquin River or into evaporation ponds located in the valley. This disposal has led to the toxicity problem associated with the valley's agricultural drainage.

For reasons discussed below, the canal originally intended to carry drainage from the Central Valley Project out of the valley ended up being constructed only as far as Kesterson Reservoir in the northern part of the valley. An alarming number of bird deaths and deformities, most likely caused by abnormally high levels of selenium in the pond water and food chain, were found at Kesterson in the early 1980s.[6] Unusually high levels of selenium and other potentially toxic trace elements have also been observed elsewhere in the valley, most notably in the evaporation ponds that serve as drainage disposal sites in the southern part of the valley, an area serviced by the State Water Project.[7] The clean-up cost of Kesterson alone has been estimated to be anywhere between $12 million and $145 million.[8]

Public awareness of the risks of selenium and other toxics found in the valley considerably increased the conflict and uncertainty over the disposal of agricultural drainage: out-of-valley options such as a master drain or pipeline, contentious even when only saline flow was foreseen, became politically unacceptable to virtually all interested parties, including agribusiness. Moreover, in-valley disposal options now include the management of minerals and other potential toxics whose properties and health impacts are little understood. Attention has therefore shifted to analyzing and assessing short-term and often technically and economically uncertain alternatives, such as improved on-farm management practices, land retirement, and various biological and physical-chemical treatment processes and facilities.

Past Policy Analysis Efforts. Over the last forty years or more, considerable policy analysis, research, and design effort has been devoted to finding better ways of disposing of agricultural drainage and managing its associated problems. Roughly three periods have been observed in this history. Between 1950 and 1975, state and federal interest focused on establishing the technoeconomic feasibility of a master drain discharging into the San Francisco Bay-Delta and serving the entire valley.[9] In the end, local, state, and federal officials proved unable to resolve their differences over financing and implementing a master drain or to reassure environmental groups of their ability to protect bay and coastal environments.

Officials did, however, agree to examine a broader range of in-valley and out-of-valley disposal options, with attention this time not only to technical and economic considerations but also to the environmental impact of implementing various options. This second phase of research and assessment revolved around benefit–cost analyses, econometric studies, environmental simulations, and environmental impact statements.[10] It ran from approximately 1975 to 1982, when the discovery of the bird kills at Kesterson raised the issue to high public concern and salience—and brought the second phase to a halt.

Following much confusion, local, state, and federal officials were able to start a third research and design effort in 1984, the San Joaquin Valley Drainage Program (SJVDP), which was to focus only on in-valley remedies to the now expanded medley of drainage problems. Unlike past efforts, this program considerably expanded its terms of reference on at least two fronts: it included members from environmental and citizen groups and its evaluative criteria explicitly broadened the earlier regard for technoeconomic and environmental factors to include other policy-analytical considerations of risk assessment, social and institutional impacts, and political and legal feasibility.[11]

Unfortunately, the SJVDP fared little better than its predecessors. By the end of the 1980s, $50 million was estimated to have been spent on research of drainage-related problems and in-valley proposals, with no technically or economically feasible and politically acceptable solution in sight.[12] The issue of how to deal with salinization and selenium toxicity in the valley's agricultural drainage still remains highly controversial and full of unknowns. Indeed, as will become clear below, the program's research effort in some cases has actually contributed to uncertainty as well as stimulating additional controversy.

The inability of the SJVDP to arrive even at a consensual problem definition can be gauged from our interviews with twenty-three experts representing the four main interest groups in the controversy—the agricultural community, planners, regulators, and the environmental community.[13] These interviews, funded as part of the third research phase, were originally to provide the basis for identifying the list of salient drainage alternatives and assessing their technical and economic features in light of different feasibility criteria. It soon became clear that this conventional policy-analytic effort, like others before it, was premature. The exercise assumed that some kind of consensus existed over problem definition. In reality, the interviewees gave different, and at times conflicting, technical, economic, social, legal, and organizational descriptions of the San Joaquin Valley drainage problem. In only twenty-three interviews, we identified ninety different drainage-related problem statements. Very few problems were mentioned by more than two interviewees (fifty-two of the ninety problem statements were recorded only once or twice; only eight problems were mentioned by seven or more interviewees).

More important, even when a number of interviewees did state the same problem, their perceptions of causality often differed widely. What was a cause or an initial problem from one expert's viewpoint proved to be an effect or a terminal problem from the perspective of another expert. Only nine problems were classified as just one type of problem (for example, as an initial or terminal problem) by all of those who mentioned it and not one of these problem statements was included among the eight most frequently mentioned in the interviews.

Nothing more clearly illustrates the failure of more than four decades of attempted policymaking than this inability of major actors in the drainage controversy to converge even on causal relationships. By and large, the problem is not clearly defined, the objectives to be achieved in terms of water quality are not agreed upon, the technical solutions in lieu of the master drain or ocean pipeline are uncertain, and little agreement exists on the criteria to assess the effectiveness of the technical solutions. The inability to agree upon causal relationships, particularly in problem definition, is made all the more salient and difficult by the one common theme that did emerge from the interviews: although no valleywide master drain or pipeline is feasible, now or in the foreseeable future, it is imperative that the valley's agricultural drainage be managed effectively, somehow. Twenty-one of the twenty-three interviewees made this point in one fashion or another.[14] We return to the point later.

The following analytic exercise was developed in response to our initial attempt to use conventional policy analysis in analyzing the drainage problem and is based on the alternative framework set out in our final report to the SJVDP. The approach takes as its central task the analysis of the controversy's fundamental lack of convergence over how problems and their causal relationships are defined. By understanding the underlying factors giving rise to this lack of convergence, new research, we argue, will be in a better position to analyze the drainage issue in ways making it more amenable to conventional analysis than has been the case so far.

The Analytic Exercise

Our starting point was the assumption that the budget to implement any proposed solution to the drainage problem would be limited but that there would be no restrictions on the kinds of solution to be reviewed and analyzed in our investigation. We were not, for example, limited to recommending building a new program on what the SJVDP considered to be "promising areas of future research" nor on the expectation that such a program would be funded at anywhere near the level of past efforts. Not surprisingly, the single most important constraint we imposed on our analysis was the need to ensure that the often differing perspectives of the major local, state, and federal irrigation officials in the drainage controversy were taken into full account.

Faced with an inability to apply more traditional policy analytical tools to compare drainage alternatives and options, we decided to analyze the stories—that is, scenarios and arguments—of the interviewees in order to identify the interviewees' underlying set of beliefs and premises about drainage problems and their causal relations. Rather than treat each interview as a test of some externally constructed model of causality said to be operating in a controversy that is taken as given, we treat each scenario or argument as an equally valid element of a larger narrative from which "reality" (in this case, the system-wide drainage controversy) is constructed. Again, such attention to stories and narratives is not new to policymaking and policy analysis. What is new is the network analysis of narratives. An integrative analysis of causality based on the interrelationships among the policy narratives of a controversy's participants has to our knowledge rarely been made the central focus of a specific policy analysis like that reported in this chapter.

Network Analysis. Given the difficulty of identifying any set of expressed causal relationships held common by any important subset of policy actors and affected parties, the question we then asked was, What were the "problems and causal relationships" specifically recounted in each interview? Since the interviewee was also a member of an interest group and since the controversy revolves around these interest groups, we also set out to determine what "problems and causal relationships" could be discerned within and among the interest groups concerned. Network analysis helped us to make rudimentary distinctions between these groupings and has several distinct advantages for the purpose of our analytic exercise.

In its simplest form, network analysis proceeded as follows. If individual X argued that problem statement 1 led to problem statement 2 ($1 \rightarrow 2$), while individual Y felt that problem statement 2 led to problem statement 3 ($2 \rightarrow 3$), then the aggregated "network" (in this case a simple chain) would become $1 \rightarrow 2 \rightarrow 3$ (assuming the only interviewees were individuals X and Y). More generally, statement 2, which is the *terminal* problem for individual X is the *initial* problem for individual Y and becomes the *transfer* problem after aggregation. When the problem networks of several interviewees are aggregated in this fashion, each reported causal relationship ($\rightarrow$) is explicit, that is, has been stated by at least one of the interviewees. The resulting aggregated networks are implicit, in the sense that no one person need actually to have described or even perceived the complete chain of problems.

The advantages of this procedure are several. First, it allows us to examine better the extent to which, if at all, the lack of convergence over problems and causality in the controversy is due to contradictory or circular argumentation at the individual or intragroup level, rather than due, say, to well-argued, but conflicting, values and perceptions between interest groups. Second, aggregation to the intergroup level might identify "causal relationships," which only become clear when the views of the controversy's participants are considered together and which are robust enough to afford possible points of departure for future follow-up. Third, *potential* sources of future conflict between interest groups might become clearer, since the aggregation exercise is our best approximation of the lines of reasoning and debate that could be displayed, were all the controversy's major participants to come around a table and argue the points raised individually in the interviews. (Obviously, "potential" has to be emphasized, since a simple aggregation exercise cannot capture the interaction effect of people modifying in public those positions they hold in private.) Fourth, and in ways that become apparent below, aggregation to the intergroup level allows us to represent the drainage controversy as a combination of individual and group perceptions that imposes system-wide problems and dilemmas across these individuals and groups. By treating individual problem statements as elements of a complex, multi-participant and multigroup "network," the resulting assemblage of connected (or in some cases, isolated) problem networks comes to represent a systemic, albeit implicit, expression of those very same causal beliefs from which the drainage controversy has in large part been constituted and through which it has been perceived by participants and the groups to which they belong.[15]

The results of the network analysis show that linear causal pathways are rare at the intergroup level. Indeed, the emergence of multiple circular networks in which there is no unique initial or terminal problem dominates the aggregation exercise. In the simplest circular network, statement 1 is said to lead to statement 2, but statement 2 is also said to lead back to statement 1 ($1 \leftrightarrow 2$). A more complex circular network could have the structure $1 \rightarrow 2 \rightarrow 3 \rightarrow 4 \rightarrow 1$. Only two interviewees were found to have made such circular argumentation in their interviews. The relative dearth of circular networks also holds at the group level (when excluding these two individuals). None can be constructed for the agricultural community, planners, regulators, or environmental community, when the problem networks of interviewees are aggregated within each interest group. This lack of within-group circular argumentation increases our confidence that these four groups are in fact fairly distinct and homogeneous.

However, at the intergroup level, where the problem statements of more than one group are considered together, the number and complexity of constructed circular networks increases markedly. The 5, relatively simple intragroup networks give way to 34 more elaborately linked circular networks in a pairwise comparison of the groups, while aggregation across all 4 interest groups yields 244 circular networks.[16] Indeed, the most striking, yet unheralded, feature of the San Joaquin Valley drainage controversy is the multiple circularity implied by, rather than made explicit in, the stories that its key participants tell as a way of articulating the drainage issue. (The next section focuses on the main noncircular narratives in the controversy.)

At first glance the emergence of so many circular networks would seem to do nothing more than confirm our earlier finding that the drainage controversy is not localized to a set of commonly perceived problems and solutions. The discovery of *circular* networks, however, was useful on two counts.

First, these networks were potentially destabilizing, positive feedback loops, where problems get worse and worse, unlike equilibrating, negative loops. Not only do the networks represent potential sources of future conflict, but they single out a complex of problems whose mutually reinforcing nature could make them even more problematic to the policymaker, as will be seen shortly.

Second, the discovery of circular networks served both to support our earlier decision to analyze the drainage controversy in narrative terms and to indicate the direction in which the narrative analysis should proceed. For as we saw in earlier chapters, an important feature of narrative policy analysis is how nonstories can enable us to generate policy-relevant metanarratives. By identifying those major narratives in the controversy, such as the circular networks, that do not conform to the definition of a story having a beginning, middle, and end, the analyst can then compare these narratives with the controversy's policy narratives to see if the comparison tells another more useful story. In our exercise, this means a comparison of the circular networks (the nonstories) with the larger networks of initial and terminal problems (the stories) in which they are embedded. If a metanarrative can be generated from this comparison of nonstory and story, the analyst then determines if or how it redefines the problem in such a way as to make that problem more amenable to the conventional policy analytical tools, which in our exercise proved to be organization theory. Narrative policy analysis provides the armature for the following analysis of major problem networks in the irrigation agencies.

Major Circular Networks—Uncertainty as a Source of Polarization. Since the views of local, state, and federal irrigation officials were of major concern in the analytic exercise, the following analysis of circular networks centers on the eighteen interviews involving the agricultural community and the planners. The two groups together are what can be termed California's "irrigation bureaucracy," that is, the interviewees represent the operational and research staff associated with the local district, state, and federal irrigation agencies working in the San Joaquin Valley.[17] When the problem networks identified by the agricultural community and planners are considered together, we find three interconnected circular networks—an "initial loop" that leads to a "terminal loop" both directly and via a "transfer loop." The initial loop revolves around the perceived breaching of state and federal water contracts that were said to have guaranteed drainage disposal for farmers in the valley, which in turn leads to a transfer loop centering around problems of water quality standards and costs said to arise as a result of the now-uncertain drainage disposal. The three circular networks and the terminal problem to which they lead are shown in figure 1.

The terminal loop best illustrates the specifics of the circularity and its important implications for exacerbating political polarization. The interviewees from the agricultural community said that the necessity of taking irrigated land out of production (because of severe drainage problems) raises in their view the need to compensate the affected irrigators. This, in turn, raises other questions in their minds about the equity of compensating these farmers for such losses and not others who remain in irrigated production and whose production costs also are rising due to drainage-related problems.

According to planners, the agricultural community's recognition that drainage-related costs are rising for all farmers, but that government compensation is not being distributed to all who deserve it, only induces further competition among the farmers for what remaining profits are to be had in irrigation. Increased competition in the view of planners pits large farms against small farms, inevitably leading to some farms going out of production. The first irrigated land to go out of production will be that suffering from the severest drainage problems. And thus the circle is completed: land is said to be driven out of production, if not because of competition between farms in the presence of compensation, then because of severe drainage problems and associated losses that would persist in the absence of compensation.

If each of the stated causal connections actually held, the impact of taking out of production those farms with severe drainage problems would be considerable; anywhere from 20 to 70 percent of the land currently under irrigation production in the valley could be affected. Market forces could, of course, forestall the worst-case scenario to the extent

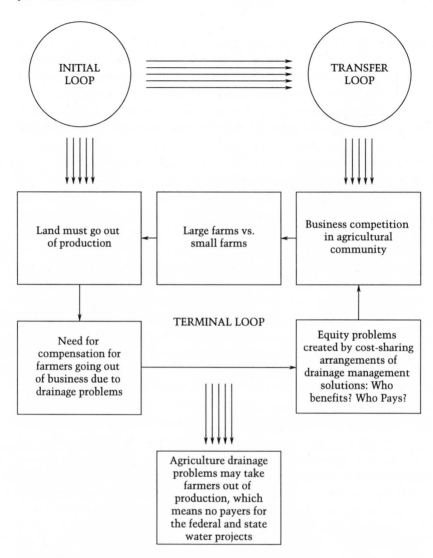

Figure 1. Circular networks of the irrigation bureaucracy.

that the declining supply of irrigable land and the growing demand for its production led to rising land and agricultural prices, thereby encouraging the development of better ways to handle the problems afflicting the remaining, poorly drained irrigated land. But that solution could come much too late and at too great a cost from the perspective of those decision makers charged with having to worry about the considerable dislocation likely to result from the loss of a million or more acres from irrigated production.

This potential cost to decision makers is evident from the major problem produced by the three circular networks. The terminal loop just described was found to lead to one terminal problem statement: "Agricultural drainage problems may take farmers out of production, which means no payers for the federal and state water projects." The irrigation bureaucracy depends on the political and financial resources of irrigators; indeed, the very legitimacy of the bureaucracy derives from the need to irrigate California farmland. Taking land out of production strikes directly at the irrigation bureaucracy's autonomy, authority, and influence. Heated comments in the interviews indicate that land retirement is an incomprehensible proposal for many irrigators and irrigation bureaucrats: "Land will NOT go out of production" and "Taking land out of production is an infeasible proposal," as some put it.

On the other hand, land retirement is no problem at all for segments of the environmental community. In fact, it is the preferred solution for many, especially those who have fought for decades against what is perceived as a federal water subsidy for agribusiness. "Concretely [the drainage problem] means that some land will have to come out of production," as one environmentalist argued. In short, even to raise the question of land retirement is rightly perceived by the irrigation bureaucracy as further polarizing the drainage controversy.

The circular argumentation implicit in the beliefs held by those in the irrigation bureaucracy helps identify several levels of uncertainty over the drainage issue that increase the potential for even greater political conflict in the controversy. One type of uncertainty arises because the empirical merits of the bureaucracy's assertions about problems and their relationships, many of them cast as the "certainties" of expert opinion, have yet to be confirmed and are sufficiently inconsistent as to give rise to some circularity at the aggregate level. If, however, the problem statements and causal relationships are proved to be as specified in the circular networks, then the certainties and uncertainties professed by experts become locked into a positive feedback loop that is mutually reinforcing and all the more persisting. For the irrigation bureaucracy, this means that the problems of land retirement and declining support will just get worse, unless something unexpected (the market? government?) intervenes. Moreover, to undertake the necessary verification exercise as to what empirically is real cause and real effect would require not only considerable additional resources, but also corroboration by those very "experts" whose statements gave rise to the circular network argumentation in the first place.

In the absence of verification, the irrigation bureaucracy is left with very real fears about what effect polarization over the land retirement issue can have on the bureaucracy's operations and legitimacy. A scenario about how "uncertainty can lead to polarization," of course, does not necessarily denote a potentially intractable problem, but it does suggest that the drainage controversy will have to be reconceived in terms that deal directly with the political polarization before uncertainties can be reduced. Unfortunately, attempts to resolve the present polarization are most likely to increase, rather than reduce, present uncertainties, as the second half of our analysis shows.

Polarization as a Source of Uncertainty: Implications of the Master Drain Assumption. Having explored the major drainage management problems in the last section, we now turn in more detail to the organizational and political implications for the irrigation bureaucracy of the widely held no-drain assumption. As noted earlier, the major parties to the drainage controversy do agree on two basic points: It is imperative that the valley's drainage be better managed and that this not be done through construction of a master drain. What though does this assumption really *mean* to the controversy's major participants?

Our starting point was to see if narrative analysis could also help in answering this question. Fortunately for our purposes, the field of semiotics has an analogue to the reciprocal causal link, ↔, found in the circular networks. Moreover, the analogue's link, which is one of mutual definition rather than mutual causation, is especially pertinent since our question revolves around defining just what the no-drain assumption means to the parties concerned. The basic notion underlying the *semiotic square* is that a term is best defined by what it is not—in this case by its contraries and contradictories.[18]

What does this mean for our controversy specifically? Within the framework of the semiotic square, the no-drain assumption draws its meaning from three possible opposing positions concerning the drain or drainage. At its most obvious level, the no-drain assumption is simply the rejection of the position that there should be a valleywide drain (in the semiotic square of figure 2, the drain and no-drain positions are essentially contraries, just as are the drainage and no-drainage positions). The drain and no-drain positions could, in turn, be opposed by those who differ not over the *drain*, but over whether *drainage* will take place at all

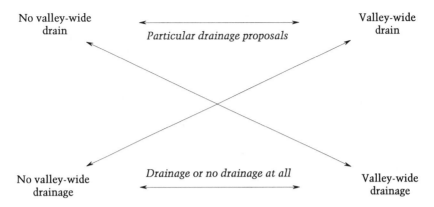

Figure 2. The implied network of drain and drainage proposals.

in the valley. Here the contrary proposals for drain or no drain are themselves contradicted by positions that basically appeal to wider boundary
conditions at variance with any particular drainage proposal. For anyone
who maintains a no-drain position as the starting point, there are others
who could assert that drainage will be maintained throughout the valley,
even if this requires the (unmentionable) master drain (in figure 2 the no-
drain and drainage positions are contradictories). In contrast, for anyone
who argues that there will be a drain, there are others who could claim
that the starting position is not merely no drain, but no drainage facilities
whatsoever in the valley (the drain and no-drainage assumptions are the
second set of contradictories in figure 2). In sum, the four positions of
contradictories and contraries define each other reciprocally, and we call
this network of mutually defining positions "the implied network."

If all four positions were evident, the debate over the San Joaquin Valley's agricultural drainage would be polarized over fairly clear-cut divisions on which the analyst could then focus attention and analysis. But
full-blown polarization is precisely what has *not* happened. Opposing
operating assumptions have yet to be fully realized or enacted. Indeed,
the lack of widespread polarization and open controversy over the master
drain greatly surprised us. What factors account for this attenuation or
truncation?

The answer is, some polarization has been internalized to the bureaucracy. Instead of only being espoused by opposing groups, two of the
opposing positions have simultaneously become an integral part of the
irrigation bureaucracy's own scenario. Many officials in the relevant federal, state, regional, and local agencies say that there will be no drain, yet

fervently argue that drainage will have to continue in the valley. They do so by formally rejecting a master drain, while still believing in it when arguing that valleywide drainage is imperative.[19] The potential for cognitive dissonance is patent.

Balancing these internal costs, however, is the fact that the bureaucracy's dual position has served the positive function of preventing a more polarized debate over the drainage issue. Against what or whom could the environmentalists argue, when both the irrigators and the irrigation bureaucrats openly say that neither a drain to the delta nor a pipeline to the ocean will be constructed? By holding what seem on appearance to be two mutually opposing positions, that is, "there will be no drain" and "drainage is required," the irrigation bureaucracy has reduced the potential for the two other opposing positions to be realized, the most threatening of which is that there will be no valleywide drainage whatsoever. Instead of four mutually opposing positions, reality presents a truncated version of the "implied network" in which real debate is frustrated by an irrigation bureaucracy which preserves the notion of valleywide drainage at the cost of conceding, rather than accepting, that there will be no master drain.

Irrigators and irrigation bureaucrats have good reason for wanting to avoid further polarization. The selenium finds at the Kesterson Reservoir transformed a primarily agricultural drainage problem into an environmental toxics one. To quote a planner in our sample, "Toxics in agricultural drainage water have shifted the nature of the problem from a 'harmless' salinity problem to one requiring policing powers." Kesterson, the "local solution to the salinity problem," became Kesterson, the "local toxics problem," threatening valley-wide drainage and irrigation as a whole.

Quick to learn by example, the irrigation bureaucracy has become very reluctant to implement further "remedies," when Californians take the major lesson of Kesterson Reservoir to be the need for constant vigilance. Who knows what new drainage "solution" will lead to even more drainage problems? Moreover, even if the "solution" actually worked, opposition would still arise from environmentalists and others to the extent that the drainage solution increases the long-term viability of irrigated agriculture as it is currently practiced by valley agribusiness. Consequently, the bureaucracy has accommodated itself to uncertainty: better to try coping with the manifold uncertainties caused by not discussing obvious problems associated with in-valley "solutions" than to run the risk of having these problems publicly discussed in a way that makes the issues just as contentious as the out-of-valley solutions of the master drain and ocean pipeline. Uncertainty over land going out of production in the absence of a remedy to the drainage problem has to be weighed against the potential for further polarizing environmentalists and others when putting forward a "solution" to forestall land retirement. Thus, the seeming certainty of the no-drain assumption engenders in the end the persistence of uncertainty for the irrigation bureaucracy.[20]

In sum, comparison of the implied and truncated networks yields its own scenario about how "polarization can lead to uncertainty" in the drainage controversy. More specifically, the potential for the controversy's polarization has led to a situation of increased uncertainty for the irrigation bureaucracy. In functional terms, the bureaucracy seems to hold conflicting positions as a way of reducing the potential for polarization, at least in the short run. Efforts to rationalize the conflicting beliefs, or to rank possible solutions to the drainage problem without addressing the underlying conflict, are likely to be actively opposed rather than accepted.

Taken together with the earlier analysis of the circular networks, our narrative approach identifies why efforts to clarify causality and options have proven so difficult. As long as the issue of drain versus no drain cannot be openly debated at the policy level, uncertainty will persist. Yet this uncertainty as to drainage options cannot be directly addressed, for fear that further polarization will occur over the matter of taking land out of production.

In contrast to the all-powerful bureaucracy painted by some authors,[21] our narrative analysis uncovers a disabling policy dilemma, whose dimensions and structure are not articulated (and perhaps not perceived) by participants to the policy process. Indeed, their suppression is part of the policy problem.

The Drainage Dilemma as a Policy Metanarrative

Irrigation agencies have little choice but to maintain the appearance of seeking resolution of the prevailing and potential uncertainties in the drainage controversy, first because agricultural drainage is perceived to be an environmental toxics problem requiring immediate remedies, and second because within the next several decades the waterlogging and salinity problems could well lead to the forced retirement of a great deal of irrigated land. If the irrigation bureaucracy does not better manage these problems, its organizational raison d'être is threatened.

On the other hand, currently proposed efforts to reduce the unknowns in the drainage controversy run the risk of eliciting opposition not just to the proposed solution, but to valley agribusiness itself. Political opposition to the master drain and the ocean pipeline, voter rejection of new large-scale water projects, such as the Peripheral Canal, more recent efforts to restrict any new diversions from the San Francisco Bay–Delta system, and now the controversy over the proposed Kesterson cleanup plans are all reminders of how irrigation-related "solutions" quickly come under attack in California. A fully polarized debate on irrigation in general and on toxics in particular is an unpalatable prospect for the irrigation bureaucracy, since it could ultimately lead to posing the issue directly as land withdrawals versus the master drain; the first is incompatible with the bureaucracy's goals and purposes, the second with its political environment.

Thus, reducing uncertainty will potentially increase polarization and political interference; reducing polarization by letting uncertainty persist or increase could ultimately force unwanted change of organizational goals and charter. Threatened from both sides, irrigation agencies are pressed to manage conflict by walking a fine line between uncertainty and polarization. This dilemma is found to persist for each of the currently proposed technical solutions to the drainage problem in the valley.[22]

Irrigation agencies attempt to resolve their dilemma in two ways. Agencies have begun to distance themselves from each other, arguing that the dilemma is more of a problem for some than others. There are those who say, for example, that the California Department of Water Resources really does not have to walk the line between uncertainty and polarization, since agricultural drainage is more of a problem for the U.S. Bureau of Reclamation, which is responsible for the Kesterson cleanup. A second tactic has been to try to create more uncertainty than polarization by not funding research on out-of-valley solutions, while at the same time conducting research on in-valley solutions. The San Joaquin Valley Drainage Program's avoidance of controversial research on out-of-valley solutions has kept alive the uncertainty over the technoeconomic feasibility of such solutions, should they become politically and legally feasible at a distant date.[23] Similarly, the program's research efforts on in-valley solutions have debunked conventional wisdoms about the drainage problem and produced new findings in areas unfamiliar to the water managers and users.[24] In so doing, irrigation agencies, such as the program, put themselves in a position where they always have more questions to ask than can be answered.

On closer inspection, these two tactics reproduce the components of the original dilemma, only in a new guise. The advantage irrigation agencies gain by arguing that the drainage problem is not their problem is only short-run, since the agencies end up confronting a different set of uncertainties. The State Water Project is in a better legal position than the Central Valley Project to reallocate water "given up" by agricultural contractors to meet the growing needs of urban contractors. But the unknowns of such a shift in allocation are considerable, and it is probable that the Department of Water Resources would exercise as much caution in making this reallocation as it is now exercising in the agricultural drainage controversy. The second approach to "resolving" the dilemma— calling for more research while avoiding funding topics that should be researched—is also a short-run expedient. Using research uncertainties to reduce the threat of further polarization will not forestall the highly polarized political debate that will ultimately surface when salinity problems have reached a scale jeopardizing wide tracts of irrigated agriculture. In short, tactically understandable but strategically unhelpful, interagency polarization and progressive research uncertainties do not in the end avoid the bureaucracy's basic dilemma.

Recommendations: Uncoupling Drainage and Irrigation

The findings of our narrative policy analysis illuminate how the bureaucracy's long-term goal of better valleywide drainage and its more immediate goal of ensuring irrigated production in the valley are irreconcilable when the bureaucracy acts as if its own self-interest precludes facing up to the political challenge of open, polarized conflict over irrigation or of persisting, unresolved uncertainties over drainage. The findings expose the degree to which the internalized bureaucratic conflict derives from and is reinforced not only by the inability of agencies to decide whether irrigation (their traditional and legitimating role) or drainage management (a relatively new goal) should have higher priority, but also by their consequent (and often implicit) rejection of the notion that the choice must be made at all. Indeed, the rejection can be explicit at times, as discussed in the following section on the agencies' response to our research findings.

In writing up the findings of our research for the sponsoring agency, we focused on the conflict over bureaucratic goals as the ultimate source of the agencies' dilemma, and its resolution as a prior condition for developing implementable drainage programs and policies. In particular, we asked whether drainage and irrigation could be administratively uncoupled as a way of resolving this goal conflict. Here narrative policy analysis proved helpful again. Going back over the results of the network analysis, we noted that while mention is made both of irrigation-related factors and of drainage-specific problems in the circular networks, the sole terminal problem statement concerns the threat that *drainage* problems in particular pose to the long-term survival of the state and federal water projects in California. Moreover, the implied network analysis pertains only to relations between drainage and the master drain. Nothing is implied with respect to irrigation *per se*. Yet drainage is commonly taken to threaten irrigation on the assumption that the former is an inseparable physical and organizational component of the latter. While this physical relationship is inherent, the organizational one is not. Even though irrigation often does lead to problems of salinity and toxic buildup, irrigation agencies not only can, but traditionally have, functioned without considering drainage. The question then becomes, Would the problems of drainage become more tractable if assigned to a specific agency not charged with concern about the future of irrigation?

With drainage responsibilities separated out, irrigation agencies would be relatively free to continue promoting and arguing for solutions most appropriate to their constituencies and historical organizational goals; it would be the task of the drainage agency (or agencies) to seek solutions for safe drainage. While the goal conflict would still exist, it would be externalized. Inner conflict and cognitive dissonance over goals would become external conflict with open political debate about goal priorities. This would clarify the terms of the debate, and allow the trade-offs to be openly argued by "advocate" agencies instead of submerged or disguised by agencies trying to avoid difficult internal choices.

In suggesting this solution, we had two objectives in mind. First, we did (and still do) believe that despite the known political and institutional problems of creating new agencies, the importance of both irrigated agriculture and safe management of drainage water to California justifies this solution, assuming we can demonstrate it to be the better alternative. Second, we hoped by this means to bring home to the policymakers and agencies following our study the significance we attached to our findings concerning the policy dilemma they faced (and will continue to face) under the current institutional structure.

We made it clear to irrigation officials that any proposal both to organizationally separate drainage and irrigation and to create an independent, autonomous agency having the sole institutional mandate of managing agricultural drainage would clearly involve issues of authority, responsibility, cost, and staffing that cannot be easily resolved and which, therefore, would have to be fully considered at the outset. The most important single issue would be assuring that those interagency differences that cannot be negotiated between them on their own will have to be settled formally, if not in the courts, then by a statutory regulatory board having this authority (for example, the State Water Resources Control Board in California).

Despite these possible drawbacks, the potential benefits are clear. First, organizational decoupling would greatly reduce the stress placed on an irrigation bureaucracy that does not have the staffing, the political mandate, or the propensity to pay full attention to the drainage problem. The tensions inherent in the internal goal conflict would thereby be reduced. Second, the new drainage agency would bear the brunt of the political debate surrounding the suggestion and ranking of various technical solutions and proposals, as well as the responsibility of developing alternatives. This would separate political conflict over further irrigation projects per se from that over the toxic and mineral loading of the agricultural drainage.

Third, organizational decoupling by function increases the prospects that the problems of toxicity and salinity will be studied as primary problems by an agency whose primary business it is to deal with them. There is a tendency for irrigation agencies to treat even such primary problems as salinization and toxics buildup as more or less "natural by-products" of irrigation, and therefore to relegate them to matters of secondary importance. Fourth, the credibility of the agency or agencies in charge of managing and disposing of drainage would be greatly increased if they were seen to be dedicated *solely* to waste management. Keeping the trade-offs between irrigation and drainage in the public arena avoids accusations of conflict of interest or private deals made in the backrooms of the irrigation agencies.

We did not suggest that such a decoupling would lead to a reduction of polarization over agricultural water in California, or directly lead to reductions in current uncertainties. What we did suggest is that the separation of function would clarify the terms of the debate, and provide avenues by which more traditional tools of policy analysis could be applied to the matters of reducing uncertainties and reconciling or resolving political conflicts.[25]

Agency Response to Recommendations

When we presented our results to the policymakers who chartered our research, we put forward two main policy points: first, the existence and persistence of the policy dilemma and the role the master drain played by its absence in the debate; and, second, the lack of any agency able to promote environmental goals without conflict with its traditional role and purpose. These were backed up with general analysis and a distillation of our data set, and only secondarily with a summary of our methodological analysis. The primary points we made were these:

—that we were unable to provide the requested comparative sociopolitical scale for comparing alternatives because of the inability of policy actors to provide a coherent, noncircular set of bounding rules, let alone goals and objectives
—that avoiding the issue of the master drain confounded attempts to rationalize policy and set priorities on options, and seriously interfered with the charter we were given
—that agencies caught in the uncertainty/polarization dilemma were unlikely to be able to reduce either
—that agencies traditionally chartered to promote agriculture and the distribution of water were unlikely agents for promotion of environmental objectives, particularly if those meant reducing irrigation water and/or taking land out of production
—that although we recognized the high political and other costs of creating a new agency, separating drainage and irrigation functions was the only course of action likely to provide an escape from the dilemma and allow policymaking to proceed towards some resolution.

When our report was sent to agencies for review, the comments we received were generally supportive, and tended to contain suggestions or critiques only with regard to specific points or sensitive areas requiring a most delicate choice of language. There were some amusing points, such as an expressed concern over our language about bureaucratic "survival" that disappeared when the manifestations of survival were reported without using this language; and a denial that agencies were distancing themselves from one another by the very people whose interviews supplied the data. Once we revised the draft to alter the "provocative" language, the written reviews were by and large quite positive.

However, when we sought to move to the scheduled next stage (a meeting between our group, our sponsor, and selected agency representatives), we received no support whatsoever. And, when we applied for the expected (and, we had thought, pre-agreed to) renewal for a second full year of research—a year to be focused on more intensive and specific data collection—it was denied. We were told that priorities had shifted, that the agency was now primarily interested in setting an agenda for action, that further institutional work was to focus on legal aspects, and, politely, that there was simply no funding to be had for work such as ours. Albeit a small consolation, our narrative policy analysis led us to understand better why our attempts to continue explicating the underlying and immediate dilemma confronting irrigation agencies were met by irrigation officials with the counterargument that we had chosen the "wrong" part of the problem to analyze, where the primary "problem" remained in the field, not in the bureaucracy.

In case it needs saying, like the rest of the policy analyst's tool kit of microeconomics, research methods, legal analysis, organization theory and public management practice, narrative policy analysis and its insights cannot *compel* policymakers to do anything.

Conclusion

Many analysts, policy or otherwise, already know that careful attention to the arguments dominating an issue of high uncertainty and dissensus can tell them something useful about how the controversy will unfold. This case study goes one step further by demonstrating that "nontraditional" procedures can be of great use to the practicing analyst not only for augmenting such conventional policy analytical techniques as organization theory and considerations of political feasibility, but also for understanding those cases where there is a seeming resistance to their application.

In particular, for complexly causal and goal-conflicted situations such as this one, our study exposes the degree to which the inability to reconcile objectives and resolve outstanding problems and indeterminacies inheres in the structure of the issue—that is, in the relationships between and among the many problems identified by the actors, given the actors' bureaucratic positions and self-definitions. In this case, the analysis was based on networks of problems and assumptions whose dimensions and linkage elude the actors themselves. The networks provide a way of disclosing the structure to the issue, and our own narrative articulates the connectivity and assumptions that structure presents, and continues to present, to policymakers.

Global Warming as Analytic Tip:
Other Models of Narrative Analysis I

We are at a point in the book where three questions readers might well have can be dealt with in one stroke. Are the preceding narrative analyses an exception, that is, are they a function of peculiarities in the case studies or the version of narrative analysis used? Are there other analysts using narrative analytical techniques like those presented here? Finally, what about the role of counterstories in a metanarrative (after all, chapter 5's semiotic square reminds us stories can be opposed by several counterpositions)?

The preceding studies are not outliers, and why this is the case is illustrated in the next two chapters. Here a different narrative analytical approach is applied, one relying on the contraposition of story and counterstory, but still directed to identifying a metanarrative that recasts a difficult policy problem in a more tractable way. The approach is that of the well-known semiotician, Michael Riffaterre. Of all the literary theorists I have read, Riffaterre comes closest in his notion of "intertext" to paralleling the metanarrative of the earlier chapters.

Riffaterre's model is introduced in this chapter and more fully discussed in the next. His model is a difficult one, and the terminology will be familiar only to readers with a literary theory background. Thus, in this chapter on global warming I have confined all references to Riffaterre, but one, to the notes, leaving to the next case study on Native American burial remains the detailed presentation of his model. Because the discussion of theory and methods has been kept to a minimum in the text, the analysis below approximates what a narrative policy analysis looks like if it were undertaken as a report for an actual client interested in fresh ways of analyzing global warming and their implications for thinking and acting on such issues.

Introduction

Global warming is one of the most contentious policy debates discussed in *Narrative Policy Analysis*. It is a subject about which not only politicians and policymakers but scientific experts, too, have staked out the widest range of opposing certainties and uncertainties.[1] Yet governments around the world are urged to join together and take action, now. How are we to respond? Atmospheric warming is said to be too important to wait for the majority of scientists to agree on the matter. Gaps in scientific knowledge must not be used as an excuse for inaction, as global warming experts repeatedly tell us. But how then are we to analyze such an issue?

One answer is to identify a policy-relevant metanarrative, in this case, the nonscientific *role* played by the controversy in analyzing global policy issues generally and environmental issues specifically. The principal feature of the global warming controversy—a feature that has yet to receive the attention it deserves—becomes clear in the process: governments will be in a better position to respond to purported greenhouse climate change once they understand how "global" is articulated as an analytic category for evaluating issues said to have worldwide implications. The controversy, we find, signals a wider "analytic tip" taking place in the examination of major public policy problems, a tip toward the notion that issues that can still be dealt with locally, regionally, or nationally must now first be addressed globally. Understanding the nature of this analytic tip and the narrative features of the global warming scenario are instrumental in telling us what we should be doing about the issue of atmospheric warming.

Certainties and Uncertainties in the Global Warming Scenario

Few scientists question the propositions that greenhouse gases produced locally disperse and build up across the atmosphere and that this accumulation can lead to atmospheric warming. Nor do many question the empirical findings that CO_2 emissions into the atmosphere, particularly from vehicles and factories, have increased substantially over the past decades or that these increases have the potential to produce climate change. Moreover, a growing number of experts believe average temperatures have risen worldwide.

The consensus, though, is not unanimous, and that lack of unanimity is reflected in widespread uncertainty and controversy. "There is little scientific doubt about the theory behind the greenhouse effect," according to Michael Glantz; "Thereafter, however, the scientific consensus begins to break down."[2] Not all respected climatologists and meteorologists agree that atmospheric warming has taken place or will in the future. One commentator reports, "There is a broad consensus among scientists that the earth is warming up. But few will claim consensus about the causes, the rate, or the future of the warming."[3] Analogies from the past to predict global warming and its consequences are widely disputed,[4] and general circulation models (GCMs) are understood, even by their compilers, to be flawed. For example, while most GCMs have assumed that clouds will increase atmospheric warming, experts continue to recognize that this effect is subject to many unknowns.[5] Modelers, too, differ in their estimates of temperature increase and in their views of the models' usefulness for predicting future temperatures.[6] Not only do meteorologists and climatologists disagree among themselves whether atmospheric warming is taking place, and if so, by how much, but the policy implications they have drawn continue to be criticized. Economists, in particular, have been critical of the dire remedies recommended by some scientists for what they see as atmospheric warming.[7] "Estimating the cost of impacts or adaptations is fraught with uncertainties," admits the recent National Academy of Science's Panel on Policy Implications of Greenhouse Warming.[8]

In sum, the atmospheric warming issue is full of uncertainties, not just because there are genuine unknowns over greenhouse climate change but because the issue is characterized both by a scientific consensus that falls short of unanimity or agreement on points that matter most for policymaking and by certainties cast up as expert, but in important respects contradictory, opinion.

The mix of certainty and uncertainty provides a natural starting point for the narrative policy analyst. For what surely is the most salient, yet largely ignored, feature of the global warming controversy has been how the *certainty of uncertainty* is used by those who argue that governments must take immediate action to avert or mitigate the more serious effects of greenhouse climate change. Since no one can predict the precise location, let alone extent, of the potentially massive impacts of atmospheric warming, everyone faces the chance of disaster, so it is argued, if appropriate efforts are not taken now to address this problem. The scenario can be summarized thus:

> Because of the unintended consequences of individual actions taken locally, regionally, and nationally, particularly in developed countries, people throughout the world now face the prospect of global warming. This warming does not respect the artificial boundaries of nation state or lesser administrative entities. The chief reason governments must act quickly and decisively is that, while global warming and massive dislocations can be expected, the exact location of local, regional, and national disasters remains a matter of great uncertainty. Thus, no one on the planet, including those in developing countries, is immune to the disastrous potential of global warming. Moreover, governments cannot expect the matter to be resolved solely through actions taken at those very levels that got them into this dilemma. Accordingly, international action must be undertaken before global warming becomes a global tragedy of the commons.[9]

The temptation is to ask of each argument in the crisis scenario, "Is it true? Can it be verified?" The first question for the narrative policy analyst is, instead, "How have the structure and logic of the scenario—like other policy narratives discussed throughout the book, this one has a beginning, middle, and end based on givens and presuppositions—affected what the scenario tells us, independently of what the scenario is describing?"[10] The short answer is that the narrative features of the global warming scenario put its proponents in a position to articulate what is admittedly a highly uncertain issue without at the same time making the scenario itself part and parcel of the uncertainty being represented. We saw how this was the case for the "nonsense" metanarrative in chapter 4, and this chapter explores why the same holds for another policy narrative, the global warming scenario. To be specific, the crisis scenario's sense of "we-are-certain-about-uncertainty-in-atmospheric-warming" is constructed not so much on the basis of representational truth as from a set of givens, descriptions, narratives, and presuppositions operating in the global warming controversy. The policy import of this is made clearer once we explore the dynamics underlying this construction.

Having said that, nothing in what follows invokes a "rhetoric of science," "paradigm shift," "discursive formation," or "social construction of reality" to debunk the global warming scenario or the seriousness of many of its supporters.[11] Nor will the scenario's detractors find here an argument questioning the empirical merits of global warming. There are good reasons why environmentalists in particular should abandon the scenario, but the reasons have everything to do with the scenario's structure and its implications for policy, not with what environmentalists take to be the case made by the scenario. Indeed, its supporters are as much a victim of the scenario's narrative structure and internal construction as we all are.

Thus, when I write of "narrative certainty" as independent of the representational accuracy of the description in question, I am not denying that the scenario refers to reality and is opened to being judged in terms of how accurately it represents that reality. Rather, it is only when the reality being described is so uncertain, as in the case of greenhouse climate change, that we must look to how the structural features of narratives enable their narrators to speak with such certainty about the policy relevance of what is so uncertain, without thereby being implicated in the uncertainty being described. It is precisely this focus on knowing how we are certain about uncertainty, rather than on persuading others that we are certain, that sets this chapter apart from the growing number of analyses on the rhetoric and rhetorical properties of the global warming scenario.[12]

The Narrative Features of the Crisis Scenario and Their Policy Implications

This section's analysis focuses on the role of atmospheric warming in climate change. The same points would hold if the focus were widened to include the effects of biomes, ecosystems, and land use on climate change as well. That said, the scenario's certainty about the uncertainties of global warming is narratively, rather than representationally, constructed in five interrelated steps.[13] Each step has been simplified to underscore its central features:[14]

Step One. The crisis scenario is based on a *given*, in this case the laws of physics. At this level of analysis, it does not matter whether the laws are paradigm-relative or universally valid. What is more important for a narrative policy analysis is that the laws are taken as given, that is, they are the subject of a consensus about the nature of reality and in this way impart to a scenario based on them the sense of certainty that comes from a consensus already encoded in scientific discourse.[15]

Step Two. The narrative construction of the crisis scenario moves from the general given to specific *descriptions* of atmospheric warming and what are frequently taken to be its operational equivalents, global warming and greenhouse warming. At the descriptive level, atmospheric warming is treated as derivative from the laws of physics, while its cognates—global or greenhouse warming—are assumed to be more or less synonymous with atmospheric warming. Laws become the input to atmospheric warming, and atmospheric warming becomes the output. In this step, *atmospheric* is a level of analysis that is broad enough to embrace a variety of atmospheric phenomena, ranging from local and regional heat island effects over major metropolitan areas to fully realized global climate change on a massive scale across the planet.[16] As a descriptive term, *atmospheric warming* does not imply a particular scale of occurrence; it simply describes what happens when greenhouse gases disperse into the atmosphere by means of physical processes alone— whether the phenomena occur locally, regionally, nationally, or globally. In this way, the scenario's original sense of certainty based on consensus over the given laws of physics is reinforced by the derivation of atmospheric warming from the laws of physics and the equation of warming to other terms said to describe the same phenomena (as when urban heat islands are said to be instances of global warming at work).

Step Three. The narrative "sense of certainty" is taken a step further when uncertainty is introduced to transform atmospheric warming and its synonyms into two separate policy narratives, *atmospheric warming as a scientific problem* and *global warming as a crisis scenario.* In the former, reference to factual uncertainty is incorporated into the descriptions of atmospheric warming. The meteorologist may subscribe to one set of uncertainties, the climate modeler another, with scientific consensus splitting up into consensuses within differing groups of experts.[17] In the case of global warming as crisis scenario, atmospheric warming is itself now treated as a given, the implications of which are extended into the argument about dire human and environmental consequences. Again, the crisis scenario uses uncertainty over the indeterminate local effects of atmospheric warming to justify immediate policy action.

At one level the incorporation of uncertainty into descriptions of atmospheric warming increases their representational accuracy. At another level the incorporation has narrative features separate from any enhanced accuracy, and with profound effect. Introducing uncertainty into the description of atmospheric warming increases the sense of narrative certainty by recasting the description into a story (or, as here, two stories) having the conventional narrative format of beginning, middle, and end. Atmospheric warming as a scientific problem is a journey starting from givens, encountering challenges along the way, and ending up with gaps in theory and fact having to be resolved or filled. The crisis scenario, by contrast, starts off with its own givens about greenhouse gas emissions, encounters its own challenges in the form of rising temperatures, and ends up with a calamity too frightening to dismiss. The two policy narratives are related (as we shall see), but what deserves highlighting here is the effect of the twofold narrativization: uncertainty as a topic is introduced into the atmospheric warming description precisely at the moment that uncertainty is bounded within a preexisting format stipulating its possible resolution. Just to tell a story about uncertainty is to raise the possibility of a beginning, middle, and end to that uncertainty, even if the end in question turns out to be that we are certain only that things are uncertain.

Moreover, uncertainty in the crisis scenario is rendered in such a way as to apportion blame for global warming, thereby making the resolution of uncertainty not only stipulated, but morally compelled.[18] We may be uncertain just where droughts and floods induced by global warming will occur, according to the scenario, but who can be in favor of the destruction, particularly as we know who the guilty parties are (said to be mostly cars and factories in the north, and land and forest abusers in the south)? Moral outrage over the unfairness of this all should be enough to spur us into action, in the view of scenario proponents.[19] Moreover, it is only within the confines of the crisis scenario that the most extraordinary conclusions make even remote sense, for example, the fuel-inefficient cars of poor drivers are more guilty of causing global warming than are the more fuel-efficient trains and subways of commuting oil executives. In short, the scenario's very specific definition and assignment of guilt enables uncertainty over the local occurrence of global warming disasters to be cast up not just as a cognitive but also as a moral basis of action. The scenario's fusion of the moral and cognitive is instrumental in enabling scientists to be both "moralizing" and "objective" at the same time, two attributes seen as very difficult to combine in science.[20]

Step Four. Becoming the subject of *controversy* not only within but also outside the scientific community has reinforced the crisis scenario's sense of "we-are-certain-of-uncertainty." The popular consensus is that scientific uncertainty is just as much a given as are the laws of physics.

To many in the public, the more controversial the scientific issue, the greater the certainty that something real and fundamentally important is at stake. The consensus over scientific uncertainty finds itself encoded in ordinary expression just as the laws of physics are in scientific discourse. Indeed, the adversarial use of the written word by environmentalists—be it a legal brief, press release, or think-tank report—to focus on risks of what was once thought to be proven science and technology (as with the environmentalists' critique of pesticide use in the Medfly Controversy) has, more than anything else, defined the very sense in which the public has become increasingly certain that science is uncertain.[21] Whatever the real risk of atmospheric warming, the ensuing controversy has certainly heightened the perception that the risk matters.

Controversializing global warming has also meant that there is not just one crisis scenario, but many versions being compared and contrasted, particularly in the form of different global circulation models for greenhouse gases discharged into the atmosphere. Debate over GCMs has tended to focus on their representational merits and the realism of their assumptions. What has been less noted is the certainty creation brought about through the metalanguage and forms of discourse for finding differences between models. Comparison itself creates narrative certainty here, as the preexisting rules and procedures of scientific discourse governing the detection of difference in models presuppose that we can be certain such differences are ascertainable and comparable.[22] Identifying differences among the models entails a framework which defines beforehand, rather than establishes, that "narrowing these differences" is equivalent to reducing uncertainty, if not increasing certainty.

Attempts of scientists to reduce controversial elements in the global warming debate serve to augment narrative certainty in other ways. Advocates of the crisis scenario have argued that their various climate models and scenarios are really nothing more than variants of the same, more basic description of atmospheric warming as a scientific problem mentioned earlier. Here the attempt is to treat what are admitted by all to be imperfectly rendered crisis scenarios as versions of a story that can always be told more simply, if not now by the scientists themselves, then in the end by scientific theories and the laws of physics.[23] In seeking to reduce the controversy to matters under the purview of the scientific community alone, a circular sense of certitude is created, whereby scientists, whether they intend it or not, have the final say on the subject, be it in the form of a description, a scientific problem, a crisis scenario, or a controversy. Indeed, it borders on the tautological to say that, while science and scientists are by no means the same thing, scientists are central to ending science controversies.[24]

To summarize, the global warming controversy as a controversy deploys metalanguage, exemplarity, and definition—not just claims to referential accuracy—to increase our certainty that what is being talked about in the scenario is real and important. The scenario's certainty about uncertainty comes about narratively, by appealing to established, higher-order rules of comparison and contrast in scientific controversies; by treating the global warming controversy as an example of science controversies and drawing the definitional implications of that exemplarity (that is, that scientists have a major role in saying when these controversies end); by redefining what is taken as given to include a broad nonscientific consensus; and by recasting the controversy as a matter whose story line always leads back to a great deal of scientific consensus.

Step Five. The global warming controversy operates within a *wider narrative framework* than that posed by science controversies alone. The larger context can best be discerned by examining the way in which "global" in the crisis scenario has more or less ceased to be synonymous with "atmospheric" at the descriptive level.

Descriptively, *global* and *atmospheric* are, as was pointed out, interchangeable terms. They are neutral equivalents that merely seek to specify a level of analysis to measure greenhouse gases that can be tracked not just globally, but locally, regionally, and nationally as well. But in the crisis scenario, "global" is used less to complement than to *reject* the appropriateness of analyzing atmospheric warming at the local, regional, and national levels. In this way, the global warming scenario becomes itself a counterargument to any position which maintains that *atmospheric* is a descriptively impartial term. Global warming represents, according to the crisis scenario, a worldwide tragedy of the commons in the making, one requiring concerted international action precisely because governments cannot expect the warming to be effectively reduced solely through actions taken at those very same local, regional, and national levels that got them into this mess in the first place. Whatever the merits of such reasoning, *global* is clearly being deployed here not as just one of the several levels of analysis for monitoring the atmospheric accumulation of greenhouse gases and their impact. *Global* has become a prescriptive, not descriptive, term in its counternarrative privileging of the supranational level of analysis over all others. Terms that are synonymous at one level are, thus, transformed into counternarrative positions at another.

It is important to be clear how and at what level *global* and *atmospheric* cease to be equivalent. In ordinary language, *global warming* and *atmospheric warming* are synonymous—and with good reason. When it comes to describing the physical processes of greenhouse gas dispersion and accumulation, it matters little whether by accumulation we mean global or atmospheric. Nothing in atmospheric warming *as a physical process* requires climate change to be measured first and foremost at one level rather than another. The same holds for the impacts of atmospheric warming. Temperature change can just as well be evaluated in terms of regional warming, or warming over the oceans, or urban heat island effects, as not. More important, nothing in the *physical processes* of greenhouse climate change entails, either logically or empirically, the global tragedy of the commons posited by the scenario. Temperature change induced by greenhouse gases has been going on for millennia without human intervention, yet most of us would be loath to call that process a tragedy of the commons in the making.[25]

What is it, then, that accounts for the affective and prescriptive connotations that *global*—but not *atmospheric*—takes on in the crisis scenario, when both terms are basically equivalent at the descriptive level? One need not search far to see that the global warming scenario, like the controversy itself, operates within the wider discourse of global change, global impact, global economy, global politics, global commitments, global conflict, global resources, global affairs, the global environment, global food supplies, global media, the global marketplace, and the global village, to name but a few. Once global warming is situated within the discourse of globalisms, it becomes clear that the crisis scenario is grist not only for a specific science controversy, but also for a broader analytic increasingly taken to govern public discourse about presumably supranational policy problems. Indeed, the rush of globalisms signals what appears to be an *analytic tip* in the examination of major public policy problems, where what used to be understood as local, regional, or national issues now have to be analyzed (or so it is increasingly accepted) as global ones.

Policy implications that follow specifically from the role played by the crisis scenario within the wider analytic tip of globalisms are discussed in the next section. It turns out that this analytic tip—what Riffaterre would call an *intertext* and what explains the (to use another term from

Riffaterre) "ungrammaticality" between the terms *atmospheric* and *global* in the crisis scenario—is precisely the metanarrative that recasts the global warming controversy in such a way as to make it more amenable to the conventional policy analysis ("ungrammaticalities," intertext, and their relation to what I have been calling, interchangeably, counter-narratives or counterstories are discussed more fully in chapter 7).

Before proceeding further, we should note how the recognition of a broader analytic context reinforces the crisis scenario's claims to being certain about uncertainty, once again irrespective of the representational accuracy of these claims. As in each preceding step, this fifth step creates its own sense of "we-are-certain-of-uncertainty" in the global warming scenario. Simply put, certainty increases because the presence of any context for analyzing global warming ensures that, while the meaning of global warming varies according to the context, global warming will thereby always ("certainly") have meaning; yet uncertainty increases because that meaning is always indeterminate, that is, the existence of even one wider analytic entails the possibility of other contexts not yet known.

This five-step narrative construction of the global warming scenario underscores why it is that the crisis scenario not only describes a physical process marked by empirical (though at times uncertain or contradictory) indicators, but also has the form of a definition articulated through a series of givens, presuppositions, and narratives. In fact, what is striking about the global warming controversy is the status of the crisis scenario as an extended definition that gets more elaborate as its narratives are constructed from descriptions that are themselves constructed from givens. What appears to be an explanation of a process taking place through time turns out on closer inspection to look like a computer program defined by a series of steps and derivations.[26] The crisis scenario, as summarized earlier, can from one perspective be viewed as a proposed explanation of what is purportedly going on in reality, while from another perspective it is equivalent to a dictionary definition of "scenario, *as in global warming. . . .*"

This narrative understanding of the crisis scenario, in turn, shows how vulnerable the scenario is to being undermined in ways that have nothing whatsoever to do with its empirical merits. Again, just as any system of budget controls is a roadmap to cheating on them, so does the global warming scenario map internally its own undoing.[27]

Leaving the policy implications for later, the following actions would have the effect, whether intended or not, of undermining the scenario's credibility, regardless of its claims to representational accuracy: displace the givens in the controversy by appealing to the "arbitrary" nature of normal science and the fickle passing of popular consensus; insist at every juncture on the lack of synonymity between atmospheric warming and global warming; denarrativize the crisis scenario by insisting that "getting the numbers right must come before knowing what the real story about global warming is," for example, by stressing the need for better-calibrated measurements of temperature change as a precondition for action; deny the exemplary role of scientists in bringing the global warming controversy to closure, for example, by arguing that this controversy, unlike others, is really an issue of analytic tip (see below); and, last but not least, assert that the number and nature of alternative contexts in which to analyze global warming are many and unknowable, thereby necessitating more uncertainty from all concerned.

Moves like these are of course already under way. Who doubts that there is another crisis scenario in the wings, even worse than that of global warming, waiting for scientific and public attention? The changing fortunes of the crisis scenarios concerning population growth, energy shortages, and nuclear winter, just to name three recent ones, have less to do with scientific merit (or political expediency) than with the fact that new crisis scenarios are themselves a judgment on the narrative priority of those they are about to displace, however temporarily. This displacement goes well beyond the fact that there will always be dissenters about global warming, that the evidence will probably never be conclusive, and that many in the public or media have a relatively low attention span when it comes to science and technology controversies.[28] The more compelling point is that there are far too many scientific givens, consensuses, terms, descriptions, and controversies for any one set of permutations and combinations, cast in the form of a single crisis narrative, to claim long-term scientific, let alone political, hegemony. Science, notwithstanding what the dictionary says, has always been a plural noun.

Policy Implications of Global Warming as Analytic Tip

To understand how and why it is likely that the global warming crisis scenario will eventually give way to another crisis narrative provides little practical help in deciding what to do about the issue of atmospheric warming. There is little consolation in recognizing the turnover in scenarios, when the physical phenomenon of atmospheric warming may be taking place regardless.

Fortunately, the role that the global warming scenario is currently playing in the analytic tip toward globalism provides specific guidance on how to respond to the issue of greenhouse climate change. In fact, once this role is recognized and its implications understood, a narrative policy analysis can be fairly emphatic and confident in its recommendations about global warming. Such confidence, while it parallels the "certainty" of those who espouse the global warming scenario, does not come from deciding one way or the other the scenario's representational accuracy, but instead from understanding what policy relevance the metanarrative—in this case, analytic tip—has for addressing the global warming issue, irrespective of whether that warming is actually taking place.

Analytic tip, as used here, is analogous to linguistic tip, where a language that has been demographically stable for generations seems to "tip" suddenly under shifting demographic pressure in favor of some other language.[29] By extension and in the same terms used to describe its linguistic counterpart, analytic tip can be conceived metaphorically as the gradual accretion of negative feelings toward conventional categories of analysis until a critical moment or period arrives when analysts seem to abruptly abandon their conventional terms and switch over to newer ones.[30]

An example of analytic tip is the change in policy discourse from the focus on means and ends, popular in public administration during the 1940s and 1950s, to the focus on benefits and costs that prevails in conventional policy analysis today. The tip occurred when a number of public administration programs and departments, then under mounting criticism, gave way to the establishment of graduate schools of policy analysis during the late 1960s and early 1970s.[31] The current wave of globalisms, in turn, can be understood as preparing the way for another analytic tip in policy discourse and the global warming crisis scenario can be seen as one, if not *the*, precipitating factor doing the actual tipping. But today's shift from the local, regional, and national to the global as the analytic point of departure is occurring less through curriculum change than through scientists assuming the role of policy analysts.[32]

Happily, the analytic tip is easier to discern than is global warming itself. The negative light in which local, regional, and national levels of analysis are cast is a prime indicator. An even better indication is the appeal by the scenario's supporters to a global analytics they in no way need in order to make their case. A number of experts agree, for example, that governments have nothing to lose in assuming atmospheric warming is taking place, since the actions needed to combat it—chiefly, reducing population growth and greenhouse gas emissions—are justified on other grounds. "Many of the measures we should begin to take to mitigate possible effects of climatic warming should be taken anyway for other reasons," advises an informed observer in *Issues in Science and Technology*. "Even were there to be a negligible greenhouse effect, we should be taking actions," adds a *Science* editorial. And, confirms *The Economist*, "conveniently, most of what would need to be done to fight a greenhouse catastrophe needs doing anyway, for other reasons."[33] In light of this "no regrets" position, there seems little prima facie reason to buy into a global analytic when its only major contribution to date—the repeated appeal to treat atmospheric warming as an urgent policy issue—is salient solely when marshaled in support of what governments should be doing locally, regionally, and nationally, period. We instead have every reason to beware of subscribing to all manner of forward and backward linkages in the analytic tip, the policy import of which may be more uncertain than atmospheric warming itself, for example, "Global Warming Means New Global Politics," promises a headline in the *New York Times*.[34]

In fact, the global analytic works *against* the improved control of greenhouse gas emissions. By and large only those who advocate the crisis scenario treat atmospheric warming as a global tragedy of the commons in the making. Remove the prop of atmospheric warming as necessarily a global commons problem, which no government can solve on its own, and those officials who have yet to do much by way of reducing population growth and greenhouse gases will have one less major reason to justify their continuing inaction. We already have sufficient scientific, technological, and public health grounds to undertake and ensure the appreciable reduction of CO_2 emissions in major U.S. metropolitan areas. These pollution abatement and control initiatives are not helped by claiming that stinting, say, by Los Angelenos is not worth the effort, given a free-riding Mexico City or industrializing China. Indeed, convincing policymakers that atmospheric warming as a local, regional, or national problem should not be confused with global warming as a tragedy of the commons may well be *the* necessary condition for getting them to do more than they have done. What chance do we have of convincing policymakers to do what is already feasible, if they and the rest believe that "No country can solve the problem [of global warming] on its own, and the actions of one can be negated if others fail to act. . . .

Universal action clearly seems required" or that the "problem of bringing about a massive reduction in worldwide emissions of carbon dioxide (and other 'greenhouse' gases) is quite clearly a collective action problem. . . . [E]very country has an incentive to encourage others to act while hanging back itself"?[35]

It is precisely at the local, regional, and national levels where the substantial learning curves remain in pollution abatement and regulation, not at the global level. It is also at these levels where scientists can be better held accountable for the remedies they recommend. It is much more difficult to falsify a theory that predicts massive flooding will take place, but not where or when, than to rebut a theory that maintains these kinds of emission control devices will work in certain kinds of cars and a certain kind of area, but not in others.[36] More generally, experience to date also suggests that what works best in terms of reducing pollution are *programs* at the local level and *policies* at the national level, with *regulations* working less well in between, and *international efforts* least effectively of all.[37] No one knows with any kind of surety, for example, if the Montreal Protocol to protect the ozone layer has had an independent effect on reducing chlorofluorocarbon (CFC) production, let alone will provide a reliable guide for controlling atmospheric warming.[38]

Already known, however, is that what works in one factory, city, or region by way of pollution control does not work everywhere. A myriad of options are now being explored and tested, with market-like emission control measures as much a part of the learning curve as more government regulation and better technology. It is difficult to see how a global analytic that casts the local, regional, and national in such a negative light as the crisis scenario does could foster anything like these "decentralized" solutions to CO_2 emissions control.

What happens, though, if local, regional, and national solutions fail, and the global warming scenario turns out to be true? The question raises a logically and empirically prior one: what reason do we have to believe that if we try—and fail—locally, regionally, and nationally, we will have any more success globally? The issue here is not what should be done or even what must be done globally, but what financial and decision-making resources allow us to do practically. Do we really believe, after four decades of trying to transfer technology and institutional arrangements from the developed countries to parts of the developing world, that we will have fewer failures when transferring even more complex technologies and arrangements across altogether wider tracts of the planet? As just noted, we already have considerable grounds for decentralized action to reduce CO_2 emissions across the United States, without waiting to settle the global technology transfer problem. In a world where the best is the enemy of the good, the bumper sticker has thus got it wrong. Better you act locally, when others feel compelled to think globally.

Such considerations lead, in turn, to a seeming paradox: the more one believes that atmospheric warming is really taking place, the more reason one has for not subscribing to the global warming scenario. Environmentalists, especially, have every reason to abandon the scenario, as its global analytic works to the detriment of what can and needs to be done locally, regionally, and nationally to counter the demonstrated and deleterious effects of excessive CO_2 emissions. Equally important, we saw (at the end of the preceding section) that the very structure of the scenario that enables its supporters to talk in a noncontradictory way about being certain about global warming uncertainties also ends up rendering the scenario vulnerable to internal undermining and external displacement by other crisis scenarios—a deplorable feature for those who believe atmospheric warming is truly taking place.

Fortunately, once global warming as a scenario is conceptually separated from atmospheric warming as a problem, trade-offs in government expenditure become much more apparent. The neutrality of the atmospheric warming description in terms of level of analysis (local and beyond) invites comparing the benefit gained from dollars spent to reduce greenhouse gas emissions at the local, regional, and national levels—something that cannot be said of the crisis scenario. It little matters if this comparison is qualitative or quantitative or if it comes by way of formal benefit/cost analysis, environmental impact statements, social impact assessments, or the like. What matters is that once trade-offs are the focus of attention, analysis can then become interdisciplinary in a way that the current controversy, dominated as it is by scientists, environmentalists, and their critics, simply is not. One has to wonder, for example, what those one-time meteorologists, the political economist W. S. Jevons, philosophers Martin Heidegger and Jean-Paul Sartre, and sociologist Raymond Aron, would say about the transformation of atmospheric warming and climate change into what for many is the Apocalypse, carried on by other means. It is only "beneath" the global level that the opportunity costs for research and deferred action are truly visible and indeed calculable for all those who want to take up their estimation.

The Use of Scientific Uncertainty by Antienvironmentalists and Other Concluding Comments

Notwithstanding the scenario's problems, those who want to believe that global warming is not taking place will find little support for their position in this chapter's narrative policy analysis.[39] Consider only the case of those libertarians who advocate across-the-board market solutions to problems associated with greenhouse gas emissions. One might expect that they would be more favorably disposed to local, regional, or national solutions, at least to the extent the solutions were market-oriented, and less favorably disposed to those international or global remedies predicated on more government planning and regulation. But in fact, supporters of market solutions are not likely to object to the crisis scenario on the grounds that its reach is global, for the very same reason they have seized on scientific disagreements in order to discredit that scenario: atmospheric pollution (at all levels of analysis, not just the global) poses a direct threat to reducing or eliminating government in favor of the market. Even "market" solutions like emissions trading schemes must be imposed by the state. Far better for the detractors to undermine the scenario by appealing to scientific uncertainty and contradictory expert opinion than to let opposition to the scenario become the rationale for local regulation that, even in market-like forms, involves increased government intervention. A thousand flowers are blooming, but not all of them will be for sale in the market.

Ideologues of at least two varieties have, then, a perverse stake in treating atmospheric warming as a "global" problem. In the case of libertarians, their ideology is preserved by turning a blind eye to the analytic tip toward globalism, even though this globalism works against site-specific market solutions. Environmentalists face the same dilemma, but from the other side. They forfeit any real hope for decentralized action against atmospheric warming, wherever it occurs, by making globalism an essential feature of their ideology. If environmentalism involves a genuine concern for remedying pollution problems, environmentalists should be expected to dissent from the drive toward globalistic consensus. By the same token, if libertarians are genuinely concerned about remedying pollution problems, they too should be expected to dissent from any consensus toward restricting government's role in imposing and supporting local market solutions to such problems. But if, as their respective detractors contend, environmentalism and libertarianism are primarily an attack on modern political life—a critique and rejection of, for one, capitalism, for the other, government—then the moral satisfaction that comes, however perversely, from their treating atmospheric warming as a global problem can be expected to win out. In so doing, these critiques, like the critique of the tragedy of the commons argument in chapter 2 and the Aerial Critique of chapter 3, end up increasing uncertainty rather than stabilizing the assumptions for decision making. We return to this point in the book's conclusion.

7

Intertextual Evaluation, Conflicting Evaluative Criteria, and the Controversy over Native American Burial Remains: Other Models of Narrative Analysis II

Michael Riffaterre's model of the intertext and intertextuality is explored and applied in much more detail here for two major policy problems, one general and long-standing in policy analysis, the other more specific and current as a public policy controversy. The dispute over the disposition of Native American burial remains housed in museums is discussed later in the chapter, after I examine the problem of what to do when there are multiple, but conflicting, criteria to choose from when evaluating a policy. Riffaterre's model is particularly helpful in addressing this more general problem, and in so doing allows the analyst to deal more effectively with specific instances of that problem, as in the case of the burial remains controversy.

First, though, a word of caution. This is the book's most difficult chapter. Most readers will find the terminology and notation unfamiliar and challenging. Here the challenge is worth the effort. Riffaterre's terms *undecidability, sociolect, idiolect, reader response, ungrammaticality, intertext,* and *intertextuality* have their exact equivalents in the chapter's two problems of policy evaluation. The underlying equivalence is, moreover, a simple one. When it comes to evaluating a policy or a literary text, the task is often the same: just as a text can be open to multiple and conflicting interpretations, so too can a policy be evaluated according to multiple and conflicting criteria. The approach Riffaterre offers for moving beyond numerous conflicting interpretations allows us, in turn, to move beyond the problem of conflicting evaluative criteria in a fundamentally new way.

This chapter should give the reader a fairly detailed understanding of what Riffaterre is doing and the way in which his approach can help the reader in her or his own policy work. To see how, let us turn to some examples.

The General Problem: Multiple and Conflicting Evaluative Criteria

Fenno Ogutu and I were arguing over how to interpret the results of his research. He had undertaken a major evaluation of the Government of Kenya's nationwide decentralization policy, District Focus for Rural Development (a program in which I had been involved).[1] There were the usual problems of carrying out a field evaluation and generalizing its results, but Dr. Ogutu had been able to assess local project development before and after the introduction of District Focus. He found that its implementation failed in a number of respects to meet the objectives and procedures set out in the original District Focus policy paper.

My counter was that evaluating a policy according to whether or not implementation matched its objectives was only one of several evaluative criteria. Alternatively, District Focus could be evaluated (1) against some ideal of government decentralization, the objectives of which the policy paper may or may not have matched; (2) against the implementation of other decentralization programs undertaken in comparable countries (as in neighboring Tanzania); (3) in terms of the counterfactual, that is, what would have happened in Kenya had District Focus not been undertaken; and (4) in terms of whether savings in staff time and funds could have been realized if District Focus had been more cost-effectively implemented. If District Focus were also assessed according to these other evaluative criteria, then its implementation would look much more mixed and far from establishing failure of the policy. Dr. Ogutu agreed that there certainly was more than one way to evaluate District Focus, but maintained that evaluation in terms of meeting original objectives had to be the priority, because those were the terms by which government and the public intended District Focus to be evaluated.

At one level, this anecdote is just another instance of that all-too-common phenomenon of multiple and conflicting, yet apparently equally valid, evaluative criteria. Even where agreement exists over problem definition and preferred solution, different and inconsistent criteria are available to evaluate policy implementation and overall performance. This includes those criteria of efficiency, effectiveness, political feasibility, people's participation, and government responsiveness.

Scarcely a volume of the leading evaluation journals—*Evaluation and Program Planning, Evaluation Review,* and *Evaluation Practice/News*—has passed in the last decade without discussing the issue of multiple criteria for evaluating policies (where, once again, "policy" embraces not just macrolevel plans, but other government interventions including field projects, agency programs, departmental strategies, and administrative reform).[2] As discussed in chapter 2, evaluation research is continually finding policies that are local successes according to one criterion, but system failures by virtue of other criteria, in a world where local policy interventions provide little advantage in correcting what are perceived to be systemic maladies. The upshot of multiple criteria is at times worthy of Alice in Wonderland. If a policy had succeeded as critics thought it would, then, according to their evaluative criteria, it would have been a disaster. The fact that its implementation frequently falls short of what the critics predicted is, however, often not enough to make the failed policy a "success" for them. In the critics' estimation, the real success would have been ensuring that government did not undertake the policy in the first place. Yet, if the criterion is one of having not done something, then why are not governments praised more frequently for all the things they fail to do?

At another level, though, Dr. Ogutu is surely correct. Government intentions should be decisive in clearing up such muddles. Here the baseball pitcher, Orel Hershiser, comes to our aid: "A mistake is a pitch I didn't execute well, one I left in an area where they could hit it. You don't call a ball a mistake because you miss the strike zone. That's not a mistake. A mistake, to me, is a ball I leave in the middle of the plate."[3] A baseball pitch can, of course, be evaluated in other ways. "It ain't nothing until I call it," or so an umpire might object. Fans, on the other hand, take a ball to be a mistake if it is tied to their team's loss. The coach thinks it is a mistake if the pitcher was signaled to throw a strike instead of a ball. And other pitchers may disagree with Hershiser. Does this mean that they are all equally valid, albeit conflicting, criteria for judging the pitcher's throw?

Clearly not, if the reason our pitcher threw the ball was because she or he didn't think it was a mistake to do so. The pitcher's intentions do matter for the evaluation of the pitch, and unavoidably so in the sense that if they didn't, we wouldn't have a pitch to evaluate. To argue that nothing per se valorizes or privileges the views of the fans, umpires, coaches, owners, and players over and against each other is to believe that a baseball game is not constituted in some irreducible way by the causal intentions of players like our pitcher. The point is made by an even better-known example. A farmer discovers the arms of the statue of Venus de Milo. To whom do they belong? To the farmer, according to common law? To the state, according to civil law? To the museum housing the statue, according to some other criterion? In the more fundamental sense, they belong to the statue, because that is where its sculptor intended them to be. Without that intention, there would be no statue having arms about which counterclaims could be made.

In short, although policy analysts and evaluation researchers have had little time for the argument that intentions rather than consequences should be the basis for evaluation, intentions do clearly have an important role when adjudicating among multiple evaluative criteria.[4] Unhappily, governments do not always know their intentions. Indeed, "government" is frequently just a rubric for loosely coupled officials contributing at different times and in complexly unpredictable ways to an outcome or decision. We saw this in chapter 1's discussion of "no-author" national budgeting. Policy, as such, may be overdetermined or underdetermined with regard to causal intentions. One could argue as easily that a variety of unstated and murky reasons converged behind initiating District Focus—breaking the stranglehold of an ethnic group, consolidating presidential power—as that senior officials and politicians did not really know what they intended until they set about working through and writing up the policy.[5] Intentions matter for policy evaluation, but often we have no reason to believe that they are in a form that can be evaluated.[6]

Literary theory has long grappled with the problem of multiple (and inconsistent) interpretations where knowledge of an author's intentions is unavailable or moot. This chapter is devoted to showing how such theory—specifically that of Riffaterre—establishes a radically different approach to addressing not only the issue of multiple evaluative criteria but also policy evaluation itself. After presenting the general outlines of the model as it applies to policy evaluation, the case study on Native American remains demonstrates how Riffaterre's model recasts the evaluation of this extremely contentious policy issue in a less intractable light.

Riffaterre's Theory and Policy Evaluation

Riffaterre's model applies to the reading of literary texts, though, as he points out, fragments "of literary discourse can be found everywhere," including newspapers, speeches, and in other public forums.[7] While the majority of texts examined are written, Riffaterre has also analyzed events and decisions.[8] Evaluation is core to his model of reading—"the literary text demands to be evaluated, to be pegged on a scale of values"— and of special interest to Riffaterre is answering the "undecidability" question, that is, how the reader (evaluator) decides what is a valid interpretation of a given text, when all seem equally valid.[9] Riffaterre underscores that his theory needs no recourse to authors' intentions in order to understand how it is that a text can say one thing, but mean quite another thing (or in our case, how a policy statement like that for District Focus can say one thing on paper, yet mean something altogether different when it is read out in implementation).[10]

The Theory and the Question. Four central elements of Riffaterre's model—*sociolect, idiolect, reader's response,* and *intertext* or *intertextuality*—have direct applicability to this chapter's policy evaluation problem of multiple criteria. Riffaterre enumerates and defines the first three components of his model as follows:

> One, language, or rather, the sociolect, that is, language not just as lexicon and grammar, but also as the repository of the myths and stereotypes with which a society organizes and allegorizes a consensus of its members about what they imagine reality to be; two, the idiolect, that is, the special usage to which the text puts the sociolect; three, the reader who actualizes in his mind the contact or conflict between the two, recognizing the sociolect under the idiolectic manipulation of it, making judgments as to the value of such transformation, interpreting their effects.[11]

The terminology is foreign, but the process whereby the idiolect follows from, but is not equivalent to, the sociolect and where the difference between the two leads to a reader response (schematically, [Sociolect ≠ Idiolect] → Reader Response) is readily illustrated in the District Focus example. Implementation represents the idiolectic rendering of a policy paper that reflects the cultural and political context in which "decentralization" means something different in Kenya (namely, less participatory and more top-down) than it does in Tanzania. The reader response to the difference between what was said in the policy (sociolect) and what was actually done by way of implementation (idiolect) was what Dr. Ogutu and I disagreed over, the criterion appropriate for evaluating the policy as it was transformed from paper to practice.

A parallel process is observed with respect to policy evaluation more generally, as the Kenya example again illustrates. Social science evaluation is itself a sociolect, a consensus (albeit by no means unanimity) over what makes for validity in evaluation, such as the use of random sampling and control groups. Dr. Ogutu's field evaluation, however, was idiolectic in the sense that he adapted social science methods to the conditions pertaining at his site, for example, his before-and-after survey of project development took place in the absence of a control group. The reader response to this difference between evaluation as it is taught and evaluation as it implemented was, again in the example, to differ over which criteria are appropriate for evaluating policy. Adopting the above schema and avoiding for the moment interaction effects (namely, that idiolectic and writerly challenges can over time change the sociolect), these relationships can be summarized as

[Policy ≠ Implementation] → Multiple Evaluative Criteria
[Evaluation ≠ Implementation] → Multiple Evaluative Criteria

That is, policy or evaluation as stated is often different from policy or evaluation as implemented, a difference that raises questions over which evaluative criteria to use. Moreover, if you believe along with the economist G. L. S. Shackle that "[p]olicy, to have meaning, must be continuously re-made by its own consequences,"[12] then policy entails evaluation and the second expression collapses into the first.

That, though, is not the end of it. On closer inspection, the first expression, like the second, is itself part of a wider sociolect that includes the preexisting and readily available narrative about how government policy is rarely implemented as planned and how this complicates evaluation considerably.[13] Indeed, there is no more potent and formulaic narrative in all of evaluation research and the policy sciences than this one of thwarted policymaking, it being one part Peter Principle (planners and implementers rise to their incompetency level), one part Pressman-Wildavsky Paradox (the conditional probability of something being implemented as planned is near zero), and one part Murphy's Law (the worst always happens), all of which are stirred together in such a way as to confuse evaluation thoroughly. If then the first expression,

[Policy ≠ Implementation] → Multiple Evaluative Criteria

is part of a broader sociolect to be responded to by further idiolectic manipulation, as in

$$\{[(\text{Policy} \neq \text{Implementation}) \rightarrow \text{Multiple Evaluative Criteria}] \neq \text{Idiolect}\} \rightarrow \text{Reader Response},$$

what are the "Idiolect" and "Reader Response" in the revised expression? Or to put it into other words: if thwarted policymaking often falls lamentably short of what was originally desired or expected, then does this tale of woe give rise to reactions and responses that are just as much at odds with the tale as are the components of that tale with each other? Answering this question entails extensive rethinking about what we mean by policy evaluation generally and the problem of multiple evaluative criteria specifically.

An Answer. Riffaterre's theory allows us to triangulate on the question from three different directions. According to his model, we will have a better fix on what the missing idiolect and reader response are in the revised expression if we first understand how the sociolect and idiolect are opposed to each other, how "ungrammaticalities" in the text we are analyzing point to the need for another text that can make sense of them, and how this other text—what Riffaterre calls the "intertext" or "intertextuality"—actually does make sense of these seeming ungrammaticalities.

The Opposition of Sociolect and Idiolect. In one way, it is fairly easy to discover the missing idiolect in the revised expression. Just find, as already noted, the narrative that, if it exists, is as much a polar opposite of the first expression as its components (policy and implementation) are to each other. This would seem, however, to lead us back to where we started. If the missing idiolect in the revised expression is the opposite of our original expression (that is, the opposite of field evaluation as implemented, which was, in turn, the opposite of social science evaluation as theorized), then doesn't this return us once again to social science evaluation as theorized? Here a closer examination of the District Focus example is helpful.

Clearly the demands of classroom social science are in tension with those of field evaluation as practiced. There is, though, a presupposition that neither Dr. Ogutu nor I questioned and which is part of the shared and wider sociolect about evaluation generally, whether taught in the classroom or tried in the trenches, namely, multiple criteria exist to evaluate the results of a policy. Our disagreement, like that of many evaluators, is over which criterion applies, not over the variety of criteria from which to choose. In fact, the variety of multiple evaluative criteria posed in the first expression—which was the end-point resulting from the gap between policy and evaluation as stated and implemented—has now become the conventional starting point and unquestioned given for many evaluators, and, as such, part of their wider sociolect. Today, more and more of us start evaluations accepting that evaluative criteria are necessarily multiple, regardless of whether or not there is a gap to be evaluated between what was planned and what was actually executed.

If, then, the wider sociolectic narrative of interest is that "multiple evaluative criteria exist to evaluate the results of a policy," its opposite, and the missing idiolect in the revised expression, is the counternarrative, *"The policy results in evaluating the multiple evaluative criteria."* Without dwelling on the matter, let it simply be said that many involved in managing a development project throughout its cycle from design through implementation to final evaluation have experienced just this sense of project implementation as the only stage where we really learn which evaluative criteria are the ones by which the project should be evaluated.[14]

Before proceeding further, it is important to be clear why the sociolect and idiolect are opposites. As defined earlier, any number of idiolectic variants of the sociolect would seem possible.[15] Why then is opposition, rather than just difference, the focus when measuring off interest in the sociolect and idiolect? Why not any variant of the sociolect as the object of attention? What is so special about its polar opposite?

The short answer is that opposites are more obvious and significant than other variants, particularly when the backdrop is an infinity of possible variants. Opposites define each other in ways that other variants do not, a phenomenon that has nothing to do with whether someone intends this to be the case or not. As Riffaterre puts it, opposition between terms "makes the guidelines for reader interpretation more obvious: it is when the description is most precise that the departures from acceptable representation" are "more conspicuous."[16] To see how this is so in the case of evaluation, ask yourself, Why of all the real-world planning scenarios has so much attention been devoted to the thwarted policymaking narrative, with its opposition between planning and implementation? What is so fascinating about a policy's unintended consequences leading to exactly the opposite of what was originally wanted? The stark contraposition of planning and implementation is significant, not because our culture, unlike others, says it is more important—the fascination it holds is too widespread across countries for that—but because the contraposition defines what we mean by "planning" or "implementation" in government and what is at stake when we talk about them. Such polar opposites are found throughout the public life and they pose the central dilemmas faced by academic and practicing policy analysts alike.[17]

The challenge to evaluation, as Riffaterre insists,[18] is sharpest and most useful in the case of such opposites. How can it be the case, for example, that multiple criteria exist to evaluate the results of a policy and *simultaneously* that the very same policy results in evaluating those criteria? If that can be answered, then there is an answer to how all other possible variations of the multiple criteria problem can also be the case at the same time, falling as they do between the poles of these two extremes.

For Riffaterre, the answer to how two opposing states are equally valid "[a]gainst all likelihood and yet with perfect logic"[19] is to be found in that fourth element of his model, the intertext or intertextuality. Extended examples of these are given below. For the moment, the intertext can be defined as one or more texts in the wider sociolect that the reader needs to know in order to understand how multiple and opposing readings of a given text are possible and even consistent.[20] Intertexts "are an implicit reference without which the text would not make sense," that is, "the text is incomplete and can be deciphered only through the intertext."[21] What is undecidable within the terms of the text can be decided only by appealing to another text. Once known, these intertextual features will help determine what our reader response is to be in the revised expression above. Since "textual ungrammaticalities" prove to be the key to identifying such features,[22] these "ungrammaticalities" must be understood before we can have a clear picture of how the intertext and intertextuality operate.

Textual Ungrammaticalities. An *ungrammaticality* is a deviant word or term in a text and stems "from the physical fact that a phrase has been generated by a word that should have excluded it, from the fact that the . . . verbal sequence is characterized by contradictions between a word's presuppositions and its entailments."[23] These ungrammaticalities—as between *global* and *atmospheric* in the preceding chapter—are important because, once they are observed, readers will try to explain them by recourse to some other text: "The urge to understand compels readers to look to the intertext to fill out the text's gaps, spell out its implications and find out what rules of idiolectic grammar account from the text's departures from logic, from accepted usage (that is, from the sociolect)."[24]

For example, consider as our "text" an abbreviated version of the earlier paragraphs introducing District Focus (which were written, with only minor changes, before I made the following analysis). This time the passage italicizes the key term *evaluation* and its cognates. Remember, the idiolect of interest is "the policy results in evaluating multiple evaluative criteria." Note, then, the asymmetry in the use of the terms like *evaluative* and *evaluated:*

> Fenno Ogutu . . . had undertaken a major *evaluation* of the Government of Kenya's nationwide decentralization policy, District Focus. . . . There were the usual problems of carrying out a *field evaluation*. . . . My counter was that *evaluating* a policy according to whether or not its implementation matched its objectives was only one of several *evaluative* criteria. . . . If District Focus were assessed according to these other *evaluative* criteria, then its implementation would . . . look much more mixed. . . . Dr. Ogutu agreed that there certainly was more than one way to *evaluate* District Focus, but maintained that *evaluation* in terms of meeting original objectives had to be the priority, because those were the terms by which government and the public intended District Focus to be *evaluated.*

With our idiolect as the context, the text's insistent message—it is policies that are evaluated and criteria that are evaluative—sounds now one-sided and downright odd. "Just why," we must ask ourselves, "isn't the reverse true as well, especially in a field evaluation of a policy's *implementation?* Why aren't policies evaluative and criteria evaluated, since that too happens when implementing policy?"

In Riffaterre's terms, the passage's repeatedly asymmetrical use of *evaluation* and its cognates constitutes an ungrammaticality, explicable only if we understand how the message and its reverse can hold at the same time. What looks undecidable solely in terms of the opposition between the sociolectic "multiple criteria exist to evaluate the results of a policy" and the idiolectic "that very same policy results in evaluating those criteria" becomes decidable, if and when another text or narrative about "evaluation" is identified, an intertext which "presupposes that the multiple meanings of the text [can] be modified together and given a common significance simultaneously, irrespective of their discrete referents" in the sociolect or idiolect.[25] To put it more concretely, the solution to the problem of how to decide among multiple evaluative criteria is to be found not in terms of the criteria themselves or their comparison, but in the intertext(s) where the multiple conflicting criteria are no problem, have already been decided upon, or are otherwise moot.

Intertext or Intertextuality. Riffaterre distinguishes three intertextual forms important to reaching a decision on what looks at first reading to be undecidable.

"[I]n the first [intertextual form], the undecidable is left entire but instead of pointing to a solution destined to remain unattainable, it becomes the representation of undecidability."[26] Riffaterre examines the deliberately ambiguous statement, "Charles makes love with his wife twice a week. So does John." In a real sense, it does not matter whether or not the triangle hinted at is true. Either way, the sentence makes its point, which is to hint and "make light of its implications": "As a sentence, the verbal sequence is referential and undecidable. As a text, it is self-sufficient and univocal."[27]

An analogue exists in policy evaluation. From one perspective, it does not matter whether criteria are used to evaluate policies or policies end up evaluating criteria. Both can be found occurring quite legitimately and at the same time—as long as, that is, evaluation is considered a *game*. A serious game, it is true, but a game nonetheless, where a variety of tactics, some of which are the mirror images of others, are justified and tolerated because of their usefulness in achieving the higher objective of winning in bureaucratic politics or at organizational survival.

"In the second [intertextual form], undecidability becomes . . . an implication of decidability, the latter being located in an actual or potential intertext."[28] Here, the intertext "is the deciding version that ends the repeated ambiguities of the text."[29] As already noted, if there is an intertext to our evaluation problem, it will be found in the sociolect (that is, the intertext is itself a commonplace), it concerns evaluation, and it must be comprehensive enough to explain how the two opposites of interest could be mutually consistent at the same time. Readers of *Narrative Policy Analysis* may know of others, but I am aware of only one intertext that fits the bill, namely, the old standby "Each case must be evaluated on its own merits." What is meant by "case" and "own merits" is sufficiently all-embracing as to enable anyone who subscribes to the commonplace to agree that (1) certain evaluative criteria, more than others, should be used for evaluating policies, while in the same breath accepting that (2) policies in practice always seem to end up determining which evaluative criteria are more appropriate than others. Indeed, this is what many evaluators mean when arguing that each case has to be judged on its own merits.[30]

"In the third [intertextual form], undecidability transfers significance from the text to intertextuality itself, rather than to an intertext."[31] Here, the analogue in the evaluation problem is what can be termed the *eval-*

uatability[32] of issues. Whether criteria are used to evaluate policies, or policies end up being used to evaluate criteria, or some position in between, the claim is that policies, criteria, and the like can be evaluated—not simply because there is an evaluator to do it, but because these issues are in and of themselves evaluatable. Evaluators evaluate issues, so it is claimed, not only because they think they know how to evaluate them, but also because the issues are themselves open to and capable of being evaluated. Thus, what looks on first reading like fractious economists disagreeing among themselves over how to evaluate a policy—for example, those who appeal to the Hicks-Kaldor compensation principle against other economists from Jevons to Shackle who maintain each policy should be judged on its own merits—ends up serving both camps. In reality their dispute reinforces and actually widens the claim of economists to issues they say are capable of being evaluated by the likes of themselves, whatever their methodological stripe.

The third intertextual feature highlights what all three features have in common, namely, the *denial* that significant issues are inherently *un*evaluatable, whether evaluation is instantiated as a game, or case-by-case, or as something falling somewhere in the middle. The assertion of evaluatability is, moreover, important precisely because more and more issues do seem unevaluatable. Evaluators are increasingly uncovering a highly contingent and indeterminate policymaking whose only "predictability" is one of learning less and less about a decision making that appears more and more prone to error (see chapter 2).

The three intertextual features put us in a position to identify what remains the missing element in the revised expression, namely, what is the "reader response" to reconceiving the problem of multiple evaluative criteria in the terms just discussed?

Reader Response: A Radical Theory of Intertextual Evaluation. The irony of the preceding analysis is that the evaluator, whether intertextual or microeconomic, starts with the same question: What is missing? In *ex post* evaluation, the economist tries to determine how the costs and benefits associated with an intervention compare to those that would have been incurred had the intervention not been undertaken in the first place. What is missing for the economist in the events being evaluated is represented, in other words, by the counterfactual. When Riffaterre asks *what is missing* in the text being evaluated, he is raising a very different set of questions, and one directed to discovering the intertext:[33] What is the ungrammaticality pointing to? What is lacking here? What is it that replaces or fills out this lack? The effect of this shift from conventional to intertextual evaluation has profound implications for what we take policy evaluation to be.

For if the above analysis is correct, then evaluators must address substantially different questions than they do now. This is particularly so for any *ex post* evaluation where there exists little or no agreement over which criteria are valid or otherwise appropriate for evaluating the results of a policy. The above analysis can be generalized into three basic sets of questions evaluators should ask of policies having conflicting evaluative criteria:

—Generalizing from the idiolect in the revised expression, did the execution of this policy in fact determine which criteria are appropriate for evaluating the results of the policy? If so, what are the implications for redesigning the policy, the evaluation process and the policymaking?
—Generalizing from the intertext of the revised expression, why should this policy *not* be evaluated on its own merits or as a game?
—Generalizing from the intertextuality of the revised expression, can the evaluator reject the hypothesis that what is taking place in the execution of a policy is unevaluatable rather than evaluatable? If the evaluator cannot, what are its implications for the policy, evaluation, and policymaking specifically?

These questions are the price we pay for our uncertainty or inability to decide which evaluative criteria among many to apply to the evaluation of a policy. If the questions can be answered in the affirmative—that is, if the policy in question determines its own evaluative criteria, can be evaluated on its own merits (if not as a game), or is inherently evaluatable and can be learned from (whether or not there is agreement over how to evaluate it)—then the issue of multiple evaluative criteria falls by the side as moot. There is no need to focus on the problem of multiple and conflicting evaluative criteria when your affirmative answers to these other questions indicate another problem is even more relevant and salient to the evaluation at hand.

Some will see such a move as sidestepping, rather than solving, the problem of conflicting evaluative criteria. On the contrary, we are solving the problem by using it to address an altogether more important problem. Multiple and conflicting criteria do not disappear in the revised expression, and, as such, they are not ignored or otherwise avoided. What does change, though, between the first and revised expressions is that the former leaves us with the seemingly intractable *end point* of having to choose between apparently equally valid evaluation criteria, while the latter takes that problem as a *starting point* to be challenged and surmounted. Moreover, as we just saw, the way to surmount the problem is to identify another set of questions which, if answered in the positive, turn the problem into a different, more imperative one. Granted, the other questions may prove as difficult as that of deciding among multiple criteria, but they do provide a way out of the dilemma of multiple conflicting evaluative criteria.

To see how the questions of intertextual evaluation can be applied to a policy issue and what implications they hold for that issue, as distinct from those of more conventional policy evaluation, let us turn now to a short case study of the controversy over the disposition of American Indian skeletal remains housed in major national and university collections. The issue is chosen because it has been evaluated and has to my knowledge no unique features making it especially appropriate for intertextual, let alone conventional, policy evaluation.

The Controversy over Native American Remains

In April 1990, the president of the University of California created a special committee to assess "University policy and practices regarding its collections of human skeletal remains and associated artifacts."[34] The committee's evaluation led it to recommend that the university develop both a policy "for the transfer (deaccession) of human skeletal remains and associated artifacts in its archaeological collections" and a "process for responding to requests for deaccession and resolving disputes."[35] The committee's report, which is the subject of the following reanalysis,[36] had state and national significance. The Smithsonian Institution and Stanford University, among others, agreed to hand over skeletal remains to Native American groups, a transfer that was strongly opposed by others inside and outside universities across the United States. Federal and California state legislation was introduced in 1990 to ensure that such remains were returned to appropriate groups under specific conditions, and this too elicited vigorous opposition. The issue is particularly salient for California, inasmuch as it has the largest American Indian population of any state, the largest number of federally recognized tribes, and the largest urban American Indian population in the nation.[37] The University of California's Lowie (now Hearst) Museum, moreover, has had the third largest archaeological collection of human remains in the United States, the vast majority of skeletal remains being those of California Indians.[38]

Native Americans, like university researchers, have their own customs and differences; both have their own sociolect and idiolect. One set need in no way be dependent on, let alone derive from, the other set. Yet the report and its informants leave little doubt about the operative sociolect and idiolect in the Indian burial remains controversy, and the nature of their opposition. Recent demands of many Native American groups for the return of their ancestors' remains have arisen as a direct (idiolectic) reaction to the long-standing and mainstream (sociolectic) position of academic and scientific communities that such remains belong to science, humankind, and a shared past. The report identifies one set of major concerns for the proponents of retaining skeletal remains in university collections and another set for their opponents (largely Native Americans), where the concerns of each group are virtual opposites of the other group (see table 1). It might be tempting to see this opposition less as polarization than as examples of ubiquitous policy trade-offs, for example, at what point is knowledge gained from research worth the cultural conflict it causes? The report, however, concedes that some of this "great diversity of opinions . . . may be irreconcilable."[39]

The report's ungrammaticalities and intertext are also readily apparent on close reading. The committee's twenty-one-page evaluation is filled with variants on terms like *consultation, communication, participation, responsiveness, dialogue,* and *information,* all of which address in one form or other the report's basic question: Who should have final say over the disposition of these remains? For example, the "University has an obligation to be responsive to the people of California," a "responsiveness [that] is especially important in the case of collections comprised primarily of skeletal remains."[40] Opponents of retention "argue that excavation of human skeletal remains is done only after parties with 'standing' in relation to the deceased have given permission, and maintain that contemporary Indian tribes and other groups have 'standing' in relation to all Indians in the past."[41] Opponents "also expressed the view, often strongly, that direct contact about these matters [in the report] should be made by the University with tribal councils and their designated representatives."[42] Proponents of retention, on the other hand, "are concerned that if some skeletal remains and artifacts at the University of California are removed, a major part of the study of California history before European contact would be limited primarily to knowledge gained to date, and that knowledge would be subject to question without possibility of verification."[43]

The committee concludes that "those with differing concerns indicate

Table 1. What Proponents and Opponents Say about Museum Retention of Remains

Proponents	Opponents
[M]aintain that archaeological skeletal remains and artifacts, unless they are the skeletal remains of known individuals with living relatives, are part of the physical and cultural remains of past peoples that are the appropriate domain of public knowledge and education (p. 7)	[B]elieve that Native Americans should be the only people to decide what can be done with Native American skeletal remains, regardless of age or relatedness. . . . They argue that secular research claims should not have precedence over the claims of Native Americans for authority over skeletal remains and associated artifacts of their ancestors (p. 5)
[B]elieve that the skeletal remains and artifacts at the University were obtained by proper and professional archaeological methods and that the preservation, conservation, and study of these skeletal remains continues [sic] to be done with consideration for ethical issues . . . They add that the same ethical and professional standards apply to research and retention of archaeological human skeletal remains of all . . . social groups, including Native Americans (p. 7)	[Believe the] existence of Native American skeletal remains at universities is symbolic . . . of past exploitation, injustices, discrimination and colonialism on the part of a dominant European culture towards American Indians . . . [, a past that] involved degradation, demoralization, decimation and genocide throughout the United States. . . . Some Native Americans believe that skeletal remains of Native Americans are treated with less respect than those of other Americans (p. 6)
[A]rgue that the spiritual beliefs of contemporary Indian people should not control the study of the past, including the right to control the study of artifacts and human skeletal remains. . . . Such control, they would argue, is an inappropriate obstruction of the nation's right to know about its total history (p. 7–8)	[H]old that only when skeletal remains are properly interred in the ground can the spirits of their Native American ancestors find peace. . . . Others argue that . . . the curation of archaeological skeletal remains constitutes an infringement of their freedom of religion and the freedom to bury their ancestors according to religious/cultural beliefs (p. 5–6)
[A]rgue that discoveries made from the study of [archaeological remains] are a public service to all of humanity, including Native Americans (p. 8)	[B]elieve that claims about the 'scientific value' of the skeletal remains are unfounded, that there is not enough evidence offered in language a lay person can understand or that can help Indians today (p. 6)

Source: University of California, Office of the President. *Report of University of California Joint Academic Senate–Administration Committee on Human Skeletal Remains.* Oakland: University of California, 1990.

a mutual interest in expanded communications and relations between the University and California Indians" and notes that "[m]echanisms for sharing information about University collections with the public, including California Indians and groups, are limited."[44] The committee goes on to observe that the "experience of other museums illustrates that respectful dialogue between all interested parties has been an effective approach to the resolution of any differences regarding the disposition of human skeletal remains" and, accordingly, recommends the establishment of a deaccession process that provides for the "initiation by the [university] of a dialogue among the interested parties for the purpose of achieving an understanding of the attitudes, beliefs and goals of all interested parties, clarifying options for deaccession, and reaching a mutually acceptable resolution of the issues."[45]

The key ungrammaticality in statements such as these, which revolve so closely around the issue of who has final say over the disposition of remains, is that those who both opponents and proponents agree should have had the first say in the matter are in absolutely no position now to tell us what they think, namely, the Native Americans whose remains are at issue. Not even an oral tradition accepted over hundreds of years can settle the matter of what Native Americans would say about disposition of their remains, when the remains are between five hundred to seven thousand years old, as were 95 percent of those in the university collections.[46] In that conundrum—those most intimately concerned by an issue are the least able to tell their own views on the matter—lies the intertext for this specific policy issue. For it turns out that the problem of determining *stewardship* (guardianship, custodianship) in the face of conflicting claims is not limited just to the controversy over Native American remains.[47] We see it reproduced in all manner of issues today. Policy debates over, for example, terminating the lives of the vegetatively comatose, using Nazi hypothermia records, and undertaking research on animals pose the same dilemma as the skeletal remains controversy: in the absence of knowing what the "objects" of the intervention would say, we are left with having to identify who, if any, among opposing claimants are the best stewards of their interests and how this stewardship is to be realized in practice.[48]

If the skeletal remains controversy is itself an example of a class of structurally similar controversies, then the policy implication would seem to be that resolution of any one of those controversies cannot be done without finding at the same time a paradigmatic solution to others in that class as well. What would such a solution look like? Fortunately, we have already identified one candidate in the form of the generalized intertext question, Why not evaluate each case on its own merits?[49]

To see how this applies within the specific intertext of stewardship identified for the skeletal remains controversy, consider one of the major recommendations of the committee on the "[d]evelopment of criteria for deaccession":

> When direct family descendants of human skeletal remains and associated artifacts cannot be identified, the University should deaccession, only on a case by case basis, the skeletal remains and associated artifacts to requesting groups.[50]

At first, the proposal seems self-serving. It is the university which determines the policy and deaccession process, and then decides to examine each case "on its own merits." But look closer now at how the intertext of stewardship identified in the controversy operates within the confines of the other intertext generalized for evaluation as a whole, namely, that of judging each case on its own merits.

Our earlier analysis found that the significance of an intertext lies in its ability to maintain and sustain the opposition of the idiolect and the sociolect. As Riffaterre puts it more formally, the "universal structure of intertextuality" is "the semiotic shuttle between polar opposites, trading them back and forth, and treating them as if they were mutually equivalent, one pole being the negative of the other."[51] Equivalencies, in other words, are created by reversals within the confines of any given intertext. Reverse, then, the components of the controversy's intertext of stewardship, keeping constant at the same time that "each case should be judged on its own merits." That is, allow ourselves to imagine a situation where Native American groups now control the disposition of all skeletal remains, where animal welfare groups have final say over all animal experimentation, and where groups of former concentration camp victims and their families have sole authority over the use of hypothermia records. Can we, in turn, imagine that these groups would not themselves adopt a "case-by-case" approach along similar lines recommended by the university committee?

Clearly, some in each group would say that never under any circumstances whatsoever should skeletal remains, animals, or hypothermia results be handed over for "research."[52] Yet, not all groups are unanimous on that point. Some animal rights advocates would, for example, allow certain kinds of experimentation on already terminally ill animals, just as some Native Americans would agree to use of skeletal remains for research if stringent and specific conditions held (for example, demonstrated or high potential of research to improving the lot of Native Americans). In fact, it is just as plausible to imagine Native American groups allowing case-by-case exceptions to the general rule prohibiting skeletal research as it is equivalently to imagine the university permitting case-by-case exceptions (that is, deaccessions) to a rule promoting that research. Thus, the committee is on the right track in suggesting each case of deaccession should be judged on its own merits. It would have had an even stronger argument had it recommended that the sought-after dialogue focus specifically on identifying those "exceptions" that both opponents and proponents agree would allow research on skeletal remains (or barring that, specifically identifying groups within the Native American community who would agree to discuss the matter of exceptions with the university).

How does this reanalysis differ from the report's approach? The committee clearly wanted to base its recommendations on what it perceived were the few areas of agreement between opponents and proponents of retention. Under "Points of Consensus," the report speaks of agreement over the need to "respect" cultural beliefs and for "expanded communications" between the parties concerned, terms that resurface prominently in the report's recommendations on developing a deaccession process around the aforementioned "dialogue" and a policy "that establishes ways of ensuring respect for human skeletal remains."[53] The committee is, of course, not alone in its search for consensus on which to base policy, even when important differences dividing parties to the controversy are recognized to be irreconcilable. As we read, evaluators everywhere are making the same search under the same imperative.

Intertextual evaluation takes a diametrically different tack in its search for "consensus." Here evaluation starts with the divisions that polarize the parties in the controversy and in no way diminishes, dispels, or otherwise dismisses their prominence. In fact, this kind of evaluation needs these polar divisions in order to be applicable and effective. The whole idea behind the intertext is not to search for a solution in spite of differences in highly polarized controversies, but rather to account for these differences in a way that makes their irreconcilability more useful for policy purposes. Thus, while conventional evaluation frequently undertakes the well-nigh impossible task of establishing common ground between opposing parties whose very definition of themselves excludes a common ground, intertextual evaluation ratchets up the analysis one level by searching instead for a shared intertext that is grounded in the very polarization observed. True, the university and Native American groups could come to some kind of consensus by virtue of agreeing to treat each case on its own merits, but such treatment not only acknowledges that polarization exists, it also derives from and in the process maintains and ratifies that polarization.

The idea behind intertextual evaluation (or, for that matter, any kind of narrative policy analysis) is not to find a way to get rid of the polarization driving a controversy, but rather to find a state of affairs whose very success depends upon having that polarization in place.[54] Judging each case on its own merits works only if all other ways of judging merit are in dispute. Where conventional evaluation treats polarization as the problem, intertextual evaluation treats it as the basis of solution. Here, the "common ground" does not lie between polar opposites, but is rather a more policy-relevant and useful story this polarization tells. Indeed, this general approach—that is, finding a metanarrative (in this chapter, a metacriterion) that rationalizes but does not slight in any way a controversy's divisions—is core to all the case studies in *Narrative Policy Analysis*.

Final Note

It should come as no surprise to evaluation researchers and policy analysts that the rewards can be high from cross-disciplinary exploration and interchange between policy evaluation and literary theory (better yet, theories). The problem of how to interpret evidence is common to both, and, more to the point, literary critics and theorists have given considerable thought to the problem of multiple interpretations for much longer than policy analysts or evaluators.

Nonetheless, the fat-to-lean ratio is fairly high for the evaluator who comes to literary theory looking for specific answers or applications to specific problems.[55] *Narrative Policy Analysis* narrows that gap by focusing on what is most applicable in literary theory to those highly controversial policy problems most in need of its application. Still, there is another problem that has to be faced. An evaluator who wants to pursue an innovative approach, such as intertextual evaluation, is probably working for a policymaker who is quite happy, thank you, with conventional evaluation research as currently deployed. Similarly, literary critics interested in these applications may well find themselves in settings that demand little more than critique and fault finding, if that.

Nonetheless, the problems that continue to challenge both policy analyst and literary critic alike—that of multiple and conflicting evaluative criteria being most prominent—are not going to go away any time soon. Polarization, along with issue uncertainty and complexity, are here to stay. The clients we serve might not encourage the cross-disciplinary exploration needed to better address these issues, but the enterprise is there for the professionals who want to undertake it. What this professionalism entails for such analysts—whether policy or literary—takes us to this book's conclusion.

Conclusion
In Shackle's Tide-Race: The Ethics of Narrative Policy Analysis

Talk is cheap, and so is criticism. Not so, though, for policy critiques discussed in this book. True, critiques are costly when they increase uncertainty under the pretext of stabilizing policymaking. Yet the narrative policy analyst puts up with critique, even when she or he has failed to get the critics to move beyond criticism and tell their own story. Why? Because it takes two to make a metanarrative, and the sense of increased uncertainty that comes with critique would not be as corrosive were there not policy narratives on the other side to be corroded. We tolerate critique, not because criticism makes our work easier, but because critique may lead to metanarrative, and that metanarrative may be more tractable to policy intervention than is critique on its own. As for uncertainty, it too is tolerated when it functions positively in a metanarrative, that is, when it promotes rather than disables decision making, as in the case of the "complexifying" metanarrative of the animal rights case study. (Obviously, uncertainty can function negatively at the metanarrative level, as illustrated in the medfly case study.)

Tolerance—this putting up with what one objects to, when one could do otherwise—needs no apology.[1] Anyone who believes that the analyst finds it easy to put up with disputants to the kinds of controversies discussed in this book has not been reading closely. The temptation always is to choose sides, to be part of the polarization being analyzed. After all, who wants to be in favor of encouraging budgetary excess, dumping pesticides, killing animals, spreading toxic irrigation, incinerating the planet, and, on top of it all, denying minorities their cultural heritage? Put that way, you have to choose sides, don't you?

No, you do not. These issues are genuinely uncertain and complex. Their truth is not obvious, their science not clear. The differences that divide parties are real, in some cases incommensurable, in all cases easier to contrast than to compromise. In such cases, choosing sides isn't the answer to uncertainty, polarization doesn't reduce complexity, and the search for consensus ends up trivializing uncertainty, polarization, and complexity altogether. Yet, decisions have to be taken in spite and often precisely because of all this uncertainty and complexity and polarization. The question thus becomes, How can we better use the uncertainty we are unable to reduce, the complexity we are unable to simplify, the polarization for which we are unable to find a middle ground? How can we use them to make our urgent and increasingly specific problems more tractable and amenable to resolution or management?

Narrative Policy Analysis shows how this can be done, but it asks analysts to put up with a great deal of ambiguity, much more than they would like, have been trained to accept, or receive incentives to bear. The kind of tolerance required of analysts means charting a course between choosing sides and thinking these sides can be bridged, if not ignored. Tolerance means resisting all manner of calls that make it trendy to be, say, for animal rights and the environment and against agribusiness and corporate universities. The narrative policy analyst first wants to know just what this trendiness is marginalizing.

What about those stories few want to hear, but many are ready to tell? Namely, the stories of those in universities, agribusiness, and the pesticides industry who have less leverage in the face of uncertainty, complexity, and polarization than their critics suppose; those in the Third World who have a life-or-death stake in whether animal research continues; those who would be left jobless in the name of environmentalism, like the Latino agricultural worker, the Asian fisher, or the white forester; those who cannot afford expensive electricity or organic food or policy critiques that do not offer them a qualitatively different future in which to survive; those, in other words, with their stories to tell. These are the stories that we, as narrative analysts, also have to hear. We listen to a multitude of voices, because it is from them that a metanarrative, if there is one, can be realized, a metanarrative whose policy relevance does not rest on slighting their stories or those others that continually tempt us with their one-sidedness. That is why this book has been written from the Left: not just because it is concerned with the marginalized, who often but not always are the poor, but because, in this century's butt end of intolerance, complacency, and reduced prospect, the insistence that policies can be analyzed for the better, that there are answers to policy problems, that uncertainty and complexity may be given, but their intractability is not, is a radicalism common to the Left, not the Right.

The intolerance of other people's stories—this rejection rather than acceptance of other policy narratives, whether in the form of a corrosive policy critique or a deeply divisive controversy—has clearly been on the rise in conventional policy analysis. "Since the 1960s," the economist Werner Z. Hirsch reminds us, "ideology-driven economic research appears to have gained in importance in the United States" and "has been accompanied by ideological polarization."[2] "Fighting fire with fire, estimate against estimate, is very much a part of the current partisan analytical scene," as Arnold Meltsner put it.[3] In fact, many take policy analysis to be itself unavoidably partisan, if simply by virtue of its client-orientation and the politicized climate in which practicing policy analysts operate.[4] Intolerance in the form of polarized analysts hired to promote or rationalize the exclusionary demands of all manner of special interests is not, however, the chief threat to toleration and narrative policy analysis. Things are not that simple or straightforward in the kinds of controversies and issues examined in this book.

For, while intolerance is never far from policy analysis, neither is the less obvious but considerably more caustic dilemma posed by indifference and its inimical effect on tolerance. Attitudinal survey information on the topic is hard to come by, but many bureaucratic analysts already know only too well that the energy they need to put up with things not approved of or liked can be sapped over time into a dispirited not caring one way or the other on their part. Something snaps in them as professionals when burnout and a jaded exhaustion make them indifferent to what comes of the advice they give—and burnout is very high in the science, technology, and environmental controversies that have been the focus of this book.[5] Analysts know a grim distortion takes place when applying in practice what one of the cofounders of the marginalist tradition in economics, Leon Walras, had argued in theory, namely, "the distinguishing characteristic of a science [like economics] is the complete indifference to consequences, good or bad, with which it carries on the pursuit of pure truth."[6] Analysts may tolerate this kind of indifference or value-neutrality in others, but they know they cannot themselves afford to be as indifferent in the high-tech, high-cost, and high-risk controversies where so much is at stake.

What explains the particularly pernicious effect of indifference toward tolerance for the analyst is the fact that indifference and tolerance are true opposites, in a way that tolerance and intolerance are not.[7] If tolerance is acceptance plus objection, then intolerance, as rejection plus objection, cannot be its exact contrary. Indifference better captures the opposing sense of neither accepting nor objecting to something.[8] This logical connection is, in turn, expressed behaviorally in the threat that always looms large for practicing policy analysts, namely, that they may turn into "professional bullshitters" who couldn't care less about what comes of their analyses, as long as that pole star in the midst of all this uncertainty and complexity—the analyst's own self-interest—is not risked in the process.[9]

Intolerance and indifference may be steadily increasing in conventional policy analysis, but tolerance, it must be stressed, has always had a place of honor in the profession. In his defense of the central role that utilitarianism plays in the evaluation of economic policies, James Mirrlees emphasizes the importance of putting up with what one objects to when undertaking analysis and implementation of such policies.[10] Albert Hirschman has underlined the values of tolerance and openness, their relation to changing economic tastes, and the conditions under which society tolerates income inequality.[11] And in his early *American Economic Review* article on policy analysis, Charles Lindblom sets out what was soon to become a received wisdom in the literature on government policymaking: public policies are frequently analyzed and evaluated by means of an incremental and fragmented decision making process, the very success of which depends upon putting up with different points of view from different groups along the way.[12]

Even earlier is the work the nineteenth century British economist, W. Stanley Jevons, another cofounder of the marginalist tradition and an early promoter of social experiments as a guide to improved policymaking. For Jevons, acting tolerantly comes about through approaching each policy problem from many different directions and disciplines in order to decide if one should intervene or not:

> We must consent to advance cautiously, step by step, feeling our way, adopting no foregone conclusions, trusting no single science, expecting no infallible guide. We must neither maximise the functions of government at the beck of quasi-military officials, nor minimise them according to the theories of the very best philosophers. We must learn to judge each case on its merits. . . . We must recog-

nize the fact clearly that we have to deal with complex aggregates of
people and institutions, which we cannot usually dissect and treat
piecemeal. . . . Tolerance therefore is indispensable. We may be
obliged to bear with evil for a time that we may avoid a worse evil, or
that we may not extinguish the beginnings of good.[13]

The same holds for today. As Jevons did before him, the economist,
G. L. S. Shackle, argues that "economic knowledge should surely be applied to each problem on that problem's merits, to each case as something singular and special."[14] Indeed, as we saw in the last chapter, analyzing each case on its own merits becomes the preeminent way an
analyst tolerates the multiplicity of conflicting criteria available for evaluation and interpretation.

When analyzing each case on its own merits is the metanarrative, then
how can analysts advise policymakers on anything? When we are asked
to tolerate situations of high uncertainty and complexity, where we do
not even know enough to distinguish satisficing from maximizing or the
second-best from the Pareto-optimal, and where no one is clearly right
or where everyone thinks they are, what are we then, as analysts, to advise about the merits of the case? Shackle's answer can be applied to all
analysts:

[W]hat of the economist's right or duty to offer counsel in the practical contingencies of the nation's life? Being sure that he does not
know everything, being certain only that nothing is certain, ought
he to be silent? The class of economists are like a ship's crew who
have been wrecked in a swirling tide-race. Often a man will hear
nothing but the roar of the waters in his ears, see nothing but the dim
green light. But as he strikes out, his head will come sometimes well
above the water, where for the moment he can see clear about him.
At that moment he has the right to shout directions to his fellows, to
point the way to safety, even though he may feel sure that next
moment he will be again submerged and may then doubt whether
after all he has his bearings.[15]

Analysts, in other words, have to see the urgency of taking decisions as
the core merit of each case. They must, in one sense, care enough about
the uncertain, the complex, the polarized to want to do something about
them, but, in another sense, be professional enough to know that their
answers are demanded by the moment and at times with considerable
personal risk. They must understand how indifference reduces personal

risk only by risking one's professionalism. There are, of course, found throughout the bureaucracy and in academe those analysts who, like half-hearted churchgoers, hurry their way through the litany called policy analysis (or literary criticism), no longer even trying to come up with anything more potent than a weary agnosticism towards getting the job done. But the job needs to be done. It needs analysts who see themselves advancing a profession, not just treading water for clients. We shout out in Shackle's tide-race, because that is the best, the absolute very best, we can do.

Graduate training, while neither a necessary or sufficient condition for professionalism, is just such an opportunity for advance. *Narrative Policy Analysis* demonstrates that policy analysts and literary theorists have a great deal to say to one another. Words can little convey how utterly sterile, even loony, I find debates in both fields: Is narratology out, deconstruction in? Does deconstruction promote the status quo or is it the vanguard of leftist adversary culture? Does policy analysis promote the status quo or is it nothing better than advocacy journalism? Is policy analysis out, public management in? This is rubbish. The proof of the pudding is in the eating. Of course, contemporary literary theory is useful in the analysis of major social and policy problems. This book nails down that point. The question is not, Is literary theory applicable? It is, rather, How can it be made even more useful for the future?

My scenario for the future runs something like this. Humanities departments and cultural studies institutes of major universities will approach schools of public policy to design and establish joint degree programs, leading to a specialization in "applied narrative analysis." During the first year of the two-year graduate program, the student would take the same core policy analysis courses as are currently offered in many masters-level programs, with one basic difference: the courses in microeconomics, statistics, legal analysis, public management practice, and organization theory would have modules and problem sets introducing the student to the variety of literary and cultural criticism concerned with public policy issues. Students might thus read, during the first year, articles on the use of rhetoric in microeconomics and the social sciences, a statistical test of some of Kenneth Burke's theories applied to a bureaucratic setting, a case study relying on the techniques and insights of ordinary language philosophy to help explicate the organizational causes of the Challenger accident, or the application of literary criticism to legal studies.[16] The program's first-year objective would be to familiarize the student with the breadth of applied criticism. During the second year, students would specialize by focusing electives on courses that apply narrative analysis in depth to specific public policy issues, such as has been done in the case studies of *Narrative Policy Analysis.*

One of the major objectives of the combined faculty involvement in both the first- and second-year courses will be to extend narrative analysis to new issues and to develop and improve their techniques and application. Public policy schools offer ideal resources to the humanities student or faculty member interested, for example, in using the computer to disaggregate, analyze, and rearrange narratives that dominate an issue (as was done in the chapter 5 case study).[17] The humanities, in turn, offer ideal resources for the policy analysis student or faculty member who wants to understand how policy relevance is narratively constructed (as was illustrated in the chapter 6 case study).

The program's joint courses need not stand or fall on "coming up with the solutions" to major policy problems. But their common theme should be the literary critic's precept that, while interpretations will differ and "true meaning" remains elusive, the act of interpretation can be defended. The courses will not find *the* answers to policy issues, but the program should enable students to defend for any given problem whether or not they are in a position to provide *an* answer for it, no matter how uncertain and complex the problem appears. The virtue of contemporary literary and cultural criticism, even when negative and adversarial, is precisely its continuing affirmation that people today are in a position to analyze major policy issues and that this matters, profoundly.

Appendix A
Methods for Narrative Policy Analysis

The basic approach to narrative policy analysis set out in the introduction and the more specific procedure developed in chapter 5's case study on irrigation are summarized here. The summary is deliberately schematic and simplified and is not a recipe. It assumes the reader is or will be familiar with the fuller, more representative narrative policy analyses presented elsewhere in this book.

The Basic Approach

A narrative policy analysis proceeds by four steps. The analyst starts with the conventional definition of stories and identifies those policy narratives in the issue of high uncertainty that conform to this definition: If they are stories, they have beginnings, middles, and ends, as in scenarios; if arguments, they have premises and conclusions. (Remember, the policy narratives of interest here are those scenarios or arguments that dominate the issue in question, namely, those used to underwrite and stabilize the assumptions for policymaking in situations of many unknowns, high intricacy, and little, if any, agreement.) The next step is to identify those other narratives in the issue that do not conform to this definition or run counter to the controversy's dominant policy narratives, that is, the nonstories or counterstories. The third step is to compare the two sets of narratives in order to generate a metanarrative "told" by the comparison (the governing precept here being that of semiotics and gestalt psychology, namely, a thing is defined by what it is not).

In the Riffaterre model, the metanarrative is the intertext that accounts for how two policy narratives, each the polar opposite of the other, can both be the case at the same time. Once the metanarrative has been generated, the analyst's last step is to determine if or how the metanarrative recasts the problem in such a way as to make it more amenable to the conventional policy-analytical tools of microeconomics, legal analysis, statistics, organization theory, and/or public management practice.

The metanarrative's relevance to policy can be specific or broad, depending on the extent to which the narrative analysis helps the analyst in addressing the seven common elements in a conventional policy analysis, namely,

—defining the policy problem of interest
—identifying data and information needed for analyzing that problem
—selecting criteria to evaluate different alternatives for addressing the problem
—formulating those alternatives
—projecting the consequences associated with each alternative
—assessing the trade-offs between those alternatives; and
—deciding among the alternatives

In some cases, as in chapter 7, the metanarrative is specific to one or two steps, that is, in the selection of evaluative criteria. In other examples, particularly chapter 5, all seven steps took the form of a narrative policy analysis. In all cases, the goal is to generate a metanarrative that functions as a policy narrative in underwriting (that is, establishing or certifying) and stabilizing (that is, fixing or making steady) the assumptions for decision making in the face of continuing (let me stress, continuing) uncertainty, complexity, and polarization. In so doing, the metanarrative finds a set of common assumptions that make it possible for opponents to act on an issue over which they still disagree (how this comes about is more fully explained in chapter 7).

It is useful here to illustrate briefly how the four steps of the approach work (using, in this case, the story/nonstory contraposition). The example below has been drastically reduced for expository purposes. It does suggest, however, ways in which narrative policy analysis can be extended to major science and technology controversies other than those discussed in the chapters. The example is from that pedagogical warhorse of public policy schools, the Cuban Missile Crisis.

The Cuban Missile Crisis. Stories about the Cuban Missile Crisis have increased considerably since Graham Allison's *Essence of Decision*,[1] and the use of multiple perspectives in its study has become so commonplace as to elicit little or no passing comment.[2] The crisis remains a subject over which there is still great uncertainty, where each new story becomes a candidate for another conflicting model or perspective.[3] "Essence of Revision" is how one article summarizes the current state of the topic.[4]

Transcripts have been published recently of the secret tapes of several of the October 1962 meetings involving key White House participants to the crisis.[5] In narrative-analytical terms, these transcripts are nonstories. They record the discussions of decision makers caught very much *in medias res*, where, if they had some idea just when the "crisis" they were holding meetings about had actually begun, they certainly did not know when it would end.[6] The transcripts' most distinctive feature is the relative dearth of stories used by the meetings' participants to articulate the high uncertainty of the events around them. The transcripts are full of speculation about why the Soviets (and Cubans) might be doing what they seemed to be doing and guesses about how they would respond, should the United States act one way or another. On the whole, though, scenarios are started but not finished, arguments are interrupted or dropped, and positions are more critiqued than countered by alternatives.

Indeed, the transcripts give the impression that if those present at the meetings had been asked at that time, "What's the story behind why the Soviets are doing what they're doing?" few would have been able to answer beyond "Who knows?" The paucity of stories illustrates a crisis that was one precisely because few people present in those meetings knew what were the "rules of engagement" by which they and the Soviets were playing. In contrast, the multitude of stories told after these meetings frequently differ over just what these rules really were. Here the Allison book is exemplary. While the differences among his three analytic models of the crisis have frequently been commented on, what deserves just as much attention is the attempt of each to set out "the rules" that were said to pertain during the crisis.

If the above is correct, then the major metanarrative generated by comparing the dearth and plenitude of stories can be summarized succinctly: The Cuban Missile Crisis is not over as long as we are obsessed with telling different stories about it. The crisis is instantiated with every new reinterpretation, or more properly, with the continuing felt need to reinterpret those October days. Telling stories about the crisis in the past tense becomes the way of our concealing that the crisis has been very much with us in the present tense. By being always preoccupied with determining which story "was" correct, we evade the more urgent exercise of having to deal with there still being no "story" to tell, or at least none with a beginning, middle, and end that we did not dread, until the end of the Cold War.[7]

The metanarrative's major implication is therefore sobering. Since so much time has been spent in trying to determine the rules of nuclear engagement since 1962 (and before), one must wonder whether even the rules of conventional warfare are any longer known. What *is* known is that the chances of misadventure increase when one or all of the major parties to a dispute do not know the rules of combat, *any* combat, by which they are playing.

When the original version of the narrative analysis of the Cuban Missile Crisis was published, the following sentences appeared after the preceding one:

> This lack of clarity among military and political leaders has likely increased in some parts of the world due to recent and otherwise positive Soviet and Eastern European regime changes. A major challenge facing practicing policy analysts and social critics is analyzing the potential for conventional warfare in the Cold War transition period with as much skill and attention as has been given to the Cold War's nuclear threat.[8]

Since those words were written, the Gulf War has more than vindicated them.[9]

An Ideal Procedure

A more formal, expensive procedure for narrative policy analysis was developed and used in chapter 5.[10] Those with sufficient resources should undertake the collection and analysis of primary data on the controversy of interest according to this procedure. Much of what is described below also applies to narrative policy analysis based on secondary data (i.e., on material that has been collected by others, though not necessarily in the form of unedited interviews).

1. As in chapter 3's medfly case study, the starting point is the interview with major actors in the controversy. Interviews should be open-ended, geared to letting the interviewee tell her or his story. No attempt

should be made to use questions as a way of constructing a putative middle ground between the controversy's opposing parties. Questions, of course, should not be used to accentuate differences either. Considerable care thus must be taken in interviewer selection and/or training. It is important for the analyst to remember that most of the major actors in a controversy do not write about their involvement (one of the few exceptions being the medfly case study). Where they can be interviewed and the analyst has the resources to do so, they should be.

2. Implicit in the interview approach is the case study format. It is always possible to discuss science, technology, and environmental disputes solely at the metatheoretical level, pitting, say, poststructuralist interpretations against those of the Frankfurt School or public choice models. I do not find such metatheoretical to-and-fro helpful. A case study approach, on the other hand, forces the analyst to see how others define a specific policy problem, identify and assess its alternatives, and then decide among them. There is nothing quite as salutary as putting yourself in a position of recommending what a policymaker or analyst should have done with respect to a problem, but did not do, when that someone is still around to argue your recommendation.

3. Once the interviews have been undertaken and transcribed, each interviewee's transcript should be disaggregated into discrete problem statements. A problem statement asserts a causal relationship or set of causal relationships, for example, problem 1 is said to lead to problem 2, which in turn is said to lead to problem 3. Attention at the disaggregation stage should be directed to what was asserted, avoiding any attempt to determine if what the interviewee said was causally related in fact. If sufficient funds are available, the analyst may want to have several people do the disaggregation and coding exercise of problem statements and their purported causal relationships, and, where there are differences over a given statement or relationship, have them adjudicated by a third party.

4. Once the transcripts have been disaggregated into coded problem statements, the analyst then proceeds to aggregate all problem statements across all interviewees. The result will be a set of frequency tables, indicating, for example, what the most commonly identified problems are, and a network of purported causal relationships said to exist among problems identified by interviewees. The tables and network will enable the analyst to ascertain several important points:

—Are more interviewees and interviews needed? By looking at the number of new problems added with each successive interview, the analyst gets a better fix on whether more interviews are needed and whether it is worth the cost at the margin to do so. It is important to canvass as many views as possible in the dispute, and to get as many different problems out on the table for analysis as resources permit.

—The frequency tables and network analysis should confirm whether the problem or controversy is really complex and uncertain. It may be that there is consensus over the problem, for example, some 70 percent of the interviewees mentioned problem 1, while the causal pathway, say, of problem 1 leading to problem 27 leading to problem 3 was mentioned by the majority of those interviewed. If this is so, the problem may well be approachable directly through conventional policy-analytical techniques.

If, however, as was the case in chapter 5's irrigation controversy, not only did the frequency tables show no agreement over what the major problems were and no dominant causal pathway, but instead what was found was a massive amount of circular and opposing argumentation, then network analysis will have confirmed for the analyst a truly complex and uncertain and polarized problem, and one suitable for narrative analytical techniques.

—Note how this concern of the narrative policy analyst to demonstrate complexity, uncertainty, and polarization as the starting point of analysis contrasts with the typical ending point of applied social science research in uncovering complexity. For the social scientist, the problem is to avoid thinking that answers are simple, when matters are discovered to be complex. For the narrative analyst, the problem in searching for answers is to avoid thinking that a problem is complex and uncertain and divisive, when it is not. The narrative policy analyst wants to be absolutely confident that the issue is truly one of many unknowns and deep divisions in order to apply those semiotic and narratological techniques based on binary contraposition (a point fully illustrated in chapter 7).

—In the absence of a formal network analysis, the only sure indication the analyst has that she or he is dealing with a complex, polarized policy problem of many unknowns is the past record of repeated, unsuccessful, and costly efforts to address it by conventional policy analytical techniques.

—The corollary of the last two points should be clear and must not be forgotten: many policy issues are not complex, uncertain or divisive. Most of the time you can get along quite well with conventional analysis alone.

5. The network analysis enables the analyst to locate the story (or stories) and the nonstory or counterstory (plural again) from which the metanarrative is (or metanarratives are) to be constructed, assuming at least one exists. With chapter 5's irrigation case study as a guide, the analyst can expect to find a great deal of implied circular argumentation as people run around trying to make sense of what they think they see in a complex and uncertain science, technology, and environment controversy. Circular arguments, just as those policy critiques discussed in chapters 2 and 3, are paradigmatic nonstories with no beginning, middle, and end of their own. Nonetheless, the question of circular argumentation is an empirical issue and its existence cannot be presupposed as the dominant nonstory in all controversies. Complexity and uncertainty could be configured as a plot of causally unrelated problems, with no connecting network, or as several dominant causal pathways, one being a point-by-point rebuttal or mirror image of the other, as in the Indian burial remains and medfly controversies.

6. By undertaking a disaggregation and reaggregation exercise in order to determine what, if any, networks form, the analyst comes to better appreciate what "objectivity" means when the policy narratives in question contain problem statements whose truth value is difficult to ascertain, is little accepted, or both. Under conditions of high uncertainty and complexity, where policy narratives seek to ensure the assumptions for decision making, the analyst approximates objectivity by identifying whose uncertainty and complexity and polarization she or he is analyzing. Is it the uncertainty of the interviewees, when they express skepticism about specific points? Is the uncertainty the analyst's or the policymaker's, when she or he tries to determine the factual merits of any interviewee's assertions? Or is it systemic uncertainty, apparent only at the aggregate level as the certainties of expert, but opposing, viewpoints?

7. With greater understanding of whose uncertainty is at issue in a controversy comes greater respect for the functional role that uncertainty can have in such disputes. In some cases uncertainty enables decision making, while reducing uncertainty paralyzes it. This dynamic is most graphically illustrated in the irrigation case study, though the best example of the positive nature of uncertainty is given in chapter 4's study on animal rights. If there ever was an issue that could profit from considerably more uncertainty and complexity than there is currently between opposing camps, it is this one between the very sharply defined animal researchers and animal welfare groups.

8. Last, but not least, writing up the results of a narrative policy anal-

ysis takes considerable care and sensitivity. Different clients have different requirements. Some policymakers may be put off by the story/nonstory or counterstory/metanarrative terminology, even though they subscribe to its logic. Some reports or journals may want references to the procedure lodged in the endnotes, others may want them up front in the text. While one should explicitly discuss the formal analytics of story, nonstory or counterstory, and metanarrative when writing for one's professional and disciplinary colleagues, it may be necessary to avoid such a discussion when writing for policymakers and specialists.

Why would you avoid it at all? For example, if I were doing the narrative policy analysis of San Joaquin irrigation and drainage over again, I would still derive our recommendation for a separate drainage agency precisely the way we did. However, in view of our subsequent problems with state irrigation officials (see chapter 5), I would not refer to the approach at all, but instead would justify the recommendation on the grounds that the irrigation and drainage literature provides a number of organizational arrangements for drainage disposal, including the one recommended. Which, by way of conclusion, is just what I did in an article for the American Society of Civil Engineers.[11]

Appendix B
Short Chronology of Medfly Controversy[1]

5 June 1980. One medfly male found in a Los Angeles trap. Sent immediately to Sacramento for verification. Two males found in a Santa Clara trap. Sent to Sacramento third class mail and received 17 June.

6 June. California Medfly Project created. First California Department of Food and Agriculture (CDFA) project leader for the Santa Clara infestation named 20 June.

25 June–5 July. Fruit stripping and collection begins.

8 July. Technical Review Committee, later known as Technical Advisory Committee (TAC), is created, consisting of scientists to advise and review project operations.

17 July. State quarantine established (approximately 96 square miles in Santa Clara County and 130 square miles in Los Angeles County).

22 July. First sterile flies released. Ground spraying and aerial release of flies begin 1 August.

31 October. The infested area in Santa Clara Valley has grown to slightly more than 175 square miles.

24 November. U.S. Department of Agriculture (USDA) reaches consensus that aerial spraying with malathion is necessary. Three days later USDA and CDFA discuss tremendous pressure being exerted by California growers and other states for aerial spraying.

3 December. CDFA and USDA hold news conference to announce proposed aerial spraying with malathion. TAC minutes show its members divided over whether or not such spraying is warranted at that time.

8–9 December. Four city councils and the Santa Clara Board of Supervisors vote to prohibit aerial spraying. A number of other cities do the same later in the month.

11 December. CDFA agrees to hold off on aerial spraying in order to see if intensified ground program will work.

Mid December. Eradication achieved in Los Angeles County. The California State Department of Health Services publishes its report on health risks associated with the aerial spraying of malathion-bait mixture.

23 June 1981. First medfly larvae collected since intensified ground spraying began. CDFA officials are, however, uncertain what caused this fresh outbreak.

7 July. TAC holds emergency meeting and recommends aerial spraying.

8 July. TAC members meet with Governor Brown and try to convince him to start aerial spraying at once. Instead, the governor announces an expanded ground program to handle the new outbreak.

9–10 July. U.S. Secretary of Agriculture John Block threatens to quarantine the entire state of California if aerial spraying is not begun immediately. Governor Brown announces aerial spraying will commence on 14 July. (Spraying begins shortly after midnight of the 13th from a secret helicopter base established in a local cemetery. Pressure for Governor Brown's impeachment mounts.)

16 July. Texas, South Carolina, Mississippi, and Florida impose quarantines restricting movement of specific California produce. Other state and international quarantines (particularly Mexico and Japan) follow later that month and the next. These quarantines are subsequently lifted through court action or by more bureaucratic channels.

August. TAC is reorganized and a permanent USDA comanager to the Medfly Project is assigned.

21 September 1982. USDA and CDFA hold news conference to officially declare eradication. TAC holds final meeting. All regulatory measures are dropped.

Appendix C

Prevalence of Stories in the Medfly Controversy

Stories were central to how key participants understood and expressed the controversy. A university entomologist actively involved in these events complained about the government bureaucracy's "same scenario and script for each [eradication] project," that is, "It is the same script— the insect is a monster; it is causing tremendous damage; the agency is right and don't question the agency."[1] A "worse-case scenario" was important for the Department of Health Services' risk assessment of the proposed aerial spraying with malathion in the winter of 1980/81. The project's state comanager complained that "[i]t was our worst case scenario" when the medflies reemerged after the spring of 1981.[2] A reporter covering the controversy proposed a "scenario" that best summed up in her mind the activities of the TAC.[3]

The pejorative sense of "merely" telling stories that were "just stories" pervades many accounts of the controversy's key participants. A senior USDA official came close to this sense when describing the response of a foreign government to his unit's assurances that importation of California produce could continue: "We had been telling them for so long that we were on top of things . . . but there were so many flies found that they felt they couldn't believe us. . . . 'Well, you don't even know where the damn thing is!' was their reaction. . . . 'What are you talking about?' "[4] A member of one city council complained: "We met with [the project's state comanager] last night at our council meeting and the thrust of his comments was 'Trust us, we know what we are doing.' People trusted the government when they used thalidomide . . . when they were using

Agent Orange . . . when they said nuclear waste disposal problems were safe and you know what happened. We are now finding out that the government didn't know what was going on or suppressed what was going on with respect to PCB and asbestos and the list goes on and on."[5] The former chair of the state assembly's agricultural committee told of one state senator's political posturing during the Medfly Controversy: "He'd go to Stanislaus County and advocate immediate aerial spraying. . . . Then in Santa Clara County he would say something different."[6] A reporter for the state's best-known newspaper gave a number of examples of where she felt TAC had made decisions and recommendations for political, rather than scientific, reasons: "On one hand, some would say, 'I am a scientist. Therefore, I have to have pure information before I can say anything.' The next thing, they'd turn around and do something that was just absolutely, blatantly political."[7] Since "true objectivity and neutrality do not exist in science," the university entomologist concluded, "those seeking technical advice can more or less shop around and get the answers they desire."[8]

The accounts of the key participants are full of instances where two or more policy positions, over which there is a great deal of uncertainty (scientific, political, organizational), are contrasted in such a way as to make them appear equally doubtful or self-cancelling as if they were "just stories." The project's state comanager recounted: "One member of the Technical Advisory Committee, a Ph.D. entomologist who had spent his whole life studying the medfly, said, 'Don't release [the sterile flies] by truck. . . . Release them by plane.' Another member, also a Ph.D. with the same kind of background, said, 'Don't release them by plane.' "[9] "You can get entirely different views from entomologists on any subject," according to one observer of the controversy.[10] A person familiar with the different factions in CDFA noted "One group [in the department] said trapping was the only way to go, another group said 'biometric' grid surveys were the only way to go, and the third group said, 'I'll follow my nose to find larvae.' "[11] One entomologist on TAC explained some of their equivocation this way: "Sometimes we [i.e., members of TAC] spoke up and said, 'Don't forget, these data are not so hot.' Other times we may have kept quiet, thinking, for example, 'Let them take the chance. Maybe it will work.' "[12]

Notes

Introduction to Narrative Policy Analysis

1 W. Kip Viscusi, *Fatal Tradeoffs* (New York: Oxford University Press, 1992), pp. 153–4.

2 Charles Perrow, *Normal Accidents* (New York: Basic Books, 1984).

3 For an extended discussion of how narratives and tropes stabilize the assumptions for economic analysis, see the work of Duke University economist, E. Roy Weintraub, *Stabilizing Dynamics: Constructing Economic Knowledge* (Cambridge: Cambridge University Press, 1991). See also Warren Samuels, ed., *Economics as Discourse: An Analysis of the Language of Economists* (Boston: Kluwer Academic Publishers, 1990).

4 Richard Neustadt and Ernest May, *Thinking in Time: The Uses of History for Decision-Makers* (New York: Free Press, 1986), p. 106. Neustadt is considered a founder of one of the major policy analysis schools in the United States, Harvard's John F. Kennedy School of Government. See J. Anthony Lukas, "Harvard's Kennedy School: Is Competence Enough?" *New York Times Magazine*, 12 March 1989, p. 68.

5 For a sampling of this literature, see Martin Rein, *Social Science and Public Policy* (Harmondsworth, Middlesex, England: Penguin Educational, 1976); Thomas Kaplan, "The Narrative Structure of Policy Analysis," *Journal of Policy Analysis and Management* 5 (2) (1990); Martin Krieger, *Advice and Planning* (Philadelphia: Temple University Press, 1981). For a discussion of the importance of argumentation in policy analysis, see Giandomenico Majone, *Evidence, Argument and Persuasion in the Policy Process* (New Haven, Conn.: Yale University Press, 1989).

6 *If You're So Smart* was published in 1990 by the University of Chicago Press. See, in particular, pp. 36, 146, and 162.

7 Instances of this insight are commonplace. Zygmunt Bauman notes that the term *intellectual* arose during the Dreyfus scandal, precisely at the moment the homogeneity and cohesiveness of intellectuals as a group was in decline. Michael Ham-

burger notes that terms, like culture, gain increasing importance and popularity, precisely at the moment things like culture are in disarray and shambles. See Zygmunt Bauman, *Legislators and Interpreters: On Modernity, Post-Modernity and Intellectuals* (Oxford: Polity Press, 1987), p. 21. See also Michael Hamburger, *Testimonies: Selected Shorter Prose, 1950–1987* (Manchester, England: Carcanet, 1989), p. 50. For the general principle involved, see John Myles's review in *Contemporary Sociology* 18:2 (1989): 219.

8   Isaiah Berlin, *The Crooked Timber of Humanity* (New York: Alfred A. Knopf, 1991), p. 80. The quotes are taken from pp. 32, 47, and 18 respectively.

1 Deconstructing Budgets, Reconstructing Budgeting

1   Aaron Wildavsky, *The Politics of the Budgetary Process*, 4th ed. (Boston: Little, Brown and Co., 1984), p. 252.

2   Aaron Wildavsky, *The New Politics of the Budgetary Process* (Boston: Scott, Foresman and Co., 1988), p. 399.

3   Wildavsky, *Politics*; Aaron Wildavsky, *Budgeting: A Comparative Theory of Budgetary Processes*, 2d rev. ed. (New Brunswick, N.J.: Transaction Books, 1986); Naomi Caiden and Aaron Wildavsky, *Planning and Budgeting in Poor Countries* (New York: John Wiley and Sons, Wiley Interscience, 1974).

4   See, for example, Allen Schick, *Congress and Money: Budgeting, Spending and Taxing* (Washington, D.C.: Urban Institute, 1980), p. 230. Rather than bring out another edition of his *Politics of the Budgetary Process*, Wildavsky published a much revised version, *The New Politics of the Budgetary Process*, in 1988.

5   Richard Goode, *Government Finance in Developing Countries* (Washington, D.C.: Brookings Institution, 1984), p. 9.

6   Wildavsky, *Politics*, p. 1.

7   See ibid., p. 252.

8   David Lamb, *The Africans* (New York: Vintage Books, 1984), p. 175.

9   Caiden and Wildavsky, *Planning and Budgeting*, pp. 289–90.

10 I have in front of me a review for the World Bank on livestock research projects in West Africa which complains of the " 'fictional' allocation of funds which do not get released by treasuries resulting in receipt of less than half of official budgets." Robert McDowell and C. de Haan, "West Africa Agricultural Research Review (WAARR): Livestock Research," draft (1986), p. 77. See also Wildavsky, *Politics*, pp. xviii–xix; Wildavsky, *Budgeting*, chap. 5.

11 Emery Roe, "The Ceiling as Base: National Budgeting in Kenya," *Public Budgeting and Finance* 6 (2): (1986). For similar gaps in the U.S. federal budgeting process, see Naomi Caiden, "The New Rules of the Federal Budget Game," *Public Administration Review* 44 (2): (1984). One reviewer pointed out how "cross-cuts" in the U.S. federal budget aid the fiction that there are subbudgets spanning conventional budget categories, as in the U.S. government's "science budget."

12 See Caiden and Wildavsky, *Planning and Budgeting*, p. 113.

13 Schick, *Congress and Money*, p. 338.

14 Wildavsky, *Budgeting*, pp. 35, 325.

15 Roland Barthes, *S/Z*, trans. Richard Miller (New York: Hill and Wang, 1974), p. 4.

16   See Goode, *Government Finance*, p. 33, and Wildavsky, *Budgeting*, pp. 176, 239, about the "seriousness" with which budgets should be read.

17   See also Caiden and Wildavsky, *Planning and Budgeting*, pp. 144–5, and Wildavsky, *Budgeting*, passim.

18   Wildavsky, ibid., p. 157.

19   Republic of Kenya, *Report and Recommendations of the Working Party on Government Expenditures* (Nairobi: Government Printer, 1982), p. 15.

20   Vincent Leitch, *Deconstructive Criticism: An Advanced Introduction* (New York: Columbia University Press, 1983), p. 98.

21   See Wildavsky, *Budgeting*, p. 352.

22   Wildavsky, ibid., pp. 12–3, 238.

23   This notion of "power" was long ago identified by James March as "different parts of the system contribut[ing] to different decisions in different ways at different times." J. G. March, "The Power of Power," in *Varieties of Political Theory*, ed. D. Easton (Englewood Cliffs, N.J.: Prentice-Hall, 1966), pp. 66–7. For budget examples in almost the same terms, see Schick, "Congress and Money," p. 320; Caiden and Wildavsky, *Planning and Budgeting*, p. 55.

24   Emery Roe, *Guide to the Government of Kenya Budgetary Process*, with editorial assistance of Anne Kamiri and Alan Johnston (Nairobi: Ministry of Finance and Planning, 1985).

25   Emery Roe, "Counting on Comparative Budgeting in Africa," *International Journal of Public Administration* 11 (3): (1988).

26   Jean-François Lyotard, *The Post-Modern Condition: A Report on Knowledge* (Minneapolis: University of Minnesota Press, 1984), p. 6.

27   See Caiden and Wildavsky, *Planning and Budgeting*, pp. 89–91; Goode, *Government Finance*, pp. 28–31.

28   Jacques Derrida, "Structure Event Context," *Glyph 1*, (Baltimore: Johns Hopkins University Press, 1977), p. 185.

29   Michael Fischer, *Does Deconstruction Make Any Difference?* (Bloomington: Indiana University Press, 1985), pp. 112–3.

30   Leitch, *Deconstructive Criticism*, p. 58.

31   See David Bromwich, "Recent Work in Literary Theory," *Social Research*, 53 (3): 447 (1986).

32   For example, the conditional probability that a government-sponsored rural water supply will be completed as originally proposed in Kenya is less than .15 for remoter areas of the country. Only half of such projects ever proposed are started, and of those that are started, slightly less than 30 percent are ever completed. See Emery Roe, "Project Appraisal: A Venture Capitalist Approach," *Development Policy Review* 3 (2): (1985). For a review of the evaluation literature on program failure in the United States, see Peter Rossi and James Wright (1984), "Evaluation Research: An Assessment," in *The Annual Review of Sociology*, Annual Reviews Inc., Palo Alto, Calif.; D. Greenberg and P. Robins, "The Changing Role of Social Experiments in Policy Analysis," *Journal of Policy Analysis and Management* 5 (2): (1986). For the literature on program failure in the Third World, see Bruce Johnston and William Clark, *Redesigning Rural Development: A Strategic Perspective* (Baltimore: Johns Hopkins University Press, 1982); Robert Chambers, *Rural Development: Putting the Last First* (London: Longman, 1983).

33 For example, L. O'Toole, "Policy Recommendations for Multi-Actor Implementation: An Assessment of the Field," *Journal of Public Policy* 6 (part 2): (1986).

34 This paragraph is a drastically reduced discussion of a very complex implementation literature. In chapter 7, for instance, evaluation criteria are introduced that are not tied to the determination of whether or not the program goals or objectives are met. I focus on implementation and evaluation problems at more length in Emery Roe, "District Focus and the Problem of Project Implementation," *Rural Development Project Discussion Paper* (Nairobi: Ministry of Finance and Planning, 1984); Roe, "Project Appraisal"; Emery Roe, "Lantern on the Stern: Policy Analysis, Historical Research, and *Pax Britannica* in Africa," *African Studies Review* 30 (1): (1987); Emery Roe, "Management Crisis in the New Class," *Telos*, no. 76: (1988).

35 As Ned Rorem, the American composer, put it of one opera director, "under [his] guidance even a world premiere would be an alternate version." Ned Rorem, *The Nantucket Diary of Ned Rorem: 1973–1985* (San Francisco: North Point Press, 1987), p. 5.

36 A good introduction to what the U.S. government calls "National Intelligence Estimates" can be found in John Macartney, "Intelligence: A Consumer's Guide," *International Journal of Intelligence and Counterintelligence* 2 (2): (1988).

37 J. G. March and Johan Olsen, *Rediscovering Institutions: The Organizational Basis of Politics* (New York: Free Press, 1989), p. 11.

2 What Are Policy Narratives?

1 For example, Goren Hyden, *No Shortcuts to Progress: African Development Management in Perspective* (Berkeley: University of California Press, 1983), p. 65; Jon Moris, *Managing Induced Rural Development*, International Development Institute (Bloomington: University of Indiana, 1981), pp. 19–22; David Korten, "Community Organization and Rural Development: A Learning Process Approach," *Public Administration Review* 40 (5): 496–501 (1980); Stephen Sandford, *Management of Pastoral Development in the Third World* (Chichester, England: John Wiley & Sons, 1983), pp. 258ff.

2 See, for instance, Robert Chambers, *Rural Development: Putting the Last First* (London: Longman, 1983), pp. 211–12.

3 Hyden, *No Shortcuts*, p. 157.

4 Caiden and Wildavsky, *Planning and Budgeting* (see chap. 1, n. 3); Bruce Johnston and William Clark, *Redesigning Rural Development: A Strategic Perspective* (Baltimore: Johns Hopkins University Press, 1982), chap. 1; for an exception, see John Cohen and David Lewis, "Role of Government in Combatting Food Shortages: Lessons from Kenya 1984–85," in *Drought and Hunger in Africa*, ed. Michael Glantz (Cambridge: Cambridge University Press, 1987).

5 The literature on the preconditions for better learning and decision making is voluminous. For a review that discusses issues of and links between learning, redundancy, uncertainty and goal stability, see Scott Sagan, *The Limits of Safety: Organizations, Accidents, and Nuclear Weapons* (Princeton, N.J.: Princeton University Press, 1993), chap. 1. It must be noted that the pressures for long-term planning remain strong, at least in Africa, notwithstanding past learning failures.

The persistence of structural adjustment and budget ceilings have become reinforcing factors. One response of African governments to the series of IMF/World Bank structural adjustment programs (SAPs) has been to call for longer-term planning horizons to counter what they see as the invariably short-term and short-sighted corrections suffered under SAPs. See, e.g., United Nations Economic Commission for Africa, *African Alternative Framework to Structural Adjustment Programmes for Socio-Economic Recovery and Transformation*, E/ECA/CM.15/6/Rev. 3 (New York: UNECA, 1989), p. 33. Moreover, the increased use of ceilings on ministry budgets as a form of year-to-year expenditure control has fitted in quite neatly with those who argue that an intermediate- to long-term macroeconomic framework is needed in part to establish just what these yearly ceilings should be. See Subramaniam Ramakrishnan, "Issues in Budgeting and Fiscal Management in Sub-Saharan Africa," discussion paper prepared for the Workshop on Economic Reform in Africa, sponsored by the University of Michigan's Center for Research on Economic Development and USAID, Nairobi, pp. 2, 26–7. For an example of ceilings used as a form of expenditure control, see Emery Roe, "Ceiling as Base" (see chap. 1, n. 11).

6 For a discussion of this phenomenon as it is found in irrigation projects, see Emery Roe, "Perspectives from Organization Theory on Irrigation Bureaucracies in East and West Africa," in *Improving Performance of Irrigation Bureaucracies: Suggestions for Systematic Analysis and Agency Recommendations*, ed. Norman Uphoff, with Prithi Ramamurthy and Roy Steiner (Ithaca, N.Y.: Cornell University, 1988).

7 For example, Korten, "Community Organization," p. 498.

8 Blueprint development is alive and well: a United Nations–sponsored publication, for example, regrets that the Lagos Plan of Action "does not provide a blueprint of the actual policies that are required for its implementation at the country level." Itsuo Kawamura, "Summary and Conclusions," in *African Development Prospects: A Policy Modeling Approach*, ed. Dominick Salvatore (report for the United Nations, New York: Taylor & Francis, 1989), p. 270.

9 This definition of narrative and story is the standard one. See the respective entries in Gerald Prince, *A Dictionary of Narratology* (Lincoln: University of Nebraska Press, 1987). For more on the importance of stories and storytelling in the policy world, see the introduction, particularly the section "What Use Are Stories?"

10 How the truth of a narrative does not necessarily derive from or depend upon the truth of its constituent parts is discussed in Paul Roth, "How Narratives Explain," *Social Research* 56 (2): 456ff. (1989).

11 Garrett Hardin, "The Tragedy of the Commons," in *Managing the Commons*, ed. Garrett Hardin and John Baden (San Francisco: W. H. Freeman and Co., 1977), p. 20.

12 Sandford, *Management*, chap. 1.

13 See Panel on Common Property Resource Management, *Proceedings of the Conference on Common Property Resource Management* (Washington, D.C.: National Academy Press, 1986). Report for the Board on Science and Technology for International Development, Office of International Affairs, National Research Council, Washington, D.C.; Bonnie McCay and James Acheson, eds., *The Ques-*

tion of the Commons: The Culture and Ecology of Communal Resources (Tucson: University of Arizona Press, 1987).

14   Garrett Hardin, "Denial and Disguise," in Garrett Hardin and John Baden, eds., *Managing the Commons*, pp. 47–8.

15   Hardin, "Tragedy of the Commons," p. 28.

16   Hardin, "An Operational Analysis of 'Responsibility,'" in Hardin and Baden, eds., *Managing the Commons*, p. 72.

17   Hardin, "Tragedy of the Commons," p. 22.

18   The survey was funded by the Government of Botswana's Ministry of Agriculture and USAID through the Center for International Studies, Cornell University.

19   Louise Fortmann and Emery Roe, *The Water Points Survey* (Gaborone, Botswana: Ministry of Agriculture, Ithaca: Cornell University, Center for International Studies, 1981); Charles Bailey, *Cattle Husbandry in the Communal Areas of Eastern Botswana* (Ph.D. diss., Cornell University, 1982).

20   Republic of Botswana, *White Paper of 1975: National Policy on Tribal Grazing Land* (Gaborone, Botswana: Government Printer, 1975), p. 1.

21   Emery Roe, "Range Conditions around Water Sources in Botswana and Kenya," *Rangelands* 6 (6): (1984).

22   Malcolm Odell and Marcia Odell, "Communal Area Livestock Development in Botswana: Lessons for the World Bank's Third Livestock Development Project" (paper presented to the World Bank, Synergy International, Amesbury, Mass., 1986), p. 7.

23   Solomon Bekure and Neville Dyson-Hudson, *The Operation and Viability of the Second Livestock Development Project (1497-BT): Selected Issues* (Gaborone, Botswana: Ministry of Agriculture, 1982).

24   Emery Roe and Louise Fortmann, *Allocation of Water Points at the Lands* (Gaborone, Botswana: Ministry of Local Government and Lands, Ithaca: Cornell University, Center for International Studies, 1981), p. 71; Animal Production Research Unit, *Beef Production and Range Management in Botswana* (Gaborone, Botswana: Ministry of Agriculture, 1980), pp. 85–6.

25   Louise Fortmann and Emery Roe, "Common Property Management of Water in Botswana," *Proceedings of the Conference on Common Property Resource Management*.

26   For an example of one such model, see Emery Roe, "Last Chance at the African Kraal: Reviving Livestock Projects in Africa," in *Proceedings of the 1987 International Rangeland Development Symposium*, ed. J. T. O'Rourke (Morrilton, Ariz.: Winrock International Institute for Agricultural Development, 1987); Emery Roe, "New Frameworks for an Old Tragedy of the Commons and an Aging Common Property Resource Management," *Agriculture and Human Values* (forthcoming).

27   Elinor Ostrom suggests eight "design principles" that help to account for the success of long-enduring common property resource systems. She cautions, however, that her list is speculative. Elinor Ostrom, *Governing the Commons: The Evolution of Institutions for Collective Action* (Cambridge: Cambridge University Press, 1990), p. 90. For a sketch of four possible countermodels to both the tragedy of the commons argument and the common property resource management literature, see Roe, "New Frameworks."

28 See, for example, Yusif Haji, "Focus on 1989 Nakuru Show—Rift Valley: Land of Plenty," *Kenya Times*, 29 June 1989, p. 20 (Mr. Haji was the Rift Valley Provincial Commissioner); Gideon Cyrus Mutiso, "Historical Perspective, Existing ASAL Programmes and Institutional Analysis," Technical Paper no. 3, in *Republic of Kenya—Arid and Semi-Arid Lands (ASAL) Development Programme: Summary of Technical Reports on the Strategy, Policy and ASAL Development Programme 1989–1993* (Nairobi: IFAD/UNDP, 1988), p. 48. The Sywnnerton Plan's policy narrative can be found in Colony and Protectorate of Kenya, *A Plan to Intensify the Development of African Agriculture in Kenya*, comp. R. J. M. Swynnerton (Nairobi: Government Printer, 1954), pp. 8–9.

29 M. P. K. Sorrenson, *Land Reform in the Kikuyu Country: A Study in Government Policy* (Nairobi: Oxford University Press, 1967); William Barber, "Land Reform and Economic Change among African Farmers in Kenya," *Economic Development and Cultural Change* 19 (1): (1970); Frank Bernard, *East of Mount Kenya: Meru Agriculture in Transition* (Munich: Weltforum Verlag, 1972); Nancy Gray, "Acceptance of Land Adjudication among the Digo," Discussion Paper no. 37, Institute of African Studies, Nairobi, 1972; Rodney Wilson, "The Economic Implications of Land Registration in Kenya's Smallholder Areas," Staff Working Paper no. 91, Institute of Development Studies, University of Nairobi, 1971; Simon Coldham, "Land-Tenure Reform in Kenya: The Limits of the Law," *Journal of Modern African Studies* 17 (4): (1979); Diana Hunt, *The Impending Crisis in Kenya: The Case for Land Reform* (Aldershot, England: Gower Publishing Co., 1984); E. H. N. Njeru, "Land Adjudication and its Implications for the Social Organization of the Mbere," Research Paper no. 73, Land Tenure Center, University of Wisconsin, Madison, 1978; David Brokensha and E. H. N. Njeru, "Some Consequences of Land Adjudication in Mbere Division, Embu," Working Paper no. 320, Institute of Development Studies, University of Nairobi, 1977; Angelique Haugerud, "Development and Household Economy in Two Eco-Zones of Embu District," Working Paper no. 382, Institute of Development Studies, University of Nairobi, 1981; Angelique Haugerud, "The Consequences of Land Tenure Reform among Smallholders in the Kenya Highlands," *Rural Africana* 15 and 16 (1983); Angelique Haugerud, "Land Tenure and Agrarian Change in Kenya," *Africa* 59 (1): (1989); Parker Shipton, "Land, Credit and Crop Transactions in Kenya: The Luo Response to Directed Development in Nyanza Province" (Ph.D. diss., University of Cambridge, 1985); Richard Odingo, "The Dynamics of Land Tenure Reform and of Agrarian Systems in Africa: Land Tenure Study in the Nakuru, Kericho and Machakos Areas of the Kenya Highlands" (Rome: Food and Agricultural Organization, 1985), cited in Joy Green, "Evaluating the Impact of Consolidation of Holdings, Individualization of Tenure, and Registration of Title: Lessons from Kenya," LTC Paper no. 129, Land Tenure Center, University of Wisconsin, Madison, 1985; Anne Fleuret, "Some Consequences of Tenure and Agrarian Reform in Taita, Kenya," in *Land and Society in Contemporary Africa*, ed. R. E. Downs and S. P. Renya (Hanover, N.H.: University Press of New England, 1988); see also Esther Wangari (Ph.D. diss. on land registration in Lower Embu District, New School of Social Research, forthcoming); Willis Oluoch-Kosura with S. E. Migot-Adholla, study on the effect of land registration in four localities from two districts in Kenya, Nairobi (sponsored by World Bank, forthcoming).

Green, "Dynamics of Land Tenure Reform," has a more detailed review and bibliography of the literature on Kenya's land registration program.

30   For related comments on contemporary insecurity of land tenure in Kenya, see Paul Collier and Deepak Lal, *Labour and Poverty in Kenya: 1900–1980* (Oxford: Clarendon Press, 1988), p. 131.

31   For example, World Bank, *Kenya: Agricultural Credit Policy Review,* Report no. 5619-KE (Washington, D.C.: World Bank, 1985).

32   See Shipton, "Land, Credit, and Crop Transactions"; Haugerud, "Land Tenure."

33   That the ministry responsible for Kenya's land registration program has been under increased pressure to better justify its expenditures is indicated by a memo from the ministry's permanent secretary to his staff: "During the past six months or so, His Excellency the President has on a number of occasions impressed upon this Ministry the need to expand and intensify our work in land surveying, land adjudication and land administration so that desired goals in land tenure, and the attendant social and economic benefits, can be realized throughout the Republic in the shortest time possible. . . . A review of the performance of this Ministry over the last few years indicates clearly that our performance and output have been below expectation and that drastic changes are needed in our operational strategies, priorities and personal attitudes if we are to fulfil the mammoth responsibilities entrusted to us by the Government. . . . While it is acknowledged that external factors such as scarcity of funds, personnel and equipment may retard the implementation of the [ministry's work] programme in certain cases, it must also be recognised that the Government does not have a limitless source of funds and, therefore, it is incumbent upon us all to optimise the utilization of the scarce resources at our disposal." Ministry of Lands and Settlement, "Programme of Work and Performance Targets for the Year 1988," Memorandum MLS 2/001 vol. 2/(16) (Nairobi, 1988).

34   John Galaty and Dan Aronson, "Research Priorities and Pastoralist Development: What is to be Done?" in *The Future of Pastoral Peoples: Proceedings of a Conference Held in Nairobi, Kenya, 4–8 August, 1980,* ed. John Galaty, Dan Aronson, Philip Salzman, and Amy Chouinard (Ottawa: International Development Research Center, 1981), p. 21.

35   Ahmed Sidahmed and L. Koong, "Application of Systems Analysis to Nomadic Livestock Production in the Sudan," in *Livestock Development in Subsaharan Africa: Constraints, Prospects, Policy,* ed. James Simpson and Phylo Evangelou (Boulder, Colo.: Westview Press, 1984), p. 61.

36   Anders Hjort, "Herds, Trade, and Grain: Pastoralism in a Regional Perspective," in *Future of Pastoral Peoples,* ed. Galaty, et al., p. 135.

37   Piers Blaikie and Harold Brookfield, *Land Degradation and Society* (London: Methuen, 1987), p. 27.

38   Galaty and Aronson, "Research Priorities," p. 20.

39   USAID, "Suggestions for the Improvement of Rangeland Livestock Projects in Africa: A Panel Report" (Washington, D.C., 1985), p. 7.

40   Sidahmed and Koong, "Application of Systems Analysis," p. 74.

41   David Leonard, "Disintegrating Agricultural Development," *Food Research Institute Studies* 19 (2): (1984).

42 The sociologist, Charles Perrow, provides an excellent description of these general properties of tightly and loosely coupled systems. Charles Perrow, *Normal Accidents: Living with High Risk Technologies* (New York: Basic Books, 1984), pp. 93–6.

43 Jon Moris and Derrick Thom, *African Irrigation Overview: Main Report*, Water Management Synthesis Report 37 (Logan: Utah State University, 1987), pp. 430–1.

44 More details on this illustration can be found in Emery Roe and Louise Fortmann, *Season and Strategy: The Changing Organization of the Rural Water Sector in Botswana*, Special Series in Rural Development (Ithaca, N.Y.: Rural Development Committee, Cornell University, 1982), chap. 6.

45 Emery Roe, "Project Appraisal" (see chap. 1, n. 32). See also John Cohen, *Integrated Rural Development: The Ethiopian Experience and the Debate* (Uppsala, Sweden: Scandinavian Institute of African Studies, 1987), chap. 7.

46 Emery Roe, "Counting on Comparative Budgeting in Africa," *International Journal of Public Administration* 11 (3): (1988); Eddy Omolehinwa and Emery Roe, "Boom and Bust Budgeting: Repetitive Budgetary Processes in Nigeria, Kenya and Ghana," *Public Budgeting and Finance* 9 (2): (1989).

47 The example comes from Timothy Sullivan, "Knowledge and Method in the Study of Public Management," paper prepared at the Graduate School of Public Policy, University of California, Berkeley, 1987.

48 For a discussion of the difficult and different contexts in which government officials administer and manage in the developed and developing worlds, see Emery Roe, "Management Crisis" (see chap. 1, n. 34).

49 Thomas Pinckney, John Cohen, and David Leonard, "Microcomputers and Financial Management in Development Ministries: Experience from Kenya," *Agricultural Administration* 14 (3): 151, 167 (1983).

50 Ibid., p. 166.

51 World Bank, *World Development Report 1988* (New York: Oxford University Press, 1988), p. 129.

52 Stephen Peterson, "Microcomputers and Institutional Development: Emerging Lessons from Kenya" (paper prepared for the Harvard Institute of International Development Conference on Economic Reform, Marrakech, Morocco, 1988).

53 Clay Wescott, "Microcomputers for Improved Budgeting by the Kenya Government," Development Discussion Paper no. 227, Harvard Institute for International Development, Cambridge, Mass., 1986.

54 Roe, "Last Chance."

55 This is not to argue against criticizing development narratives for their lack of realism. For examples of conventional wisdoms, puzzles, myths and folktales in rural development that deserve much greater scrutiny, Emery Roe, "Lantern on the Stern" (see chap. 1, n. 34); Emery Roe, "Individualism and Community in Africa? The Case of Botswana," *Journal of Modern African Studies* 26 (2): (1988); Emery Roe, "Six Myths about Livestock Rangeland Development South of the Sahara," *Rangelands* 11 (2): (1989); Emery Roe, "Folktale Development," *American Journal of Semiotics* 6 (2): (1989).

3 Stories, Nonstories, and Their Metanarrative in the 1980–1982 California Medfly Controversy

This chapter relies heavily on quotations and verbatim extracts cited from a draft volume prepared on the Medfly Controversy, *A Fly in the Policy Ointment: The 1980 California Medfly Program in Multiple Perspectives*, ed. Hilary Lorraine, Percy Tannenbaum, and Martin Trow. The volume was based on transcripts of papers and discussions presented by a number of the major actors in the Medfly Controversy at a faculty seminar series in the Survey Research Center, University of California, Berkeley. The seminar was supported by the Survey Research Center, with a grant from the William and Flora Hewlett Foundation, and by the University of California's Graduate School of Public Policy, with a grant from the Alfred Sloan Foundation. Portions of this chapter appeared in a paper, "A Case Study of the 1980/82 Medfly Controversy in California," that I prepared for the Committee on Risk Perception and Communication, National Academy of Sciences, Washington, D.C., 1987. Hilary Lorraine deserves special thanks for compiling the draft volume used for this chapter.

1 Martin Krieger, *Advice and Planning* (Philadelphia: Temple University Press, 1981), pp. 12, 83.
2 We shall see this more clearly in chap. 5.
3 Quoted in John Patrick Diggins, "Sidney Hook," *Grand Street* 7 (1): 189 (1987).
4 See the summer 1986 issue of the *Journal of Policy Analysis and Management* (*JPAM*) vol. 5, no. 4). See Thomas J. Kaplan, "The Narrative Structure of Policy Analysis," *JPAM*, 5 (4): (1986) and Martin Krieger, "Big Decisions and a Culture of Decisionmaking" *JPAM*, vol. 5, no. 4: (1986).
5 Gideon Doron, "A Comment: Telling the Big Stories—Policy Responses to Analytical Complexity," ibid., p. 799.
6 Cost and coverage figures are from Erik Larsen, "A Close Watch on U.S. Borders to Keep the World's Bugs Out," in *Smithsonian* (June 1987): 110. Unless otherwise stated, all figures and quotes in this case study are from the draft volume, *Fly in the Policy Ointment*, ed. Lorraine et al.
7 Jerry Scribner, "The 1980 California Medfly Program: A View from Management—The State Perspective," p. 13.
8 Quoted in Greg Rohwer (1985), "The View from Washington," p. 24.
9 Steve Dreistadt (1985), "A View from the Community," pp. 7, 9.
10 Donald Dahlsten (1985), "The Scientist as a Source of Technical Advice to Large Action Programs," p. 9.
11 K. S. Hagen (undated), "Potential Fruit Fly Pests of California: A Technical Overview," p. 25.
12 Rohwer, "View from Washington," p. 21.
13 Derrell Chambers (1985), "Technical Advisors: Wise Men, Wizards, Wind Vanes or Wimps," p. 16.
14 Dreistadt, "View from the Community," p. 9.
15 Scribner, "1980 California Medfly Program," p. 8.
16 Kathleen Rassbach (1985), "A Medical Overview of the Health Debate," pp. 9ff.
17 Donald Dilley (1985), "The Technical Advisory Committee: Use and Abuse," pp. 11–2.

18   Ibid.
19   This research is described in detail in Rassbach, "Medical Overview."
20   Rohwer, "View from Washington," p. 20.
21   Dilley, "Technical Advisory Committee," p. 8.
22   Hilary Lorraine (1985), "Medfly: An Historical Overview: Tag-Team Wrestling in the Technical Arena," p. 10.
23   John Thurman (1985), "Medfly Politics," p. 7.
24   Scribner, "1980 California Medfly Program," p. 3.
25   For example, see Cherryl Churchill-Stanland (1985), "Quality Control: Management's Forgotten Resource," p. 17.
26   Dahlsten, "Scientist as a Source," p. 14.
27   Lorraine, "Medfly," pp. 28–30.
28   Dick Jackson (1985), "A View from Management—The Federal Perspective," p. 20.
29   Ibid., pp. 12, 13.
30   Churchill-Stanland, "Quality Control," p. 11.
31   Chambers, "Technical Advisors," pp. 5, 10.
32   Marc Lappe (1985), "Technical Dissent," p. 9.
33   See Hilary Lorraine (undated), "Man the Master or Sorcerer's Apprentice," p. 17.
34   For survey research information on community attitudes toward aerial and ground spraying at the time of the Medfly Controversy, see Glenn Hawkes and Martha Stiles (1985), "A Survey of the Public's Assessment of Risk," particularly p. 3.
35   Scribner, "1980 California Medfly Program," pp. 33–4; Thurman, "Medfly Politics," pp. 4–5.
36   Tracy Wood, "Medfly and the Media," p. 8.
37   Scribner, "1980 California Medfly Program," pp. 11, 33–4.
38   Dilley, "Technical Advisory Committee," pp. 15–16.
39   Rohwer, "View from Washington," p. 9.
40   Dilley, "Technical Advisory Committee," p. 16.
41   Ibid.
42   Chambers, "Technical Advisors," p. 19.
43   Wood, "Medfly and the Media," p. 27.
44   I owe this point—i.e., that good public managers are those bureaucrats who are able to engage preexisting narratives in the public discourse—to Timothy J. Sullivan, "Knowledge and Method in the Study of Public Management," Graduate School of Public Policy, University of California, Berkeley, 1987.
45   See, for example, Scribner, "1980 California Medfly Program," p. 16.
46   Lorraine, "Man the Master," p. 8.
47   Ibid., pp. 23–4.
48   Scribner, "1980 California Medfly Program," p. 28.
49   Ibid., p. 27. The governor's remark is not unusual. "You give me the perfect plan and I'll worry about the politics," so said President Carter to his Health, Education, and Welfare secretary during the design of their ill-fated welfare reform proposal. Lawrence Lynn and David Whitman, *The President as Policymaker: Jimmy Carter and Welfare Reform* (Philadelphia: Temple University Press, 1981), p. 89.

50 Thurman, "Medfly Politics," pp. 12, 14, 15.
51 Jackson, "View from Management," p. 17.
52 Thurman, "Medfly Politics," p. 8.
53 Jackson, "View from Management," p. 16.
54 A good example of how one kind of narrative analysis illuminates what was once the most compelling public policy issue in the West—Nazism—can be found in the chapter entitled "Narratives of National Socialism: An Analysis of the Work of Jean Pierre Faye," in John B. Thompson, *Studies in the Theory of Ideology* (Berkeley and Los Angeles: University of California Press, 1984). The first work in narrative analysis—Vladimir Propp's *Morphology of the Folktale,* 2d ed., trans. Laurence Scott (Austin: University of Texas Press, 1968)—details what he took to be the typical structure of a folktale, a structure that can still be found in all manner of public affairs, both here and overseas. For an application of Propp's model, see my "Folktale Development" (see chap. 2, n. 55). See also Claude Bremond, "The Logic of Narrative Possibilities," *New Literary History* 11 (3): (1980). Readers interested in how literary critics apply narrative analysis should turn to three books from Cornell University Press, Ithaca, N.Y.: Seymour Chatman, *Story and Discourse* (1978); Gerard Genette, *Narrative Discourse: An Essay in Method,* trans. Jane E. Lewin (1980); and Tzvetan Todorov, *The Poetics of Prose,* trans. Richard Howard (1977). Two helpful books on narrative in disciplines related to policy analysis are Donald Polkinghorne, *Narrative Knowing and the Human Sciences* (Albany: State University of New York Press, 1988); and Bernard S. Jackson, *Law, Fact and Narrative Coherence* (Roby, England: Deborah Charles, 1988).
55 The narrative side of microeconomics has been discussed in Donald N. McCloskey, "The Rhetoric of Economics," *Journal of Economic Literature* 21:481–517 (1983).

4 Constructing the Metanarrative in the Animal Rights and Experimentation Controversy

1 For ease of exposition, the terms "nonhuman animal research" and "human animal research" have been shortened to "animal research" and "human research."
2 Johns Hopkins University has had a center for testing purposes, while other universities, such as the University of California and the University of Minnesota, were at the time of writing contemplating their own alternatives centers. Schools of veterinary medicine have been under particular pressure to develop programs for animal alternatives.
3 The subsequent quotations are taken from the compendium of letters and articles assembled in the University of California Animal Alternatives Study Task Force, *The Animal Alternatives Study Task Force: Information Received by the Task Force,* vol. 2, Office of Research and Public Policy, the University of California, Berkeley, 1988. Material from the following organizations or groups has been quoted or used: American Diabetes Association, California Affiliate; American Heart Association, California Affiliate; Animal Protection Institute of America; Association of Veterinarians for Animal Rights; Friends of Animals, Inc.; Incurably Ill for Animal Research (iiFAR); In Defense of Animals; Johns Hopkins Univer-

sity Center for Alternatives to Animal Testing; Medical Research Modernization Committee; Physicians Committee for Responsible Medicine; Psychologists for Ethical Treatment of Animals (PSYETA); Scientists Center for Animal Welfare; and the University of Wisconsin's Research Animal Resources Center. Page numbers are not referenced as the volume is not consecutively paginated.

4 See material in ibid. from PSYETA.

5 Reprinted in the Friend of Animals material in ibid.

6 See the iiFAR and the Medical Research Modernization Committee material in ibid.

7 Richard Stevenson, "A Campaign for Research on Animals," in the Media Business section of the *New York Times*, 20 January 1989. As one might expect, the many newspaper and magazine articles focusing on alleged abuses by animal researchers have been matched by investigative reporting on alleged lies, glitz, and deception in the animal rights movement. For an example, see Katie McCabe, "Beyond Cruelty," *Washingtonian* 25 (5): (1990).

8 The Johns Hopkins University Center for Alternatives to Animal Testing has encouraged the development of a number of alternatives to the Draize test (which relies on rabbits' eyes to test the toxicity of certain compounds), but resources have remained relatively scarce to evaluate which is the better alternative.

9 See Goldie Blumenstyk, "With State Legislatures as the Battleground, Scientists and College Officials Fight Animal-Welfare Groups," *Chronicle of Higher Education*, 5 April 1989.

10 For a discussion of topsy-turvydom as a characteristic of literary nonsense, see Wim Tigges, *An Anatomy of Literary Nonsense*, Costerus New Series vol. 67 (Amsterdam: Rodopi, 1988), especially chaps. 1, 2. Tigges's epigraph in the following section comes from p. 47 of that book. The sense of a fundamental disagreement that allows for no middle ground of compromise is neatly epitomized in a statement from a senior university administrator: "The controversy over animals and animal research is seen [by the public] as a sharp two-sided issue, with staunch antagonists at both extremes . . . [and our] deeply ingrained values tell us to eschew extremes and search for the truth in the middle, to search for a moderate solution between the two extremes. . . . Yet, the plain truth is that the biomedical community . . . advocates and accepts all the tenets that are urged by moderate spokesmen: preference for the use of non-animal models whenever possible, minimization of pain and suffering, regulation and inspection by qualified officials, and participation by lay persons on animal care committees. . . . The inevitable pressure to find the truth in the middle, to reach an accommodation between the two extremes, therefore results in the steady drift from true moderation." Larry Horton (associate vice president for Public Affairs at Stanford University), "The Use of Environmental Issues as a Political Tactic of the Antivivisectionist Movement," October 1988, pp. 15–17. While animal rights groups would disagree with the particulars, many readily share the premise that there is precious little middle ground on this issue.

11 This focus on the relationship between the detailed catalogue of differences among opponents and proponents of animal research and the comparatively simpler proresearch and antiresearch scenarios that each camp currently offers up to the public has been guided by Jerome J. McGann, "Some Forms of Critical Dis-

course," in his *Social Values and Poetic Acts: The Historical Judgment of Literary Work* (Cambridge, Mass.: Harvard University Press, 1988). In narrative analytical terms, the scenarios of the controversy's parties are the stories they tell, while the catalogue of differences is another nonstory in the controversy, i.e., as McGann puts it, the text of such a catalogue lacks "narrativized completion" and "does not have a beginning-middle-end structure" as do more conventional stories (pp. 137, 139). What McGann goes on to call the kind of criticism arising as a result of "dialectic" between such stories and nonstories (pp. 145–9) is functionally equivalent to the metanarrative generated by comparing stories and nonstories in narrative-analytical terms.

12 Identification of the opposing groups discussed in this paragraph has relied on the semiotic square of A. J. Greimas. The square takes on even more importance in the narrative policy analysis of chapter 5. For a discussion of the semiotic square, see Ronald Schleifer, *A. J. Greimas and the Nature of Meaning* (Lincoln: University of Nebraska Press, 1987), pp. 25–8.

13 For a good introduction to the issue of human subjects experimentation, see Stuart Spicker, Ilai Alon, Andre de Vries, and H. Tristram Englehardt, eds., *The Use of Human Beings in Research with Special Reference to Clinical Trials* (Dordrecht, Netherlands: Kluwer Academic Publishers, 1988).

14 One of the central aims of the complexifying exercise is to make manifest the differing claims of guardianship or stewardship over laboratory animals. Is their rightful guardian "science" or "the public" or some other entity? Does, for example, the average pet owner better represent the interests of animals than, say, the average animal researcher? This theme of ascertaining the claims to guardianship is primary, as it is the distinguishing feature of a class of particularly disturbing controversies. The debates over the use of Nazi hypothermia records and over Native American claims to remains presently stored in museums share the same dilemma posed in the animal rights controversy, namely, those most intimately concerned are unable to tell us their own views on the matter. In the absence of knowing what the objects of "research" would say, we are left with having to determine who best are the guardians of their interests. We return to the issue of guardianship in chap. 7's case study of the Native American burial remains controversy, where the issue operates at the metanarrative level.

15 See Richard Hilbert, "Approaching Reason's Edge: 'Nonsense' as the Final Solution to the Problem of Meaning," *Sociological Inquiry* 47 (1): (1977).

5   A Salt on the Land

The chapter draws material from Janne Hukkinen, "Unplugging Drainage: Toward a Sociotechnical Redesign of San Joaquin Valley's Agricultural Drainage Management" (Ph.D. diss., University of California, Berkeley, 1990); and from Janne Hukkinen, Emery Roe, and Gene I. Rochlin, *When Water Doesn't Mean Power: How Government Can Better Handle Uncertainty and Polarization Related to Agricultural Drainage in the San Joaquin Valley,* report prepared for the California Department of Water Resources, Sacramento, 1988. An earlier version of this chapter was awarded the Lasswell Prize by the journal, *Policy Sciences.*

1 B. Delworth Gardner, Raymond H. Coppock, Curtis D. Lynn, D. William Rains,

Robert S. Loomis, and J. Herbert Snyder, "Agriculture," chap. 2, in *Competition for California Water: Alternative Resolutions* ed. Ernest A. Engelbert with Ann Foley Scheuring (Berkeley and Los Angeles: University of California Press, 1982), p. 12.

2   California Department of Water Resources (DWR), *California Water: Looking to the Future*, DWR Bulletin 160-87 (Sacramento, 1987), pp. 9, 11.

3   California Department of Water Resources, *The California Water Plan: Projected Use and Available Water Supplies to 2010*, DWR Bulletin 160-83 (Sacramento, 1983), pp. 117, 123; California Department of Finance, *California Statistical Abstract 1987* (Sacramento, 1987), p. 110. It has been estimated that "agriculture contributed $62 billion of the state gross product of $593 billion in 1987," when taking into account the employment, processing, transportation, and other activity generated by agriculture in California. William DuBois, letter to the editor, *Issues in Science and Technology* 5 (3): 7 (1989).

4   San Joaquin Valley Drainage Program (SJVDP), *Developing Options: An Overview of Efforts to Solve Agricultural Drainage and Drainage-Related Problems in the San Joaquin Valley* (Sacramento, SJVDP, 1987), p. 8.

5   San Joaquin Valley Drainage Program, *Developing Options*, p. 8; San Joaquin Valley Interagency Drainage Program (SJVIDP), *Agricultural Drainage and Salt Management in the San Joaquin Valley*, Final Report (Fresno: SJVIDP, 1979), p. 4–6; California General Assembly, *California 2000: Paradise in Peril—Making Issues in Natural Resources* (Sacramento, 1987), 14.

6   Harry M. Ohlendorf, "Aquatic Birds and Selenium in the San Joaquin Valley," in *Selenium and Agricultural Drainage: Implications for San Francisco Bay and the California Environment*, proceedings of the Second Selenium Symposium, 23 March 1985, Berkeley, Calif. (1986), p. 18; Kenneth Tanji, André Läuchli, and Jewell Meyer, "Selenium in the San Joaquin Valley," *Environment* 28 (6): 6–7 (1986).

7   Roger Fujii, *Water-Quality and Sediment-Chemistry Data of Drain Water and Evaporation Ponds from Tulare Lake Drainage District, Kings County, California, March 1985 to March 1986*, Open-File Report 87-700, U.S. Geological Survey, Sacramento, 1988; Roy A. Schroeder, Donald U. Palawski, and Joseph P. Skorupa, *Reconnaissance Investigation of Water Quality, Bottom Sediment, and Biota Associated with Irrigation Drainage in the Tulare Lake Bed Area, Southern San Joaquin Valley, California, 1986–87*, Water-Resources Investigations Report 88-4001, U.S. Geological Survey, Sacramento, 1988; *San Francisco Chronicle*, "High Levels of Selenium in Nature Areas," 11 May 1988.

8   *Press-Enterprise*, "UCR Toxic Cleanup Method 'Superior,'" 7 November 1988; *San Francisco Chronicle*, "$24.6 Million Plan: Water Board OKs Kesterson Cleanup," 18 August 1987; *San Francisco Chronicle*, "U.S. Kesterson Cleanup Plan—More Chemicals," 17 May 1988.

9   Among the several reports on the master drain are U.S. Bureau of Reclamation, *Central Valley Basin: A Comprehensive Departmental Report on the Development of the Water and Related Resources of the Central Valley Basin, and Comments from the State of California and Federal Agencies*, 81st Cong., 1st sess., 1949, S. Doc. 113; California Legislature, *Drainage Problems of the San Joaquin Valley of California: Tenth Partial Report by the Joint Committee on Water Prob-*

lems (Sacramento: California State Printing Office, 1957); California State Water Resources Board, *The California Water Plan*, Bulletin no. 3 (Sacramento, 1957); San Joaquin Valley Drainage Advisory Group (SJVDAG), *Final Report* (Fresno: SJVDAG, 1969).

10 San Joaquin Valley Interagency Drainage Program, *Agricultural Drainage*.

11 San Joaquin Valley Drainage Program, *Developing Options*.

12 Steven Hall, "My Turn," *West Valley Journal* (April 1989): 3.

13 During the summer of 1987, interviews were conducted with twenty-three individuals representing the main interest groups in the San Joaquin Valley agricultural drainage controversy. Each interviewee was classified into one of four groups: twelve were associated with the agricultural community (local water, irrigation, and drainage district managers); six were grouped as planners (staff from the San Joaquin Valley Drainage Program, the California Department of Water Resources, and the Department of Fish and Game); three were state and federal regulators (staff from the State Water Resources Control Board, the Central Valley Regional Water Quality Control Board, and the U.S. Environmental Protection Agency); and two were from the environmental community (the Natural Resources Defense Council and the San Francisco Bay Institute). The state's views on the valley drainage problem were sampled through interviews with staff in the California Department of Water Resources, while interviews with the San Joaquin Valley Drainage Program helped to capture federal perspectives on this problem, that is, its staff includes representatives from, among others, the U.S. Bureau of Reclamation. Lawyers as a group were not specifically interviewed, but their views on the drainage problem were reflected in the interviews with the various agency representatives, particularly the state and federal officials whose offices rely on large legal staff.

Overall, the twenty-three interviews identified most probably what are perceived to be the major problems associated with the valley's agricultural drainage from the perspectives of the parties most involved in the controversy. The cumulative frequency distribution curve of problems mentioned in the interviews shows that the number of new problems added by individual interviews tapers off considerably after the 18th interview. For more details on the network methodology developed by Janne Hukkinen, see Hukkinen et al. *When Water Doesn't Mean Power.*

14 Some of those interviewed expressed this view forcefully: "A drainage water bypass to the Delta is out of the question. This means not only that the [master drain] is unacceptable, but also that a bypass for drainage into the San Joaquin River is out." Others mentioned the "no drain" assumption with something approaching regret: "On certain farm areas the groundwater level must be lowered down, out of the root zone. This water must be taken out, and the question is where to put it. . . . Personally I still feel that the drain is the way to do it in the long run. However, it will probably not be built within the next twenty or thirty years." The consensus was clear and common for the vast majority of the interviewees: there will be no drain, but proper drainage is needed.

15 As noted earlier, the twenty-three interviews most likely captured the prevailing major problems associated with agricultural drainage in the valley.

16 The computer program developed for this research identified a feedback loop as the residual problem network left after initial and terminal problems were truncated from the larger network. As such, a circular argument can be seen as a problem network consisting only of transfer problems.

17 Sample size limitations in the number of interviewees from the regulatory and environmental communities raise issues concerning the reliability of intergroup comparisons of feedback loops that are not discussed in this chapter.

18 Semiotic squares have been derived in several ways. Our application of the square follows Schleifer, *A. J. Greimas*, pp. 25–8 (see chap. 4, n. 12).

19 Some in the irrigation bureaucracy operate under the assumption that there *will* be no valley-wide drain in the foreseeable future, but at the same time think that the drain *should* be constructed during that time period. "The main drain is politically out at the moment, but it would be the best solution," as one irrigator put it. Others find nothing contradictory in holding these two positions, since in-valley solutions and/or master drain might be found feasible *beyond* the foreseeable future. Unfortunately, belief in either option only exacerbates the drainage controversy, as will be seen shortly.

20 As such, the starting assumption, "There will be no drain," turns out to be the real problem in the final analysis. This is underscored by another example. A pattern of interconnected loops similar to the one found in the irrigation bureaucracy is produced when the problem networks of the agricultural community and regulators are aggregated together, only this time the single terminal problem produced does not relate to the loss of payers for the water projects, but to the lack of the master drain specifically: "Need for agricultural drainage outlet and discharge point, which do not exist (such as master drain to Bay-Delta)."

21 See Marc Reisner, *Cadillac Desert: The American West and Its Disappearing Water* (New York: Penguin Books, 1987), p. 486.

22 For more details on how the dilemma is replicated in each of the specific technical solutions proposed for the drainage problem, see chap. 4 of Hukkinen et al., *When Water Doesn't Mean Power*.

23 A letter from the National Research Council's Committee on Irrigation-Induced Water Problems to the San Joaquin Valley Drainage Program criticizes the program's management for restricting its scientists to those options considered "politically feasible." It will be interesting to see whether their advice, much of which is congruent to our own, is heeded, or whether, as seems probable, the California irrigation bureaucracy will continue to walk the line between uncertainty and polarization in neither mentioning the unmentionable, nor admitting to their own inability to set and hold priorities.

24 Personal communication, Ed Imhoff, manager, San Joaquin Valley Drainage Program, 1988.

25 The focus on organizational and management approaches to handling what in California seem to be technical and political problems, such as salinization of irrigated land, is consistent with the literature on irrigation systems and associated problems in other countries. See Emery Roe, "Overseas Perspectives for Managing Irrigation Drainage in California," *Journal of Irrigation and Drainage Engineering* 117 (3): (1991).

6 Global Warming as Analytic Tip

1 A good introduction to the pervasiveness and importance of uncertainty in the global warming controversy can be found in Eugene Skolnikoff, "The Policy Gridlock on Global Warming," *Foreign Policy* (1990) 79. Skolnikoff was a member of the Mitigation Panel on Policy Implications of Greenhouse Warming (PPIGW), working under the auspices of the Committee on Science, Engineering, and Public Policy of the U.S. National Academy of Sciences, National Academy of Engineering, and Institute of Medicine.

2 Michael Glantz, "The Use of Analogies in Forecasting Ecological and Societal Responses to Global Warming," *Environment* 33 (5): 12 (1991).

3 M. Jimmie Killingsworth and Jacqueline S. Palmer, *Ecospeak: Rhetoric and Environmental Politics in America* (Carbondale: Southern Illinois University Press, 1992), p. 138.

4 Glantz, "Use of Analogies," p. 13.

5 Eleven of the fourteen general circulation models reviewed in a *Science* article predict that clouds will have a net positive effect on warming, even though the consensus in the scientific community has been that cloud-climatic interactions are one of the least understood set of phenomena in the atmospheric warming debate. See R. D. Cess et al., "Interpretation of Cloud-Climatic Feedback as Produced by 14 Atmospheric General Circulation Models," *Science* 245:515, table 2, fig. 1 (1989). More recently, the Mitigation Panel on Policy Implications of Greenhouse Warming found "a recent examination of available [GCM] computer runs shows considerable difference in the treatment of clouds. Although all runs yield similar results for a 'clear sky' without clouds, their results vary substantially when clouds are included." PPIGW, Committee on Science, Engineering, and Public Policy, National Academy of Sciences/National Academy of Engineering/ Institute of Medicine, *Policy Implications of Greenhouse Warming: Mitigation, Adaptation, and the Science Base* (Washington, D.C.: National Academy Press, 1992), p. 21.

6 Dr. Cess (see n. 5) is reported to have concluded that "as presently formulated" the computer models cannot be used to predict future global warming, and that "whether they can ever be used for that purpose is problematical" (quoted in William K. Stevens, "Skeptics Are Challenging Dire 'Greenhouse' Views," *New York Times*, 13 December 1989, p. A 18.

7 See Peter Passell, "Economic Watch: Curbing the Greenhouse Effect Could Run into Trillions," *New York Times*, 19 November 1989, p. 1; and the letters to the editor, *New York Times*, 30 November 1989, p. A 30. See also S. Fred Singer, "Global Warming: Do We Know Enough To Act?" in *Environmental Protection: Regulating for Results*, ed. Kenneth Chilton and Melinda Warren (Boulder: Westview, 1991), pp. 44–8.

8 PPIGW, *Policy Implications*, p. 541. For a critique of the panel's report from within the policy analysis profession, see John D. Montgomery, "Policies without People: On Deciphering the Operational Implications of an NAS Report," *Journal of Policy Analysis and Management* 11 (4): (1992).

9 Parts of this argument can be found in Roberta Balstad Miller, "Global Change: Challenge to Social Science," Division of Social and Economic Science, National

Science Foundation, Washington, D.C. (1988); John Harte, "Global Warming: Causes, Consequences, Cures," paper presented to the Commonwealth Club of California, University of California, Berkeley, 1989. For global warming as a collective action problem (i.e., a tragedy of the commons), see Brian Barry, "Modern Knowledge and Modern Politics," *Government and Opposition* 24 (4): 388–9; and Skolnikoff, "Policy Gridlock," p. 84.

10 The notion that a story is defined as having a beginning, middle and end is an old one, dating from at least Aristotle. See Gerald Prince, *A Dictionary of Narratology* (Lincoln: University of Nebraska Press, 1987), pp. 58–9.

11 For an article that explicitly treats global warming and climate change as part of the rhetorical framework of the environmental movement, see Frederick H. Buttel, Ann P. Hawkins, and Alison G. Power, "From Limits to Growth to Global Change: Constraints and Contradictions in the Evolution of Environmental Science and Ideology," *Global Environmental Change* 1 (1): 57–66.

12 Recently published and undoubtedly the best book on the rhetoric of global warming and indeed of the environmental movement generally is Killingsworth and Palmer's *Ecospeak*. The authors are at pains to show how the rhetorical features of an argument—e.g., active voice sentences, strong action verbs, concrete and specific nouns, the use of skepticism and irony—can be and are deployed to persuade people to accept that argument. Such features, however, do not play a role in this chapter's narrative analysis. The focus here is not on how the global warming scenario is used to convince people that global warming is happening and what we should do about it, but rather on how the global warming scenario puts its proponents in a position to be certain about what is uncertain. I thank David Feldman for pointing me to *Ecospeak* as well as other references used in this chapter.

13 The following five subsections draw heavily from Michael Riffaterre, *Fictional Truth* (Baltimore: Johns Hopkins University Press, 1990). His explanation of how the appearance of truth is constructed in fictional narratives is directly applicable to how the sense of certainty is constructed in scientific narratives about uncertainty. For a different application of the *Fictional Truth* model, see Dell Hymes, "Notes toward (an Understanding of) Supreme Fictions," in *Studies in Historical Change*, ed. Ralph Cohen (Charlottesville: University Press of Virginia, 1992), pp. 128–78.

14 The simplifications are, however, no more unusual than those found in general circulation models. My objection to GCMs is not their simplifying assumptions, but their entailment of the global level of analysis.

15 See Riffaterre, *Fictional Truth*, p. xiv.

16 Ibid., p. xiv.

17 See Richard Norgaard, "Environmental Science as a Social Process," paper presented at a workshop on environmental information held at the University of Ottawa, University of California, Berkeley, p. 2.

18 This paragraph paraphrases and draws heavily from the narrative analysis of James Ettema and Theodore Glasser, "Narrative Form and Moral Force: The Realization of Innocence and Guilt through Investigative Journalism," in *Methods of Rhetorical Criticism: A Twentieth-Century Perspective*, 3d ed., ed. Bernard Brock, Robert Scott, and James Chesebro (Detroit, Mich.: Wayne State University Press, 1989), p. 269.

19   For more on this point of fairness, see Steve Rayner and Robin Cantor, "How Fair Is Safe Enough? The Cultural Approach to Societal Technology Choice," *Risk Analysis* 7 (1): (1987).

20   See Ettema and Glasser, "Narrative Form," pp. 269–71.

21   "The public has become used to conflicting opinion on health issues and position reversals on topics ranging from dietary recommendations to the depletion of the ozone layer. Many have come to feel that for every Ph.D. there is an equal and opposite Ph.D." (quoted in Killingsworth and Palmer, *Ecospeak*, p. 145). For an example of how environmentalist critiques increased public uncertainty and risk perception in a major science controversy, see chapter 3.

22   Riffaterre, *Fictional Truth*, p. xvi.

23   Ibid., p. xv. On the search by scientists for past analogues to global warming and its consequences, see Glantz, "Use of Analogies," pp. 14–5, 27–32.

24   See H. Tristram Englehardt, Jr., and Arthur Caplan, eds., *Scientific Controversies: Case Studies in the Resolution and Closure of Disputes in Science and Technology* (Cambridge: Cambridge University Press, 1987); and Peter Galison, *How Experiments End* (Chicago: University of Chicago Press, 1987).

25   Some say past examples of a tragedy of the commons resulting from climate change already exist, e.g., the collapse of the Anasazi civilization in the area of southwestern Colorado. That collapse would, however, be a tragedy of the commons only if the Anasazi themselves caused the climate change or if that change had been caused by other people, far or near, who did not bear the full cost of their destructive behavior. It may be true that relative overpopulation made the Anasazi more vulnerable to drought. It may even be the case that their overutilization of land (if that is what it was) contributed to locally lower rainfall averages. It is quite another thing to say, however, that this behavior adds up to a tragedy of the commons through climate change induced by humans. As for the argument that the Anasazi caused a tragedy of the commons, not through climate change per se, but through exceeding the carrying capacity of their land, that too remains an empirical question. Suffice it to say, since Garrett Hardin's tragedy of the commons article in *Science* (see chap. 2, n. 11), a growing body of case material suggests local populations can and do manage their common property resources and most certainly do not always overutilize them, even under conditions of climate change. This case material is discussed in chapter 2. For a brief discussion of the Anasazi case, see Stephen H. Schneider, *Global Warming: Are We Entering the Greenhouse Century?* (San Francisco: Sierra Club Books, 1989), pp. 62–3.

26   A similar point is made in A. J. Greimas, "Basil Soup or the Construction of an Object of Value," in *Paris School Semiotics*, vol. 2, *Practice*, ed. Paul Perron and Frank Collins (Philadelphia: John Benjamins Publishing Co., 1989), pp. 1–2.

27   The simile is from J. G. March and Johan Olsen, *Rediscovering Institutions: The Organizational Basis of Politics* (New York: Free Press, 1989), p. 11.

28   On the latter point, see Killingsworth and Palmer, *Ecospeak*, pp. 270–1.

29   Nancy Dorian, *Language Death: The Life Cycle of a Scottish Gaelic Dialect* (Philadelphia: University of Pennsylvania Press, 1981), p. 51.

30   The phrasing comes from Nancy Dorian, "Abrupt Transmission Failure in Obsolescing Languages: How Sudden the 'Tip' to the Dominant Language in Communities and Families?" in *Proceedings of the Twelfth Annual Meeting of the*

Berkeley Linguistics Society, ed. V. Nikiforidu, M. Van Clay, M. Niepokuj, and D. Feder, Berkeley Linguistics Society, Berkeley, Calif. (1986), pp. 74–5. As Dorian notes (p. 75), the change only *appears* sudden: "Yet when the tip has occurred and one begins to examine the period which led up to it, the tip is seldom if ever so sudden as it appeared."

31 The tip, and its apparent suddenness, from public administration to policy analysis programs is described in Joel L. Fleishman, "A New Framework for Integration: Policy Analysis and Public Management," in *Divided Knowledge: Across Disciplines, Across Cultures*, ed. David Easton and Corinne Schelling (Newbury Park: Sage Publications, 1991), pp. 219–20 and 223–25.

32 Analytic tip represents the displacement of one set of terms and constructs by a different set within a preexisting public discourse. Since the terms involved are only some among many, there is no presumption that public discourse is itself undergoing a paradigm shift in the process. It should go without saying that the analysis of means and ends has never really disappeared and there are those who now recommend means/ends analysis over benefit/cost analysis. See, e.g., Giovanni Sartori, "Undercomprehension," *Government and Opposition* 24 (4): 398 (1989).

33 Robert Cowen, "Forceful Yet Balanced Communication," *Issues in Science and Technology* 6 (2): 88 (1989/90); Philip Abelson, "Uncertainties about Global Warming," *Science* 247 (4950) 1529 (1990); *The Economist*, "Rethinking the Greenhouse," vol. 313, no. 7633 (16–22 December 1989), p. 14.

34 Allan Gold, "Global Warming Means New Global Politics," *New York Times*, 12 November 1989, p. E 5.

35 The quotes are from Barry, "Modern Knowledge," pp. 388–9; and Skolnikoff, "Policy Gridlock," p. 84.

36 As a senior scientist with the Natural Resources Defense Council put it, atmospheric warming is likely "to be punctuated by more powerful hurricanes, more frequent severe droughts, pest outbreaks, forest diebacks, millions of environmental refugees fleeing their flooded homelands and other impacts we cannot now imagine." Daniel Lashof, "A Net Saving," letter to the editor, *New York Times*, 8 December 1989, p. A 38.

37 A representative menu of global climate control proposals—ranging from international treaties, plans, and agencies to international protocols, agreements, and control regimes—can be found in World Resources Institute, *Greenhouse Warming: Negotiating a Global Regime* (Washington, D.C.: World Resources Institute, 1991).

38 The argument has been made that CFC production would have declined anyway in the absence of the protocols.

39 I am indebted to Jeffrey Friedman, editor of *Critical Review*, for the following remarks.

7 Intertextual Evaluation, Conflicting Evaluative Criteria, and the Controversy over Native American Burial Remains

1 For more on the District Focus policy, see Fenno Ogutu, *District Planning in Kenya: A View from the Bottom* (Ph.D. diss., Department of City and Regional

Planning, University of California, Berkeley, 1989); and David Leonard, *African Successes: Public Managers of Kenyan Rural Development* (Berkeley: University of California Press, 1991), especially chap. 10.

2   See, for example, Rudolf Klein, "Evaluation and Social Planning: Some Reflections on Ideas and Institutions," *Evaluation and Program Planning* 5 (2), (1982); William Shadish and Roberta Epstein, "Patterns of Program Evaluation and Practice Among Members of the Evaluation Research Society and Evaluation Network," *Evaluation Review* 11 (5): (1987); and Stephanie Shipman, "General Criteria for Evaluating Social Programs," *Evaluation Practice* 10 (1), (1989).

3   Quoted in George Will, *Men at Work: The Craft of Baseball* (New York: Macmillan Publishing Co., 1990): p. 81.

4   The focus on consequences, rather than intentions, comes to policy analysis and evaluation by way of Herbert Simon's *Administrative Behavior* and its roots in American pragmatism. Those who study the public must "start from acts which are performed, not from hypothetical causes for those acts, and consider their consequences," John Dewey informs us. It is when we analyze "causal forces instead of consequences" of government activity that "the outcome of the looking becomes arbitrary. There is no check on it. 'Interpretation' runs wild. . . . Existence of a multitude of contradictory theories of the state . . . is readily explicable the moment we see that all the theories, in spite of their divergence from one another, spring from the root of shared error: the taking of causal agency instead of consequences as the heart of the problem." John Dewey, "The Public and Its Problems," first published in 1927, reprinted in *John Dewey: The Later Works, 1925–1953*, vol. 2, ed. Jo Ann Boydston (Carbondale: Southern Illinois University Press, 1984), pp. 243, 248.

5   As others have long noted, we frequently do not know what we really intend until we set about writing "it." E.g., Aaron Wildavsky: "I do not know what I think until I have tried to write it. Sometimes the purpose of writing is to discover whether I can express what I think I know; if it cannot be written, it is not right. Other times I write to find out what I know; writing becomes a form of self-discovery. . . . [F]ew feelings compare with the exhilaration of discovering a thought in the writing that was not in the thinking." T. S. Eliot: "I have often found that my most interesting or original ideas, when put into words and marshalled in final order, were ideas which I had not been aware of holding. . . . I have always discovered that anything I have written—anything at least which pleased me—was a different thing from the composition which I had thought I was going to write." I. A. Richards: "Often one doesn't seem at all to know what one is going to say and then, in the midst of turning a few sentences over experimentally, a whole line of development, that one never seems to have thought out, opens up." W. H. Auden: "How do I know what I think till I see what I've said?" Robert Penn Warren: "A writer doesn't know what his intentions are until he's done writing. . . . Intention is closer to result than to cause." See, respectively, Aaron Wildavsky, *Craftways: On the Organization of Scholarly Work* (New Brunswick, N.J.: Transaction Publishers, 1989), p. 9; T. S. Eliot, "Scylla and Charybdis," *Agenda* 23 (1–2): 5 (1985); I. A. Richards, *The Selected Letters of I. A. Richards, CH*, ed. John Constable (Oxford: Clarendon Press, 1990), pp. 47–8; W. H. Auden quoted in Robert Heilman, *The Southern Connection: Essays by Robert Bechtold*

Heilman (Baton Rouge: Louisiana State University Press, 1991), p. 112; and Robert Penn Warren, *Talking with Robert Penn Warren*, ed. Floyd Watkins, John Hiers, and Mary Louise Weaks (Athens: University of Georgia Press, 1990), p. 84.

6   Having said this, I should stress that the study of intentions does take us some way in understanding social behavior. An exciting development in social theory is the move beyond methodological individualism to the "plural subject" and "we-intentionality." See, e.g., Margaret Gilbert, *On Social Facts* (London: Routledge, 1989).

7   Michael Riffaterre, "Relevance of Theory/Theory of Relevance," *Yale Journal of Criticism* 1 (2): p. 168 (1989).

8   See Michael Riffaterre, "Hypersigns," *American Journal of Semiotics* 5 (1): 5–7 (1987).

9   The quote comes from Riffaterre, "Relevance of Theory," p. 166. On the issue of undecidability, see Michael Riffaterre, "Undecidability as Hermeneutic Constraint," in *Literary Theory Today*, ed. Peter Collier and Helga Geyer-Ryan (Ithaca: Cornell University Press, 1990).

10 See Michael Riffaterre, "Fear of Theory," *New Literary History* 21 (4): 922 (1990). Riffaterre's theory is ambitious in its claim to comprehensiveness, i.e., it is "a radical theory of literature . . . based on literature's ability to represent all other systems, all forms of reality; that is, its ability to integrate them and treat them as if they were parts of the literary event." Riffaterre, ibid., p. 929. See also the preface of Michael Riffaterre, *Semiotics of Poetry* (Bloomington: Indiana University Press, 1978).

11 Riffaterre, "Fear of Theory," p. 930.

12 G. L. S. Shackle, *An Economic Querist* (Cambridge: Cambridge University Press, 1973), p. 121.

13 Another aspect of this wider sociolect is the intertext discussed below.

14 A longer chapter would detail the special and at times highly useful role the counternarrative has in policy evaluation. Suffice it to say, if the evaluator observes what appears to be causally a case of $(a \to b \to c)$, is there a credible explanation that could account for (not-$a \to$ not-$b \to c$) or ($a \to b \to$ not-c) in the situation being evaluated? The virtue of imagining reversed causality is threefold: (i) doing so focuses on precisely the variables of observed interest (i.e., a, b, and c) and, in the process, provides the most robust test of their linkage; (ii) even if a plausible counternarrative cannot be envisioned, trying to imagine one can suggest other possible explanations of the observed phenomenon; and (iii) even when the evaluation concludes that indeed $a \to c$ via b, if the evaluator has made a plausible case for the counternarrative, she or he has identified an alternative that might be worth pursuing, should it be found that the observed outcome of $a \to b \to c$ is unacceptable. Point (iii) is especially important. To think counternarratively is to conceive of a rival hypothesis or set of hypotheses that could plausibly reverse what appears to be the case, where the reversal in question, even if it proved factually not to be the case, nonetheless provides a possible policy option for future attention because of its very plausibility.

15 Riffaterre notes that the idiolect can be "in conformity or in contradistinction to the sociolect." Riffaterre, *Fictional Truth*, p. 130 (see chap. 6, n. 13). The vast majority of his examples are, however, devoted to cases of opposites, and the

opposition of sociolect and idiolect is explicitly treated in theoretical terms by Riffaterre. See Michael Riffaterre, "Compulsory Reader Response: The Intertextual Drive," in *Intertextuality: Theories and Practices*, ed. Michael Worten and Judith Still (Manchester, England: Manchester University Press, 1990), especially p. 76.

16   Riffaterre, *Semiotics of Poetry*, p. 6.

17   To take one of many examples, consider the argument made by Warren Samuels. He identifies eight principal approaches in the literature to the economic role of government, which characterize government as (1) an exogenous black box; (2) a neutral extension or aggregation of private choice; (3) a nonneutral decision-making or preference-aggregating process; (4) an instrument of the powerful; (5) an instrument with which to check the power of the powerful; (6) the source of problems, if not of evil, in society; (7) the source of progress; and (8) part of the necessary framework of the market. Assuming Samuels is correct, then there are not eight, but really three, or possibly four, basic approaches: an approach centering on the dimension of neutrality and its opposite (numbered 2 and 3 in Samuel's list), another around that of the instrumentation of power and its counter (numbers 4 and 5), and the third around retrogression and progress (numbers 6 and 7). Numbers 1 and 8 are not quite mirror images, but some contraposition can still be observed between the known market and the unknown. No one need have intended that these approaches be the case. From a semiotic view, to have one always entails having recourse to the other by way of stating what the former is not. See Warren Samuels, ed., *Fundamentals of the Economic Role of Government* (New York: Greenwood Press, 1989), pp. 214–6. Another example of definition through binary contraposition is given in the case study below on Native American remains.

18   Riffaterre, "Compulsory Reader Response," p. 71.

19   Riffaterre, *Fictional Truth*, p. 28.

20   See Riffaterre, "Compulsory Reader Response."

21   Riffaterre, "Relevance of Theory," p. 169.

22   Riffaterre, *Fictional Truth*, p. xviii.

23   Riffaterre, *Semiotics of Poetry*, p. 5.

24   Riffaterre, 1990, "Compulsory Reader Response," p. 57.

25   Riffaterre, ibid., p. 71.

26   Riffaterre, "Undecidability," p. 111.

27   Riffaterre, ibid., p. 112.

28   Riffaterre, ibid., p. 111.

29   Riffaterre, ibid., p. 113.

30   Independent, albeit indirect, confirmation of this approach to identifying an intertext that reconciles opposing evaluative criteria is provided by the most celebrated analysis of multiple interpretations and the rules said to generate them, namely, the analysis by Wittgenstein in his *Philosophical Investigations*. According to Wittgenstein, we can readily admit that multiple and opposing interpretations are associated with a given rule without admitting that the rule is itself an interpretation: "[T]here is a way of grasping a rule which is *not* an *interpretation*, but which is exhibited in what we call 'obeying the rule' and 'going against it' in actual cases." Ludwig Wittgenstein, *Philosophical Investigations*, trans. G. E. M.

Anscombe, (New York: Macmillan, 1953), p. 81e. Or to put it for our case, we can readily admit that "policies evaluate criteria" and "criteria evaluate policies" are alternative interpretations of the rule, "Evaluate each case on its own merits," without admitting at the same time that this rule is itself an interpretation—at least as long as we can tell the difference between what is "evaluating each case on its own merits" and what is not. For Wittgenstein (pp. 80e, 81e), our ability to tell the difference depends ultimately on practice and custom, or on what we have been calling the sociolect, of which the intertext, "Evaluate each case on its own merits," is a part.

31 Riffaterre, "Undecidability," p. 111.

32 The term is used to distinguish it from the more specific "evaluability assessment" in the evaluation literature.

33 Riffaterre, "Fear of Theory," p. 929.

34 This section is based on University of California, Office of the President, *Report of University of California Joint Academic Senate–Administration Committee on Human Skeletal Remains* (Oakland: University of California, 1990). The terms, "Native American" and "American Indian" are used interchangeably in the report and below. The quote is from ibid., p. 1.

35 Ibid; pp. 18–9.

36 The report is divided into two parts: a twenty-one-page assessment of the committee, including analysis, conclusions, and recommendations; and a much lengthier series of appendices. The analysis below focuses only on the first part, the committee's evaluation.

37 Russell Thornton, "The California Indian Population," in ibid., app. 7, pp. 12–4.

38 Ibid., p. 11.

39 Ibid., p. 9. As one Native American informant to the committee put it about research based on skeletal remains, "*any* knowledge was gained at the expense of spiritual, cultural and political integrity of the tribes and was not worth that price" (my italics); see Bonnie Guillory, "A Report on the California Indian Tribes Opinion Survey," in University of California, *Report*, app. 4A, pp. 1–9.

40 Ibid., p. 4.

41 Ibid., p. 5.

42 Ibid.

43 Ibid., p. 8.

44 Ibid., pp. 9, 16–7.

45 Ibid., pp. 18, 19.

46 Ibid., p. 12.

47 The vexed issue of custodianship and "collective ownership" of skeletal remains is explicitly addressed in Robert Henry Stevens, "Research Project Report on California Indians: Advisement to the University of California Regarding Indian Ancestral Remains and Tribal Articles in University Museums," in ibid., app. 4B, pp. 1–20.

48 For more on these lines on the animal experimentation issue, see chapter 4.

49 A more thorough analysis would deal with the other questions as they apply to the skeletal remains controversy. Suffice it to say, the issue appears evaluatable, if simply because it is too early in the controversy to say no learning is going on. It is also too soon to determine how, if at all, the criteria for evaluating the retention or

return of skeletal remains will evolve out of the controversy. As for the possibility that the controversy really is only a game, clearly there has been gaming strategy and bureaucratic politics behind the promotion of various pieces of legislation concerning the disposition of Native American remains. Yet nothing in the report or its appendices indicates that this issue is a game, even a serious one, to those involved.

50 University of California, *Report*, p. 20.
51 Riffaterre, "Compulsory Reader Response," p. 74.
52 For an example of this attitude, see note 39.
53 University of California, *Report*, pp. 9, 18–9.
54 This point is developed in different context in Emery Roe, "Analyzing Subsaharan Livestock Rangeland Development," *Rangelands* 13 (2): (1991).
55 The evaluator is counseled to look for methods and techniques from contemporary literary theory, not for policy advice. One fairly representative example of misleading poststructuralist criticism will have to suffice. A recent poststructuralist critique of nuclear weapons argues that smart weapons have made soldiers obsolete in modern warfare:

> In his *Critique of Cynical Reason*, Peter Sloterdijk better situates the demise of the warrior. . . . [T]echnology finishes the task of displacing the heroic subject: "There are modern artillery systems that in strategic jargon are called 'intelligent munitions' or 'smart missiles,' that is, rockets that perform classic thought functions (perception, decision making) in flight and behave 'subjectively' toward the enemy target." The "human factor" present with "the self-sacrificing kamikaze pilots" or the manned bomber is "fully eliminated." This is an elimination of special status: "With the 'thinking missile,' we reach the final station of the modern displacement of the subject."
> William Chaloupka, *Knowing Nukes: The Politics and Culture of the Atom* (Minneapolis: University of Minnesota Press, 1992), p. 27.

Happily, this argument is wrong. Indeed, it is exactly opposite of what occurred in the Gulf War. Many people believe, misleadingly it turns out, that "continuing the trend toward a high-tech military using primarily 'smart' weapons will allow the United States to fight and win with minimal U.S. casualties," according to Gene Rochlin and Chris Demchak, *Lessons of the Gulf War: Ascendant Technology and Declining Capability*, Policy Papers in International Affairs 39 (Berkeley: Institute of International Studies, University of California, 1991), p. 2. What the Gulf War actually demonstrates, in their view, is the "necessity for establishing and maintaining an immense social organization in order to provide the degree of support necessary for effective use of the newer weapons" (pp. 5–6). They go on to argue:

> If the focus on high tech continues to be directed at the weapons themselves, the massive social system behind these weapons will remain invisible to public debate. One possible consequence is a political belief that wars can be fought with smaller forces by continuing to substitute technology for people. The cycle of the past decade of American defense budgets would then be replayed, with purchases of weapons given priority over the operations,

maintenance, and personnel budgets to sustain them. But without the massive support provided in the Gulf, there is every likelihood that the next war will be quite a bit more costly in lives—unless the opponent is smaller and less capable than Iraq was presumed to be. (pp. 31–2)

In other words, not only is the poststructuralist observation wrong, but if we believed it, we would likely increase the chances of lives lost in the next "smart" war! Fortunately those sympathetic to elements of poststructuralism have begun to address how inaccurate some of its criticism has become, e.g., Christopher Norris, *Uncritical Theory: Postmodernism, Intellectuals and the Gulf War* (London: Lawrence & Wishart, 1992). For an exceptionally acute analysis of nuclear war informed by contemporary literary and cultural theory, see Jeff Smith, *Unthinking the Unthinkable: Nuclear Weapons and Western Culture* (Bloomington: Indiana University Press, 1989).

Conclusion

1   Some argue that tolerance is acceptance irrespective of dislike or disapproval, and there has been at least one empirical attempt to discredit the notion that dislike is a necessary condition for tolerance, Paul Sniderman, Philip Tetlock, James Glaser, Donald Philip Green, and Michael Hout, "Principled Tolerance and the American Mass Public," *British Journal of Political Science* 19 (part 1): (1989). There is, however, a long tradition of defining tolerance as putting up with what one dislikes or disapproves, when she or he could do otherwise. See, for example, Bernard Crick, "Toleration," *Government and Opposition* 6 (2): (1971); Preston King, *Toleration* (New York: St. Martin's Press, 1976); Peter Nicholson, "Toleration as a Moral Ideal," in *Aspects of Toleration: Philosophical Studies*, ed. John Horton and Susan Mendus (New York: Methuen, 1985); and Mary Warnock, "The Limits of Toleration," in *On Toleration*, ed. Susan Mendus and David Edwards (Oxford: Clarendon Press, 1987). Some authors, such as Warnock, distinguish between disapproval and dislike. For a discussion of tolerance as one of many types of acceptance, see Emery Roe, "The Zone of Acceptance in Organization Theory: An Explanation of the Challenger Accident," *Administration and Society* 21 (3): (1989).

2   Werner Z. Hirsch, "Economists' Role in Government at Risk," in *Fundamentals of the Economic Role of Government*, ed. Warren Samuels (New York: Greenwood Press, 1989), p. 92.

3   Arnold Meltsner, *Policy Analysts in the Bureaucracy* (1976; paperback edition, Berkeley: University of California Press, 1986), p. 298.

4   The notion that policymakers and analysts are necessarily partisan has long been associated with Charles Lindblom's work. See Charles Lindblom, *The Intelligence of Democracy: Decision Making through Mutual Adjustment* (New York: Free Press, 1965), pp. 28–30; and Charles Lindblom and David Cohen, *Usable Knowledge: Social Science and Social Problem Solving* (New Haven, Conn.: Yale University Press, 1979), pp. 62–6.

5   Robert Golembiewski and his colleagues have studied burnout among professionals in complex organizations, including those in the public sector. See, e.g.,

his "Differences in Burnout, by Sector: Public vs. Business Estimates Using Phases," *International Journal of Public Administration* 13 (4): (1990).

6 Leon Walras, *Elements of Pure Economics*, translated by W. Jaffe (London: George Allen and Unwin, 1954), p. 52.

7 Crick, "Toleration," pp. 149, 162.

8 Preston King, "The Problem of Tolerance," *Government and Opposition* 6 (2): 189–91 (1971).

9 For an elegant essay by a leading philosopher on how not caring about what one is saying has led to too much bullshit in the world, see Harry Frankfurt, "On Bullshit," in his book *The Importance of What We Care About: Philosophical Essays* (Cambridge: Cambridge University Press, 1988).

10 Mirrlees argues, "There are many reasons why a utilitarian should not, in practice, insist that the utility functions he has come to believe in must govern economic policy, even if he has the power to do so. . . . I may have a tendency to be biassed in favour of, or even against, people like myself. . . . In order to gain influence for my evaluations . . . it may be necessary to agree to some degree of influence for considered valuations, or even the tastes, passions and whims of others. All of these are reasons for taking account of the views of others." See J. A. Mirrlees, "The Economic Uses of Utilitarianism," in Williams, eds., *Utilitarianism and Beyond*, ed. Amartya Sen and Bernard Williams (Cambridge: Cambridge University Press, 1982), p. 81.

11 See, respectively, Hirschman's "Notes on Consolidating Democracy in Latin America," in his book *Rival Views of Market Society and Other Recent Essays* (New York: Viking, 1986), pp. 178–9; Albert Hirschman, "Having Opinions— One of the Elements of Well-Being?" *American Economic Review* 79 (2): 77–8 (1989); and Albert Hirschman, "The Changing Tolerance for Income Inequality in the Course of Economic Development," in his book *Essays in Trespassing: Economics to Politics and Beyond* (Cambridge: Cambridge University Press, 1981). I am grateful to Professor Hirschman for pointing out the first two references.

12 Charles Lindblom, "Policy Analysis," *The American Economic Review* 48 (3): 306 (1958). At a later point in his article, Lindblom seems to be saying that incremental analysis is favored by the analyst because it allows him or her to avoid having to choose between tolerating or not tolerating different policies (e.g., p. 308). For a somewhat different gloss on toleration from a Nobel Laureate economist, see F. A. Hayek, "Individual and Collective Aims," in Mendus and Edwards, eds., *On Toleration*: "I am afraid I rather doubt whether we can tolerate a wholly different system of morals within our community, although it is no concern of ours what moral rules some other community obeys internally. I am afraid that there must be limits even to tolerance" (p. 47). Tolerance as a limit is modeled in Thomas Schelling, *Micromotives and Macrobehavior* (New York: W. W. Norton and Co., 1978), pp. 155–66. For a discussion of Keynes's (early) views on toleration, see R. M. O'Donnell, *Keynes: Philosophy, Economics and Politics* (London: Macmillan, 1989).

13 W. Stanley Jevons, *The State in Relation to Labour* (London: Macmillan, 1882), p. 166.

14 G. L. S. Shackle, *Epistemics and Economics: A Critique of Economic Doctrines* (Cambridge: Cambridge University Press, 1972), p. 448.

15 G. L. S. Shackle, *Uncertainty in Economics and Other Reflections* (Cambridge: Cambridge University Press, 1955), pp. 239–40.

16 For example, Donald McCloskey, "The Rhetoric of Economics," *Journal of Economic Literature* 21, (1983); essays in *The Rhetoric of the Human Sciences: Language and Argument in Scholarship and Public Affairs*, ed. John S. Nelson, Allan Megill, and Donald McCloskey (Madison: University of Wisconsin Press, 1987); Phillip K. Tompkins, Jeanne Fisher, Dominic Infante, and Elaine L. Tompkins, "Kenneth Burke and the Inherent Characteristics of Formal Organizations: A Field Study," *Communication Monographs [Speech Monographs]* (42): (1975); and Martha Minow, "Law Turning Outward," in *Telos* 73: (1987). For the Challenger accident, see Roe, "Zone of Acceptance."

17 For an article on how a computer program aided in identifying the narrative structure of a fresco that has long puzzled art historians, see Marilyn Aronberg Lavin, "Computers and Art History: Piero della Francesca and the Problem of Visual Order," *New Literary History* 20 (2): (1989).

Appendix A

1 For a fraction of this literature, see David Welch and James Blight, "The Eleventh Hour of the Cuban Missile Crisis: An Introduction to the ExComm Transcripts," *International Security* 12 (3): (1987).

2 See, for example, William Medland, *The Cuban Missile Crisis of 1962: Needless or Necessary* (New York: Praeger, 1988).

3 We now have, for example, what purports to be a Russian version of the crisis: Raymond Garthoff, "Cuban Missile Crisis: The Soviet Story," *Foreign Policy* 72, (1988). If the past is any indication, Garthoff may be a bit optimistic in using "the" in his title.

4 Bruce Allyn, James Blight, and David Welch, "Essence of Revision: Moscow, Havana, and the Cuban Missile Crisis," *International Security* 14 (3): (1989).

5 See "White House Tapes and Minutes of the Cuban Missile Crisis," *International Security* 10 (1): (1985); and "October 27, 1962: Transcripts of the Meetings of the ExComm," *International Security* 12 (3).

6 Bruce, Blight, and Welch, "Essence of Revision," p. 158, record the "considerable surprise and confusion in the transcripts" of some of these meetings.

7 This interpretation owes much to the notion of simulation proposed by Jean Baudrillard. See Vincent Pecora, "Simulacral Economies," *Telos*, no. 75: 128 (1988).

8 Emery Roe, "Applied Narrative Analysis: The Tangency of Literary Criticism, Social Science and Policy Analysis," *New Literary History* 23 (3): 565 (1992).

9 One continuing legacy of Vietnam has been the flight of first-rate policy analysts and social critics on the Left from analyzing the U.S. Department of Defense's specific programs and policies with anything approaching the same kind of rigor that analysts on the Right have done for years. For a deconstructionist reading with a story, nonstory, and metanarrative that resonate with those of the Cuban Missile Crisis, see Richard Klein and William Warner, "Nuclear Coincidence and the Korean Airline Disaster," *Diacritics* 16 (1): 3ff (1986). These authors, for example, argue that "[t]otal nuclear war does not refer to anything that is or ever has been, so far; its real referent is in some still hypothetical future. . . . We are left to

become the historians of the future, to invent its history before it happens, because if it happens, it may never have a history" (p. 3).

10   Much of what follows in this section was developed originally by Janne Hukkinen
or is the result of discussions with him.

11   Emery Roe, "Overseas Perspectives" (see chap. 5, no. 25).

Appendix B

1   Abstracted from The Lorraine, Tannenbaum, and Trow summary of U.S. Department of Agriculture and California Department of Food and Agriculture, *Medfly
Eradication Project Chronology of Events, June 1980–September 1982* (n.d.).

Appendix C

1   Dahlsten, "The Scientist as Source," pp. 5, 7. All sources cited in this appendix are
from *A Fly in the Policy Ointment*, ed. Lorraine, Tannenbaum, and Trow (see
unnumbered endnote, chap. 3).

2   Scribner, "1980 California Medfly Program," p. 9.

3   Wood, "Medfly and the Media," p. 11.

4   Rohwer, "View from Washington," p. 13.

5   Lorraine, "Man the Master," p. 11.

6   Thurman, "Medfly Politics," p. 11.

7   Wood, "Medfly and the Media," p. 12.

8   Dahlsten, "The Scientist as Source," p. 1.

9   Scribner, "1980 California Medfly Program," p. 4.

10   Ibid., p. 20.

11   Jackson, "View from Management," p. 11.

12   Chambers, "Technical Advisors," pp. 17–8.

Index

Analytic tip. *See* Global warming controversy

Animal rights controversy, 73, 76–85; principal features, 77–81; proponents vs. opponents of animal research, 77–81. *See also* Complexity

Aron, Raymond. *See* Global warming controversy, meteorologists

Assumptions for decision making: underwriting and stabilizing, 3, 5, 9, 30, 36–37, 40, 125, 156. *See also* Critiques; Metanarrative; Policy narratives

Barthes, Roland, 24
Berlin, Isaiah, 19
Brown, Jerry, 56, 60, 70–71, 164
Budgeting: and Angola, 22, 48; in Botswana, 28, 48; and computerization, 49–50; effectiveness in, 5, 31–33; in Kenya, 23–25, 28, 48, 49–50; key features, 22–27; readerly versus writerly, 24–25, 32; repetitive, 25, 27–33; as textual reading, 21, 31–33; in United States, 21–23. *See also* Intertext

California Department of Motor Vehicles, 49

Complexity: in animal rights controversy, 82–83, 147; and coupling, 45–48; definition, 2; givenness, 10, 66, 112. *See also* Irrigation controversy

Controversies. *See* Animal rights controversy; Global warming controversy; Irrigation controversy; Medfly controversy; Native American remains controversy

Conventional policy analysis, 1–2, 4, 13, 16–18, 55, 75, 84, 89–91, 107, 118, 156, 160. *See also* Polarization

Counterstories (counternarratives), 3, 5, 41, 50, 108, 189 n.14. *See also* Semiotic square

Cranmer, Bishop, 45

Critiques: problem of, 5, 40, 53, 57–58, 69, 74, 124–125, 147. *See also* Medfly controversy; Nonstories

Cuban Missile Crisis, 7, 157–158

Decision making. *See* Assumptions for decision making

Deconstruction, 21–33 *passim*

Derrida, Jacques, xiii, 29

Dewey, John, 188 n.4

District Focus (in Kenya), 127–130, 134

Emery Roe is a practicing policy analyst at University of California, Berkeley. He has published widely on African rural development, livestock rangeland management, comparative policy analysis, budgeting, program evaluation, and domestic science and technology controversies.

Library of Congress Cataloging-in-Publication Data
Roe, Emery.
Narrative policy analysis : theory and practice / Emery M. Roe.
Includes bibliographical references and index.
ISBN 0-8223-1502-5 (cl). — ISBN 0-8223-1513-0 (pa.)
1. Policy sciences—Case studies.   2. Decision-making—Methodology—Case studies.   3. Discourse analysis, Narrative—Case studies.   I. Title.
H97.R638   1994
321'.0—dc20   94-7248 CIP